Re-Imagining the War on Terror

New Security Challenges Series

General Editor: **Stuart Croft**, Professor of International Security in the Department of Politics and International Studies at the University of Warwick, UK, and Director of the ESRC's New Security Challenges Programme.

The last decade demonstrated that threats to security vary greatly in their causes and manifestations, and that they invite interest and demand responses from the social sciences, civil society and a very broad policy community. In the past, the avoidance of war was the primary objective, but with the end of the Cold War the retention of military defence as the centrepiece of international security agenda became untenable. There has been, therefore, a significant shift in emphasis away from traditional approaches to security to a new agenda that talks of the softer side of security, in terms of human security, economic security and environmental security. The topical *New Security Challenges series* reflects this pressing political and research agenda.

Titles include:

Jon Coaffee, David Murakami Wood and Peter Rogers
THE EVERYDAY RESILIENCE OF THE CITY
How Cities Respond to Terrorism and Disaster

Christopher Farrington *(editor)*
GLOBAL CHANGE, CIVIL SOCIETY AND THE NORTHERN
IRELAND PEACE PROCESS
Implementing the Political Settlement

Kevin Gillan, Jenny Pickerill and Frank Webster
ANTI-WAR ACTIVISM
New Media and Protest in the Information Age

Andrew Hill
RE-IMAGINING THE WAR ON TERROR
Seeing, Waiting, Travelling

Andrew Hoskins and Ben O'Loughlin
TELEVISION AND TERROR
Conflicting Times and the Crisis of News Discourse

Michael Pugh, Neil Cooper and Mandy Turner *(editors)*
CRITICAL PERSPECTIVES ON THE POLITICAL ECONOMY OF PEACEBUILDING

Brian Rappert
BIOTECHNOLOGY, SECURITY AND THE SEARCH FOR LIMITS
An Inquiry into Research and Methods

Brian Rappert *(editor)*
TECHNOLOGY AND SECURITY
Governing Threats in the New Millennium

New Security Challenges Series
**Series Standing Order ISBN 978 0–230–00216–6 (hardback) and
ISBN-978 0-230-00217-3 (paperback)**

You can receive future titles in this series as they are published by placing a standing order. Please contact your bookseller or, in case of difficulty, write to us at the address below with your name and address, the title of the series and the ISBN quoted above.

Customer Services Department, Macmillan Distribution Ltd, Houndmills, Basingstoke, Hampshire RG21 6XS, England

Re-Imagining the War on Terror

Seeing, Waiting, Travelling

Andrew Hill
Research Fellow, Centre for Research in Socio-Cultural Change,
The Open University, UK

First published 2009 by
PALGRAVE MACMILLAN

Palgrave Macmillan in the UK is an imprint of Macmillan Publishers Limited, registered in England, company number 785998, of Houndmills, Basingstoke, Hampshire RG21 6XS.

Palgrave Macmillan in the US is a division of St Martin's Press LLC, 175 Fifth Avenue, New York, NY 10010.

Palgrave Macmillan is the global academic imprint of the above companies and has companies and representatives throughout the world.

Palgrave® and Macmillan® are registered trademarks in the United States, the United Kingdom, Europe and other countries.

ISBN-13: 978 -0-230-20008-1   hardback
ISBN-10: 0-230-20008-7   hardback

This book is printed on paper suitable for recycling and made from fully managed and sustained forest sources. Logging, pulping and manufacturing processes are expected to conform to the environmental regulations of the country of origin.

A catalogue record for this book is available from the British Library.

Library of Congress Cataloging-in-Publication Data

Hill, Andrew, 1974–
   Re-imagining the War on Terror : seeing, waiting, travelling /
   Andrew Hill.
       p. cm. — (New security challenges)
   Includes bibliographical references and index.
   ISBN 978 0 230 20008 1
   1. War on Terrorism, 2001– 2. Terrorism—United States—History—
   21st century. 3. Terrorism—History—21st century. I. Title.

HV6432.H56 2009
973.931—dc22   2008035163

10 9 8 7 6 5 4 3 2 1
18 17 16 15 14 13 12 11 10 09

Printed and bound in Great Britain by
CPI Antony Rowe, Chippenham and Eastbourne

Contents

Figures

Preface

Work on this project commenced in 2004, evolving alongside the unfolding of the conflict. What follows is an attempt to make sense of what has taken place.

For their help and support throughout the writing of this book, I would like to thank: all my family, Pamela Church Gibson, Marie Gillespie, Janus Avivson, Amanda Windle, and Claudia Aradau.

AH

Introduction

In the midst of the Babelic profusion of discussion and debate that has accompanied the War on Terror there has been a broad consensus that what is taking place constitutes a new type of conflict. While it would be wrong to take such claims as locating the War on Terror beyond comparison with other conflicts, in a number of its fundamental features it can indeed be understood as presenting something new.

Underpinning this sense of newness is the scope or breadth of the War on Terror – as suggested by its very name. At one level, the War on Terror constitutes a campaign against an enemy that, under the rubric of 'Al Qaeda', presents a loosely organised network of terrorist groups and cells that criss-cross the globe. At the same time though it has taken the form of more 'conventional' wars – against allies of Al Qaeda, as in the case of Afghanistan, the Taliban, as well as other purported threats to the security of the United States and its allies, as in the case of Iraq. (The latter was also prior to the invasion of the country, identified, at least by the Bush administration, as an Al Qaeda ally.)

In the form of Al Qaeda – the West's principal opponent in the War on Terror – the conflict has witnessed the emergence of a new type of enemy. While in certain respects Al Qaeda might be compared with earlier terrorist groups, its distinctiveness has been integral to the conception of the War on Terror constituting a new type of conflict. At the heart of Al Qaeda's distinctiveness stands the looseness of its structure and the terms in which it has provided an ideological template for groups and cells from across the globe to claim affiliation with it. Indeed, the global dimensions of these networks, and their irreducibility to any distinct territory, have been crucial to the sense of indeterminacy

1

surrounding Al Qaeda's ontological status, and the extent to which its activities are shrouded in uncertainty.

The scope of the War on Terror and the profile of Al Qaeda intersect with a further distinctive feature of this conflict: its spatial dimensions (in addition to its global scale). While it is possible to identify quite definite 'theatres of operation' – in the case of Afghanistan and Iraq – the range and reach of this conflict extends well beyond these locations, refusing to be reduced to a clearly demarcated territory (or series of territories), boundaries, or frontlines.

Rather, this is a conflict that is marked by a what at times appears to be near constant shifting of focus around the globe: from New York, to Afghanistan, to Bali, to Madrid, to Pakistan, to London, to Iraq, to Saudi Arabia, and so on ... (to name only a selection of the locations which have figured as the focus of the War on Terror).

The distinctiveness of the War on Terror is also evident in another of its fundamental dimensions – its temporality – and above all the uncertainty around its perceived duration. While it can be argued that this is a feature of conflicts in general – who could have predicted much prior to 1989 that the Cold War would end in that year? – in the context of the War on Terror such calculations are imbued with an added degree of unpredictability by the United States and its allies appearing to possess little sense of how, let alone when, it will be clear victory has been achieved. Indeed, as President Bush admitted in August 2004,[1] such a victory may never be forthcoming – a statement that was taken as implying the War on Terror has become a conflict without end.

It is this sense that the War on Terror constitutes a new type of conflict that in turn suggests the need for new approaches to interrogating its shifting dynamics and unfolding structure.

In taking the processes of seeing, waiting, and travelling as its organising themes, this book is concerned with processes that do not belong to any discreet academic discipline, but rather transcend disciplines, raising new questions and demanding innovative ways of reimagining and reconceptualising the nature of this conflict. (Such an approach contrasts with the desire to make the object of study conform to a specific disciplinary gaze and to reproduce disciplinary knowledge, that is the remit of discipline-based approaches.) As Roland Barthes has asserted, 'Interdisciplinary studies ... do not merely confront already constituted disciplines (none of which, in fact, consents to *leave off*) ... Interdisciplinary study consists in creating a new object, which belongs to no one' ([1972] 1989: 72).

Why then the choice of these particular 'objects' or processes of seeing, waiting, and travelling? What issues and questions do they raise that are so integral to the War on Terror? And in particular, in regard to this book's concern above all with the way in which this conflict has been experienced and perceived in the West – how do these themes serve to illuminate the terms in which the War on Terror has been perceived and comprehended here?

Of the three it is the theme of seeing that leads this book. The War on Terror is a conflict in which questions of visuality have been fore-grounded and discussed, debated and scrutinised with an unprecedented intensity. This attentiveness to the visual is apparent in the nature of the conflict's instigating event – the September 11 attacks – the spec-tacular dimension of which was fundamental to the impact the attacks achieved. And yet, it has been reiterated time and again since that day, in, to cite a number of the most obvious instances: the 'Shock & Awe' assault that opened the Iraq War, the images of torture and abuse that emerged from Abu Ghraib jail, the videos of western hostages seized in Iraq, and Bin Laden's video appearances.

The significance accorded to the act of seeing in the War on Terror derives in no small part from the scope of media coverage (driven by developments in media technology) the conflict has been subject to – as evoked by the then Secretary of State for Defense Donald Rumsfeld, in a speech to the Council of Foreign Relations, in February 2006, in which he described the War on Terror as the 'first war' to be fought:

> In an era of e-mails, blogs, cell phones, BlackBerrys, Instant Messaging, digital cameras, a global internet with no inhibitions, hand-held videocameras, talk radio, 24-hour news broadcasts, satellite television. There's never been a war fought in this environment before.[2]

Rather though than focusing on the 'representability' of media coverage of the conflict – of how closely this coverage correlates with what 'actually' occurred and attendant issues of how this coverage is framed and 'manipulated' by different actors (issues that are well rehearsed and have been analysed elsewhere) – the concern of this book is with other aspects of seeing. The latter, derived above all from psychoanalysis and Lacan's work in particular, include questions of scopic desire, the instability of vision, techniques of intimidation, the relations between the seen and the unseen, exhibitionism and display, and the type of knowledge of the world seeing provides the spectator with.

If seeing constitutes this book's lead theme, then the themes of waiting and travelling provide a focus for interrogating the temporal and spatial dimensions of this conflict.

For many in the West experiences of waiting have come, if not to define, then to figure as central to the temporal dynamics of this conflict – finding a focus in the experience of awaiting 'the next attack' – whose imminence publics are repeatedly reminded of, but the details of which (where and when it will take place and the form it will take) remain deeply uncertain. At the same time the War on Terror has been crosscut by a host of other instances of waiting, as in, waiting for news of Bin Laden's capture or killing, waiting for loved ones to return from serving in Afghanistan, or waiting for the release of the next video showing a hostage seized in Iraq. And yet, such has been the lack of attention accorded to waiting, not only in regard to conflict situations, but as a form of experience more broadly, that this aspect of the War on Terror has been accorded relatively little attention. Indeed, in the Cold War, waiting constituted a central dynamic of this conflict for publics, in regard to awaiting the possibility of nuclear confrontation between the superpowers and their allies. Where the experience of waiting in the War on Terror differs from the Cold War is in terms of the degree of uncertainty that pervades this process in regard to the form a future attack might take, where it might occur, its scale, and who might and might not be harmed. At the same time present in the War on Terror is an awareness that even if an attack does occur, this need not be final, with further attacks still possible. An awareness of the latter points towards the duration of the War on Terror, and the sense in which what has been embarked upon is an endless war that gives rise to an endless process of waiting, with no conclusion in sight, and with little sense, in regard to even the most clearly defined theatres of operation – Afghanistan and Iraq – of when these locations might be regarded as sufficiently 'stable' for western forces to be withdrawn.[3]

As the War on Terror has been imbued with a pervasive sense of mobility, so the theme of travelling appears and reappears in multiple guises across the subsequent chapters. The conflict's instigating event – the September 11 attacks – witnessed passenger jets used as weapons, and in both Madrid and London public transport has figured as a target of attacks. At the same time, a key characteristic of the enemy is its mobility, as in the case of groups and individuals receiving training in Pakistan or Afghanistan before moving on to undertake operations in the West, and with fighters arriving from a host of countries to participate in the insurgency in Iraq. Such developments have resulted in travelling having become a focus of security concerns in the West, as evinced in the increased security around air travel and in regard to the movements of people across national borders. At the same time though processes of travelling have figured as integral to the measures employed by the United States against this enemy – as evinced in the transporting of detainees from across the globe to Guantanamo Bay, and in the use of extraordinary rendition to move suspects across international borders for 'interrogation'. Beyond examining travelling as a process of physical movement though, the chapters that follow are concerned with another type of travelling – the way in which images travel – a type of travel invoked by the quotation from Rumsfeld cited above, and the terms in which developments in media technologies have served to transform the means in which this type of travelling occurs. In particular the chapters that follow are concerned with the way in which images from other parts of the world travel back to audiences in the West, and the terms in which these images figure as integral to western publics' conception of the War on Terror.

The approach to these three themes taken in this book is informed above all by the work of Jacques Lacan. (And yet rather than constituting a perpetual point of reference, his work is foregrounded at various points in the subsequent chapters, while forming a broader background presence.) Although this book does not require prior knowledge of Lacan's work – concepts where used have been defined as succinctly as possible without it is hoped losing their nuances – it is worth briefly elucidating the ontological schema developed across his work, as this figures most centrally in the chapters that follow.[4] Lacan develops a tripartite ontological schema made up of the intersecting orders of the Imaginary, the Symbolic, and the Real. The Imaginary is the order of seeing, of visuality and images actual and imagined. The Symbolic is the order of language, the significance of which is highlighted – and here the influence of structuralism upon Lacan's thought is most apparent – in it serving to constitute the legal – linguistic dimensions of the social order: 'the law'. While the Real constitutes the raw, unmediated dimension of experience, which stands beyond symbolisation or representation, and exists in a state of tension with the previous two orders which, in one respect, seek to regulate and control it. (The dimensions of these orders and their relationship to one another will become clearer as the book unfolds.) Taken together – and in relationship to one another and to other of Lacan's concepts – these orders provide a consistently illuminating means of configuring not simply questions of ontology, but multiple dimensions of the political and the social.

Lastly, while each chapter focuses upon a different aspect of the War on Terror, the chapters are ordered in broadly chronological terms – opening with the September 11 attacks and moving towards the ever receding present of the book's completion (in early 2008). As such, while engaging with the themes of each chapter the intention is that the reader should also obtain a sense of the terms in which this conflict has unfolded over time.

1
September 11, 2001: Spectacularity, the Ruse, the Blot

> Images never wounded any man.
>
> Aeschylus, *Seven against Thebes*

Untitled (2001)

In early September 2001, Wolfgang Staehle's *Untitled* (2001) opened at Postmasters Gallery, New York, showing a triptych of live webcam feeds, updated every four seconds, of a monastery near Stuttgart, the Fernsehturm in Berlin's Alexanderplatz, and a view of Lower Manhattan as seen from South Williamsberg across the East River. Very little appeared to happen:

> All three projections – at least on cloudless days, at moments when the boat traffic abated – seemed perfectly tranquil. They dared us to find them boring, or even to mistake them for stills. Only a periodic shiver, like a transparent curtain stirring, indicated that they were live-feed webcam transmissions.
>
> (Worth 2001: 129)

At 8.48 a.m. Eastern Daylight Time on Tuesday, September 11, the camera trained on Lower Manhattan was to capture the Boeing 767 of American Airlines flight 11, Boston to Los Angles, hitting the North Tower, to be followed 15 minutes later by United Airlines flight 175, scheduled to fly a similar route, exploding into the North Tower. A work that might previously have been positioned as a commentary on the experience of watching time passing and 'nothing happening' had transformed into a record of the way in which 'great' historical events shatter our perception of the world, and the capacity such events

7

possess for altering the terms in which we see. From providing a medita-
tion on the way in which the slow movement of time typically remains
unacknowledged and unseen in the course of everyday life – remaining
overlooked by 'the glance' that prevails in much of the way we observe
the physical environment at the level of the quotidian (Bryson 1983:
94–7; Elkins 1996: 206–7) – Staehle's piece had come to be invaded
by an event that in its startling spectacularity would be subject to the
repeated scrutiny that prompts a reassessment of the nature of seeing.

'A trap for the gaze'

Yossef Bodansky, in his account published prior to the September 11
attacks of Bin Laden's metamorphosis into the United States' most
wanted adversary, records the priority accorded by Al Qaeda to sustain-
ing 'a series of spectacular operations' against the United States (1999:
358). In fact, prior to this date, Al Qaeda-linked groups had already
been engaged in operations of this nature in the shape of the bombing
of United States' embassies in East Africa in August 1998, a strike on the
USS *Cole* in October 2000, and an attack upon the World Trade Center
itself in February 1993. The desire to mount such strikes accords with a
primary objective of terrorist acts – to maximise attention for the perpe-
trator's aims and to emphasise the capacity to cause harm in the pursuit
of their objectives, a tactic that reached its apotheosis (to date) with the
September 11 attacks, and in particular the focus of this chapter: the
strikes on the World Trade Center.

On 16 September, five days after the attacks, at a press conference
at the Hamburg Music Festival, the composer Karl-Heinz Stockhausen
responded to questions about what had taken place in New York by
describing the events of that day as 'the greatest work of art', achieving in one act something 'which we couldn't even dream of in music'.[1]
Performances of Stockhausen's work programmed for the festival were
cancelled, while the composer insisted his comments had been taken
out of context. Then, around a year later, in a series of video interviews
the BBC news website commissioned to mark the first anniversary of
the attacks, the artist Damien Hirst described the strikes on the World
Trade Center as 'an artwork in its own right' that had been 'devised visually' and was 'visually stunning' – an assessment that generated a storm
of controversy, with Hirst issuing an apology a week later.[2]

In one sense both sets of comments can be read as indicative (trou-
blingly so) of contemporary attitudes towards the conception and function of art; at the same time though they are revealing about the impact

registered by the attacks at a specifically visual level (as Hirst's remarks make explicitly clear). While distancing myself from the moral myopia of Stockhausen and Hirst's comments, I want to take up and reconfigure the analysis opened up in their assessments by interrogating how the visual spectacle of the strikes on the World Trade Center featured as a fundamental dimension to the attacks – with, as will become clear in later chapters, significant consequences for the future shape of the War on Terror – in terms of Jacques Lacan's discussion of questions of visuality in *Seminar XI: The Four Fundamental Concepts of Psychoanalysis*. Here, Lacan presents a conception of a painting as 'a trap for the gaze' ([1964][3] 1994: 89) – functioning as a means by which the artist seeks to attract, hold, and pacify the spectator's vision. As Stockhausen and Hirst's remarks suggest, the spectacle of the September 11 attacks can be configured in similar terms – as deliberately intended to produce a spectacle that would function as a trap for the gaze of audiences across the globe, with an awareness that what took place on that morning in New York would create a sight so compelling that it would be watched by audiences in the West and around the globe over and again.

Recognition of the visual appeal of the attacks is predicated upon the acknowledgement that audiences possessed a desire to witness the type of spectacle produced on that day, that, to apply Norman Bryson's (1983: 7) conception of the supposed perceptual relations between artist and spectator, these audiences constituted 'a site of reception eager for perceptual satisfaction' of the type produced by the attacks. The desire to witness the type of spectacle generated by the attacks should come as no particular surprise, though. As Slavoj Zizek (2002: 15–16) has noted, such a desire was intimated in the disaster movies that came to prominence in the 1970s and underwent something of a revival in the 1990s, with the phantasies of destruction enacted in these films coming to be realised on September 11.[4] Indeed, as James Elkins attests (1996), the nature of scopic desire is marked by an – what might be called 'disconcerting' – amorality, and as Edmund Burke ([1757] 1998: 43–4) argues in *Origin of Our Ideas of the Sublime and Beautiful*, historically spectators have demonstrated a deep desire to witness the sublime spectacle of great acts of destruction. Burke contrasts his conception of the sublime with the beautiful, yet the idea of the attacks as imbued with a type of beauty has been suggested in one instance by the photographer Thomas Hoepker, who has referred to the attacks' 'sinister beauty', adding that what happened on that day was 'beautiful on one side and on the other it's sheer horror'[5] – a statement that both echoes Yeats's ([1916] 1990: 203) vision of the 1916 Easter Rising as giving birth to 'a terrible beauty' (an assertion that has become something of a paradigmatic statement on the aesthetics of violence and conflict) and invokes the way in which images of war have exerted an ongoing aesthetic appeal (Zelizer 2004: 121–3).

There exists another dimension to these assessments though, the sense – as Don DeLillo has repeatedly examined in his novels, most explicitly in *Mao II* (1991) – that terrorist acts have since the 1960s come to overshadow and threaten to subsume the work of art, in their capacity to shock and to produce a radical disruption of everyday life: objectives that figured among the principal drives of art in the twentieth century (coming to the fore in the century's second half). Indeed, Frederic Beigbeder (2005: 8), in his novel-reflections on the attacks, *Windows on the World*, wonders at once how, in the wake of the attacks, it is possible to write about what took place and yet how it is possible to write of anything else. This subsuming of the work of art can also be traced in the tendency for art to directly mimic terrorist activity, as evident in, to take two examples pertinent to the War on Terror and anxieties about the dissemination of WMDs and hostage taking in Iraq: Gregory Green's manufacture of bombs and warheads and New York artist Brock Enright's kidnapping and 'abusing' of those willing to pay thousands of dollars for the privilege. It might also be detected in the rising demand for and price of expressionist works.[6]

'All warfare is based on deception'

Beyond the attention the attacks generated among a global audience, in what terms can the spectacular nature of the strikes on the World Trade Center and the 'trap for the gaze' they functioned as be understood as figuring as a fundamental dimension of the attacks?

To return to Lacan's commentary on visuality in *Seminar XI*, the discussion of the way in which techniques of intimidation function at the level of the Imaginary (a relatively neglected aspect of his work) serves as a valuable point from which to develop a response to this question. Lacan (1994: 100) outlines the way in which certain animals work to manipulate their appearance: 'the phenomenon known as intimidation [also] involves this over-valuation that the subject always tries to attain in his appearance', a process that is deployed by animals in stages of sexual competition and combat in which the, usually male, animal may expand or swell up – namely, create a spectacle at the Imaginary, intended to supersede or achieve an 'over-valuation' of their presence at the Real (ibid.: 107). Such a model provides an approach to understanding the spectacular nature of the September 11 attacks. While recognising the impact the attacks registered at the level of the Real – in the death and destruction they wrought – in strategic terms they did not constitute (or come close to constituting) a 'decisive' strike against the United States, in terms of inflicting serious damage on the ability of the hyperpower to function, or indeed to hit back against those who had attacked it. Instead, the essential strategic impact of the attacks can be understood as reaching beyond the Real, to be fundamentally bound up with the impact they achieved at the Imaginary – as evident in regard to two outcomes.

Firstly, the spectacular nature of the attacks served to demonstrate – to put on display at the Imaginary – the strength and capabilities of Al Qaeda, in terms that Nietzsche has noted by which an attack itself comes to figure as a means through which a group 'becomes aware of its own strength' ([1878] 1994: 179). As the BBC correspondent Jane Corbin makes clear in her account of the development of Al Qaeda,

> It was in a Jalalabad house in mid-November [2001], as al-Qaeda fled the city, that the videotape was found which showed a relaxed Bin Laden sitting with a Saudi Sheikh, smiling about the September 11 attacks, saying how he had surprised even his closest confidants with his daring plot: 'They were overjoyed when the first plane hit the building,' said Bin Laden, 'but I said to them – be patient ... We stayed until four in the morning listening to the news. Everyone was most joyous'.
>
> (2003: 263)

As Mohamed Sifaoui (2003) indicates in his report on infiltrating an Al Qaeda cell in Paris in 2002, claims that Al Qaeda were not capable of mounting the type of attacks seen on September 11 disgruntled the cell's members, who were moved to state in interviews with Sifaoui that their associates 'are capable of that sort of operation and even more than that' (ibid.: 53). At the same time, the footage of the attacks was identified as a powerful recruiting video for Al Qaeda. As an 'unnamed sheikh' in a video that showed Bin Laden laughing and boasting at a house in Kandahar about the September 11 attacks said to Bin Laden, 'Hundreds of people used to doubt you and few only would follow you until this huge event happened. Now hundreds of people are coming out to join you.'[7]

Secondly, and perhaps even more significantly, the spectacular nature of the attacks can be understood – beyond demonstrating to Al Qaeda's opponents their ability to mount an attack of this nature – as having had a carefully calculated impact upon the United States. As Sifaoui (2003: 23, 41) noted, one of the favourite slogans of the group he infiltrated in Paris was 'War is a ruse' – a statement that can be read as implying that outright violent conflict functioned as only one conduit for Al Qaeda to pursue its version of global jihad, and a distraction from the other methods through which this might be achieved – including gaining new followers and winning popular support for its message across the Muslim world. Such an utterance takes one stage further one of the defining maxims of Sun Tzu's *The Art of War* ([6th century BC] 2003: 91) that 'All warfare is based on deception.' For this Paris group, warfare (or violent acts more broadly) had itself become a means of deceiving one's opponents, and a ruse behind which other objectives might be pursued.

The visual dimension to this tactic of deception is illuminated by Lacan's comments on painting in *Seminar XI*. Lacan (1994: 111–2) speaks of a painting's capacity to operate as a 'lure' for the spectator – to draw the spectator into responding to the illusion of what they see. The September 11 attacks can be conceived of as operating in similar terms. As James Fallows has argued in *The Atlantic* in the autumn of 2006, with the benefit of the period which has passed since the attacks occurred, it has become increasingly clear that the intention of the attacks was to act as a lure or bait to draw the United States into the type of conflict of global proportions the War on Terror has developed into, with the intention that this would increase the hyperpower's vulnerability and provide Al Qaeda with a better chance of achieving victory.

Such a plan can be seen to have been based upon a calculation of how the United States would be likely to respond to a spectacular attack of the type carried out on September 11. In 2004, in an interview for a supplement ('Spotlight on Terror') of the Jamestown Foundation's *Terrorism Monitor*, the Saudi exile and opposition group leader Saad al Faqih argued that the attacks figured as part of a long-term strategy to lure the United States into this type of conflict, with Ayman al Zawahiri (typically identified as Al Qaeda's 'number two' and 'strategic master-mind') having told Bin Laden a version of the following:

The American mentality is a cowboy mentality – if you confront them ... they will react in an extreme manner. In other words, America with all its resources and establishments will shrink into a cowboy when irritated successfully. They will then elevate you, and this will satisfy the Muslim longing for a leader who can successfully challenge the West.

(Abedin 2004)

Such an assessment can – as subsequent developments have shown – be said to have been broadly correct. The likelihood of the United States responding in such a way can be located in terms of what Victor Davis Hanson (2001) identifies as a defining feature of 'the western way of war' – namely, a reliance upon heavy and superior firepower to defeat one's opponents. The United States has displayed a particular proclivity for this form of combat (Huchthausen 2004: 55),[8] as evident in the month following the strikes on the World Trade Center in the assault on Afghanistan and the 2003 Iraq War (both of which will be scrutinised in later chapters). Indeed, Bin Laden himself directly invoked the United States' proclivity for this type of action in his declaration in a video broadcast days before the 2004 US Presidential Election: 'All we have to do is to send two mujahideen to the furthest point east to raise a piece of cloth on which is written "al-Qaeda" in order to make the generals race there.'[9]

Fallows's (2006: 69) assessment of 'terrorist warfare' (in general) is that 'The most dangerous thing it can do is to provoke you into hurting yourself.' Echoing this contention, David Kilcullen, a senior adviser at the State Department, has asserted, 'It is not the people al-Qaeda might kill that is the threat ... Our *reaction* is what can cause the damage' (ibid.: 62). Such warnings are not new; Bernard Lewis, writing in 1990 (commenting on the history of Islamic hostility to the West) in a piece that first raised the notion of a forthcoming 'clash of civilizations', warned, 'It is crucially important that we on our side should not be provoked into an equally historic but equally irrational reaction against that rival.'[10]

And yet, despite these warnings, this was indeed the type of reaction that was forthcoming from the Bush administration. If, prior to the attacks, the administration was widely perceived as lacking in identity and purpose, the attacks provided it with a clear raison d'être[11] (that became 'the Bush Doctrine'): to defeat 'global terrorism' (for which can be read 'Islamic terrorism') and the states which harbour terrorists. As Christopher Layne (2006: 204–5) has argued, while realists (in international relations terms) would have shied away from embarking on a conflict of the nature and scale of the War on Terror, the Bush administration's vision of the world (or the vision it found in the aftermath of the attacks) was, as Walter LaFeber (2002: 558) has dubbed it, 'so self-righteous that it could not check itself'. The 'trap for the gaze' the attacks were intended to function as had become a trap for a hyperpower.[12]

Catastrophe, the hard Real, Horror

Having focused upon the spectacularity of the attacks, I want now to shift emphasis for a moment to scrutinise the 'other side' of the attacks – what is left behind and remains unseen in focusing upon their visuality. In so doing I want to turn my attention to the Real – that realm of the raw, unsignifiable, and unrepresentable dimension of experience that stands beyond the Symbolic and the Imaginary and exists in a constant state of tension with these orders.

In terms of Lacan's schema, catastrophe (in general) can be conceived as entailing a rupture in the Symbolic – here in the guise of the linguistic underpinnings of the social order – brought about by the intrusion of the Real.[13] As Jonathan Rutherford has commented[14] on watching from close by as the second plane hit the World Trade Center:

> When United Airlines Flight 175 crashed into the south tower I felt *the symbolic order*[15] of the world I had grown up in reverberate in shock. As the twin towers crashed to the ground something in my unconscious seemed to fall with them.
>
> (2005: 624)

The breakdown in the Symbolic produced by the attacks might also be read in a figure (a symptomal figure) in Larry Towell's photograph, who, in the immediate aftermath of the attacks, stood in a dust- and paper-strewn street, seemingly frozen in place as he reads one of the pieces of paper – as if attempting to cling to the Symbolic – as the police yelled at him, 'Get back. More buildings may collapse' (Magnum Photographers 2001: 42).

However, the attacks can, I want to suggest, be said to entail not only a rupture in the Symbolic, but at the same time, a breakdown or col-lapse in a certain dimension of the Real. Mark Wigley (2002: 71) locates the collapse of the physical environment and the faith in the security of the built environment this served to undermine as fundamental to the impact registered by the attacks. Wigley's analysis points towards a specific dimension of the Real that emphasises the material rawness or raw physicality of the material world, that I want to term the 'hard Real' – a dimension that while not directly elaborated upon by Lacan is neither precluded from the conception of the Real he develops.[16] Indeed, one aspect of Lacan's definition of the Real is 'that which is always in its place' (1966: 25) and 'that which always comes back to the same place' (1994: 49), and it is precisely this fundamental aspect of that which we presume is always going to be in place – our physical environment – which was destabilised by the attacks.[17]

An alternative name given to Ground Zero by those who worked there was 'the hole'. For Lacan ([1955–6] 1997), the presence for the individual subject of 'holes' (as he terms them) in the Symbolic constitutes a fundamental feature of psychosis and the source of those hallucinations which serve to fill these holes through a process in which 'what has been rejected from the symbolic reappears in the real' (ibid.: 46). Such a process helps to explain the desperate desire, Susan Willis (2005: 21–4) highlights, to recover the bodies of the dead killed in the attacks. Beyond an attachment to the hard Real of the victim's bodies – 'all that is left' (in material terms) of them – this desire can be read as an equivalent to the process of hallucination, in which these bodies might be used to 'fill in' the holes in the Symbolic opened up by the attacks.

The status of the victims of the attacks raises the question of how to think about these dead. As Zizek (1996: 112) discusses, the ghostly can be closely related to this mechanism of hallucination, with the ghostly constituting the return of the Real, 'in the guise of spectral apparitions', that arrive to plug the holes in the Symbolic – such as those created by the attacks. As Avery Gordon (1997) has suggested, the ghostly provides a way of thinking about the dead, and the way in which they return to haunt the living, when we begin to consider the status of those who have 'disappeared' from history – in the immediate instance the victims of the attacks. These ghosts will be joined by a succession of others across the chapters that follow, with the purpose of scrutinising what it is they might reveal about the nature of the War on Terror – in particular in regard to questions of seeing and ontology, and how we think about and perceive the dead.

At the same time the ghostly stands as a central dimension of the Gothic, and its more recent manifestation, Horror. As Fred Botting (1999) attests, writing prior to the attacks, there is a sense that Horror has come to function as a key referent in contemporary Western societies (so much so that it threatens to disappear as a distinct genre) – as evinced in, for example, the commonality of plastic surgery, the flippancy with which contemporary cinema deals with acts of intense violence, and the graphic attention accorded in sections of the media to bodies in states of trauma, dismemberment, and decay. In addition, Mark Neocleous (2005) has asserted the ties between the Gothic and 'the politics of fear' – connections that have, as Richard Devetak (2005) adumbrates in regard to the field of international relations, been exacerbated by the September 11 attacks and the focus upon fighting 'terror' they have generated. Indeed, Joseba Zulaika and William Douglass (1996: 4–5, 27) have emphasised how terrorism constitutes a source of horror. As all genres do, Horror provides a means of configuring and seeing the world, playing an epistemological function that in the case of this genre provides an approach to depicting and engaging with a tenebrous realm of experience that might otherwise be marginalised or shut out. Indeed, in providing a means of bringing into focus aspects of the War on Terror that might otherwise be occluded, this genre will be invoked at various points in the chapters that follow.

The black screen, non-representation, 'the blot'

To return to the spectacularity of the attacks – what light might an attentiveness to the Real cast on the questions of seeing the September 11 attacks raised in the first part of this chapter?

As Adorno (2003) and Maurice Blanchot (1986) have asserted, the representation of catastrophe foregrounds a series of issues in regard to the terms in which the work of art (and the realm of representation more broadly) attempts to depict disasters of such magnitude that they threaten to throw into doubt the very possibility of representation – let alone how such depictions might provide a means of comprehending or coming to terms with what has taken place. In regard to Lacan's ontological schema, such concerns can be said to centre on the question of the terms in which, when the twin orders of representation – the Imaginary and the Symbolic – have undergone the radical disruption instigated by catastrophe, it is possible to re-present this rupture.

One response to this question – that is worth elaborating upon here as it opens up a series of important issues for addressing the terms in which the September 11 attacks have been seen and understood – is offered by the Mexican director Alejandro Gonzalez Inarritu's[18] contribution to the collection of short films, *11'09"01* (2002).[19] Inarritu's film is dominated by a plain black screen broken only by glimpses of figures falling from the Twin Towers, followed by brief footage of the World Trade Center collapsing (accompanied by a soundtrack that takes the form of a complex bricolage of sounds and voices). In interview Inarritu acknowledged that 'the magnitude and complexity' of the September 11 attacks presented him with profound difficulties in formulating a response to what had taken place, noting how 'on that day, reality killed fiction'.[20] Inarritu's film – most clearly in its use of black screen – suggests that such an event cannot simply be represented in realist terms, by seeking to reproduce the Imaginary 'as it was' or 'as it appeared', and that another strategy that does not (re)confirm the stability of the Imaginary, but rather responds to what has taken place by calling into question its stability, is needed. In its use of a black screen the film can be understood as employing a strategy of 'non-representation', one that serves to limit what the spectator sees of the attacks and their aftermath.

Rather than 'simply' serving to acknowledge the difficulties (or impossibility) of adequately representing the attacks, the film, in its foregrounding of Lacan's notion of 'the blot' (or 'stain') introduced in *Seminar X: Anxiety* (1962–3),[21] serves to raise broader questions about the terms in which the attacks were seen. The blot constitutes the presence of the Real in the spectator's field of vision, that which presents in Zizek's (1999: 127) words the 'remainder of the Real that "sticks out"' – assuming the form of that aspect of this field which is obscured, unclear, or does not seem to accord with what is depicted in the rest of the scene.[22] In so doing – in drawing attention to the nature and limits of seeing – the blot comes to figure as a key source of interrogative scrutiny (an issue that will be returned to in subsequent chapters). In the limits placed upon seeing the attacks through its use of a black screen, Inarritu's film can then be seen to radically foreground the blot, forcing the spectator to consider the terms in which the attacks can and cannot be seen, and how we might make sense of what has occurred.

In choosing to deny the spectator a view of the planes hitting the Towers, or indeed much else beyond brief glimpses of the aftermath of the attacks, Inarritu's film can be understood as working to negate and deny the spectacularity of the attacks and the impact achieved by this dimension to them – namely, 'the trap for the gaze' they were intended to function as. Indeed, in place of the spectacle of the planes hitting the Towers, the film emphasises the horrific human consequences of the events of that morning. In so doing Inarritu's film invokes Marguerite Duras's assessment of the relations between cinema and the imagination. Duras's film *L'Homme Atlantique* (1981) makes use of a similar technique of non-representation to Inarritu; for half of the film's 40 minutes the spectator is presented with a black screen while listening to a reading of the film's script. As Renate Günther (2002: 24), in her study of Duras's cinema, has argued, the film articulates Duras's awareness of how 'the filmic image tends to restrict the imagination, precisely because whatever is visually present in the front of the spectator, on the cinema screen, cannot be imagined', or, as Duras herself has put it, 'The cinema stops the text and kills its offspring: the imagination' (ibid.: 24).

Conceived in these terms Inarritu's film opens up the space for re-imagining, reflecting upon and thinking critically about what it is that has occurred – an opening up that presents a gesture in defiance of what Lacan identifies as 'the pacifying' effect of the image – the way in which 'the trap for the gaze' leads to the spectator's '*laying down*, of the[ir] gaze' (ibid.: 101). In foregrounding the blot – and in so doing drawing attention to the presence of the Real and the terms in which it might be represented, perceived, and comprehended (in the midst of catastrophe) – Inarritu's film works to provide a counter to the lure set in place by the attacks. In so doing the film provides a means for (re)considering how best the attacks might have been responded to in a way that is not blinded by their spectacularity.

It is the very failure of the Bush administration to wait and consider the attacks in a way that is not taken in by their spectacularity (the failure to, it might be said, think beyond the spectacular and the Imaginary) that led to the type of response that became the War on Terror – the first stage of which will be scrutinised in the next chapter.

2
'Acting Out': Afghanistan, Autumn 2001 and since

On 7 October 2001, less than a month after the attacks on New York, the United States and its allies commenced their aerial assault on Afghanistan – the first military action of the War on Terror – aimed at paving the way for the toppling of the Taliban and destruction of Al Qaeda's use of the country as a base.

The assault took on an epic scale, combining the full range of the United States' 'conventional' weapons arsenal, continuing deep into November, and bringing further destruction to a country already ravaged by decades of war. This aerial campaign was accompanied by the Northern Alliance – the grouping of Afghan forces opposed to the Taliban – launching a ground offensive that by mid-November had resulted in the capture of Kabul, with the Taliban ousted from their last major stronghold, Khandahar, in early December.

Acting out ...?

Commenting on the aerial assault on Afghanistan, Zizek has made the following observation:

> If the greatest power in the world bombards one of the poorest countries, in which peasants barely survive on barren hills, is this not the ultimate case of impotent acting out? Afghanistan is ... an ideal target: a country that is already reduced to rubble, with no infrastructure, repeatedly destroyed by war for the last two decades.
>
> (2002: 35)

The Freudian ([1914] 2001) conception of acting out refers to those instances when a subject, in the grip of their unconscious desires, performs an act as a substitute and diversion from acknowledging the impact of a past trauma and attempting to engage with or 'work through' it. The immediate incident the bombardment presented a response to was of course the September 11 attacks (although as will be suggested, the assault is shadowed by other earlier traumas that continue to haunt the United States). Elsewhere Zizek (1996: 104) has argued that all violence fundamentally constitutes a form of acting out, 'that emerges when the symbolic fiction that guarantees the life of a community is in danger' – a contention that can be challenged in its occlusion of protagonists' differing degrees of comprehension as to their recourse to violence – but which in regard to the War on Terror serves to illuminate the sense in which, in declaring 'war' on Al Qaeda, this campaign has failed to address the causes of Islamic terrorism, and as such, is limited in its capacity to defeat it.

While the assault on Afghanistan was identified by the US government with certain strategic objectives – above all as paving the way for the defeat of the Taliban and the removal of Al Qaeda from Afghanistan – in what terms can this assault be seen to constitute an instance of acting out, that reached beyond and was directed towards something other than these objectives?

Such a diagnosis is most obviously suggested by the assault's magnitude. As Zizek contends, the scale of the assault (detailed by Robertson (2003: 422–48)) went far beyond that needed to defeat the forces it was directed against. As John Simpson (2003: 300–1, 393–9), the BBC's World Affairs Editor, emphasises in his account of the bombardment of the country and the fall of the Taliban – contrary to the pervasive perception in the West of the Taliban constituting a formidable fighting force, beyond a relatively small, committed core, they were in the main poorly organised, ill-disciplined, lacked much in the way of heavy armour or weaponry, and contained numerous fighters who had recently transferred over from opposing groups and possessed a high propensity to transfer back once they found themselves on the defensive,[1] Such was the gap between the two sides that for Simpson the bombardment was 'like watching the RAF bomb John Ball's army in the Peasants' Revolt of 1389. It was a ludicrous mismatch' (ibid.: 399).

At the same time, the scale of the assault reached well beyond that needed to destroy the infrastructure used by the Taliban to maintain their hegemony over Afghanistan. (Indeed, the notion that this infrastructure needed to be destroyed for the Taliban to be defeated can itself be read as pointing towards the assault as an instance of acting out.) As Simpson contended in regard to the bombing of Kabul, 'The Americans and (to a far lesser extent) the British were firing missiles at a city whose infrastructure was so primitive it might have been easier and a great deal cheaper to have left it unbombed. How would we have noticed the difference?' (ibid.: 327). This question is also raised by Simon Norfolk in an essay accompanying his photographic work *Afghanistan: chronotopia* (2002), taken in the aftermath of the assault, in which he documents a country pummelled by years of continuous warfare:

> Afghanistan is unique, utterly unlike any other war-ravaged landscape. In Bosnia, Dresden or the Somme for example, the devastation appears to have take place within one period, inflicted by a small gamut of weaponry. However, the sheer length of the war in Afghanistan, now in its 24th year, means that the ruins have a bizarre layering; different moments of destruction lying like sedimentary strata on top of each other.
>
> (ibid.: 3)

In a similar context, a report in the UK newspaper *The Guardian* from October 2001 referred to, 'one former and highly decorated general' from the UK confessing, 'he finds the aerial bombardment of an already benighted land like Afghanistan a little "strange". He fears, "we are turning big bits of rubble into small bits of rubble"'.[2] Rather then than being directed 'solely' towards the toppling of the Taliban, in these terms the assault indicates an acting out of the anger provoked by the September 11 attacks directed towards the hard Real of the physical environment, no matter the already battered state of the country – an analysis echoed by Zizek (2002: 35) in his question, 'Is not the ultimate irony that prior to the US bombing, the whole of Kabul already looked like downtown Manhattan after September 11?'.

Beyond its excessive scale though, a second dimension to the assault that is suggestive of it constituting an instance of acting out is evident in the inappropriate application of tactics against an enemy of the type it was directed against. The choice of undertaking a sustained, heavy, aerial bombardment against an enemy that was in the main made up of lightly armed, small groups of fighters, lacking much in the way of heavy weaponry, and that in swathes of the country were hiding out in a rugged, mountainous terrain, can be adjudged inappropriate in tactical terms (Black 2004: 162). The questionable efficacy of such tactics was confirmed by the fact that despite the bombardment those members of the upper echelons of the Al Qaeda hierarchy (including Bin Laden) that the campaign was supposed to destroy remain at large, and that the Taliban have never disappeared as a presence in Afghanistan. Indeed, the period since the summer of 2006 has witnessed their reappearance as a significant threat to the stability of the country and the re-establishment of their suzerainty over swathes of the east and south of Afghanistan.[3] As Simpson (2003: 399) has suggested, 'There is such a thing as being too sophisticated for your enemy', too sophisticated perhaps, but also too ready to rely upon airpower to defeat one's opponents.[4]

Airpower, the unlocatable enemy, Revelations

Why then did this acting out take the form that it did? Why an aerial assault stretching out for weeks on end? And in turn – what might such questions reveal about the then nascent War on Terror?

To answer these questions it is necessary to return to what it was the assault presented a response to – most immediately and obviously the September 11 attacks. In discussing conceptions of acting out in *Seminar X* (1962–3, 30 January 1963), Lacan stresses the signifying dimension of acting out – how this process is always addressed towards an Other to whom it presents a 'call for interpretation' intended to elicit the desired response – despite the lack of comprehension of what is required from the Other by the subject engaged in the acting out. If, as was argued in Chapter 1, the attacks were directed above all towards achieving a spectacular impact at the Imaginary, the assault upon Afghanistan can be located in similar terms – as intended to show not simply that the United States was ready and able to respond to the September 11 attacks with such spectacular and overwhelming force, but to elicit the 'call for interpretation' that Al Qaeda had not achieved a victory 'even' at this level. As such the spectacle of military strength enacted in the bombardment can be conceived as presenting a response 'in kind' to that staged on September 11, demonstrating the unassailable strength of the United States' military to its opponents and a global audience that included its own public – as such serving to sustain 'an absolute representation of military superiority' which Alain Badiou (2004: 228) has identified as vital to the United States' self-image. Indeed, in the words of a former UK diplomat and government minister, the bombardment resembled above all 'a firework display'.[5] Such was the build-up to the bombardment that by the time of its commencement on 7 October the world's media were already engaged in cycles of speculation about precisely when – to the day and then to the hour, the assault might commence – and were in place, primed and ready to cover the assault once it had begun. At the same time though, the 'call for interpretation' presented by the assault can be conceived as being directed towards the United States itself – constituting a means of reassuring the US public, along with the Bush administration and the US military, that in the wake of the September 11 attacks the United States still possessed the will and capacity to respond in such terms. (In so doing, the bombardment accords with Melanie Klein's ([1932] 1997: 114) assessment of violence serving as a means of confirming that one is not a victim.)

In another respect though the decision to launch an assault upon Afghanistan from the air can be understood as intended to limit the casualties likely to be incurred by the United States and its allies from a ground assault. Beyond reports of 'special forces' operating in Afghanistan, the fighting on the ground, including the capture of Kabul, was undertaken by the Northern Alliance. (Although once Kabul had fallen the allies began to deploy ground forces.) This desire to avoid incurring even comparatively limited casualties can be seen to reflect the traumatic effects of a series of US military incursions since (and including) the Vietnam War, most notably the Iran hostage crisis (1980), Lebanon (1982–4), and Somalia (1993), that had resulted in the loss of US personnel – an alarm that would return with the occupation of Iraq. In the skies over Afghanistan the United States and its allies were all but untouchable. The decision to launch a sustained aerial assault can however be understood as extending beyond such 'rational' practical-operational objectives. An aerial assault, utilising aircraft and missiles arriving from hundreds and thousands of miles away, generated the type of spectacle for the world's media that went well beyond that which would have been possible through the deployment of ground forces. As Robertson discusses, since World War I, in the United States (and elsewhere in the West), a particular glamour has been attached to aerial combat that has fed a 'fantasy of winning the war from the air' (2003: 3). While the focus of this may have migrated from a fascination with individual pilots as 'knights of the air', to the fetishisation of new technology, this phantasy has retained a good degree of its lustre, not least thanks to the feeling for the 'technological sublime' that as David Nye (1994) has traced weaves its way through the history of the United States.

Beyond the desire to stage a spectacular response to the September 11 attacks, the form the acting out of the assault took can be seen to be structured by a further desire, one that Wolfgang Schivelbusch

(2003: 294) addresses towards the end of his study of 'the culture of defeat' – namely, that the bombardment of Afghanistan presented an attempt to situate the enemy in a locatable territory that could be bombarded until they were destroyed. Such a desire can be traced back beyond the September 11 attacks to the still unresolved, or – to apply the notion Freud introduces in the same paper he discusses acting out – 'worked through', legacy of the Vietnam War:

> The nation attacked though [on September 11], is still limited to a traditional response: to nominate another nation as a terrorist within a concrete territorial enemy, a target. Thus the United States responded by taking action against Afghanistan, much as thirty years earlier when, tired of fruitlessly battling the Vietcong guerrillas, the United States trained its sights on North Vietnam.
>
> (ibid.)

Such an analysis overlaps with Teresa Brennan's (1993: 41) more broad ranging assessment of the desire to control the physical environment foregrounded in modernity: a 'territorializing imperative' that in one manifestation takes the form of the division of the world into locatable spaces that can be regulated and acted upon. It is in such terms that the destruction of the hard Real of Afghanistan enacted in the assault becomes clearer – constituting the desire to destroy the physical territory within which the enemy 'should' be able to be located.

That Al Qaeda has refused to conform to this type of spatial ordering, that it has refused to be reduced to a locatable territory that could be obliterated, has presented a primary obstacle in the struggle against it (the ramifications of which will be explored in Chapter 8). The western approach to war (and particularly the United States') has been marked by a desire to bring opponents into 'decisive battle', where the West's typically superior firepower can be brought to bear upon its opponents. As Davis Hanson elucidates, the notion of decisive battle has accumulated a moral force that underpins, and can even be said to have encouraged, the assault upon Afghanistan as a means of defeating the enemy:

> We in the West call the few casualties we suffer from terrorism and surprise 'cowardly', the frightful losses we inflict through open and direct assault 'fair'. The real atrocity for the Westerner is not the number of corpses, but the manner in which soldiers died and the protocols under which they were killed.
>
> (2001: 97)

And Davis Hanson alludes to quite recent United States military engagements to illustrate this assertion:

> Americans consider it honourable and effective to bomb the Libyans when they have committed a terrorist act ... or to rain down enormous battleship projectiles upon Palestinian villages openly and 'fairly' from offshore when a few of their residents are alleged to have bombed in a 'cowardly' fashion American marines asleep in their barracks ... As long as Westerners engaged the enemy in an open contest of firepower, the ensuing carnage was seen as relatively immaterial: terrorists who shamelessly killed a few women and children, or states that surprised us on a Sunday morning in a bombing attack on our fleet, usually found mechanized murderous armies of retaliation on their soil and daylight fleets of bombers over their skies.
>
> (ibid.: 97)

In such a context the bombardment of Afghanistan takes on the complexion of the acting out of a moral right as a response to the 'evil' of the September 11 attacks through this righteous act – no matter the disparity between the forces attacking from the sky and their opponents on the ground.

Here Maria Warner's (2005) discussion of 'The Book of Revelation', with the account it offers of the Apocalypse and the Last Judgement, and the place the book occupies in contemporary US culture, is illuminating. Warner emphasises the significance of Biblical interpretation to the Bush administration and its conception of the War on Terror, a theme evident in the notion that the conflict presents an end of the world struggle between good and evil, as central to conceptions of the conflict in the United States and to Islamic fundamentalists.[6] In such a context it is possible to conceive of the assault on Afghanistan as a mimicking of the angels and horsemen of Revelations striking from the air in an act of divine retribution. As Norfolk (2002: 3) states in a comment on his photographs, the 'landscapes of Afghanistan' have, since the assault, indeed come to resemble something of the 'Apocalypse or Armageddon'.

Bin Laden: 'the anamorphic ghost', Al Jazeera

The angels and horsemen of Revelations points us in the direction of the ghostly, a realm that I want to invoke a little longer in turning to examine the weaknesses, vulnerabilities and problems generated by the assault and the compulsion to act out the anger provoked by the September 11 attacks that lay behind it.

On the opening night of the bombardment, as news of the assault began to be broadcast around the world, this coverage was interrupted to show video footage of Bin Laden sitting somewhere in mountainous terrain – his first broadcast response to the September 11 attacks. In his statement Bin Laden praised the attackers, and stated that the United States had now declared war on the Muslim world as a whole, linking the United States' actions to the persecution of the Palestinians by Israel and Iraqis by United Nations' sanctions. As he added, 'These events have divided the world into two camps, the camp of the faithful and the camp of the infidels'[7] – and he urged Muslims to hit back.

Such an intervention can be located, in the words of one commentator, as 'An essential part of his [Bin Laden's] strategy, almost as important as the September 11 terrorist attacks themselves'.[8] The opening of the bombardment provided Bin Laden with both the evidence and attention he needed to attempt to rally the Muslim world against the United States and its allies. More than this though the broadcasting of this video served to radically disrupt the acting out staged by the bombardment and the demonstration of military strength it sought to convey, by inserting at its commencement the very figure above all held responsible for the September 11 attacks.

In the western media Bin Laden has repeatedly been portrayed via recourse to a lexicon of the ghostly (as scrutinised in the following chapter). His appearance at this juncture – and the dynamic this established with the spectacle of the bombardment – is suggestive of a specific type of spectral presence: a version of 'the anamorphic ghost' Lacan (1994: 85–9) in *Seminar XI* reads in Holbein's painting *The Ambassadors* (1533). Much as the intended subject of Holbein's work appears at first sight to be the two Renaissance gentlemen with their tools (globes and navigational devices) for ordering and dominating the world, the spectacle of the assault (itself an attempt to order and dominate) was intended to provide the focus of attention for audiences across the globe. At the bottom of Holbein's painting though stands a mark or blot – an anamorphic device, that appears blurred when viewed from in front of the work, but from a position to the right reveals itself as a skull, a *momento mori*, the presence of which, once realised, serves to radically disrupt the picture's meaning, shifting an image that appears to be about the assertion of power to one haunted by death. It is this which Lacan designates 'the anamorphic ghost', and it is the position of the skull in relation to the rest of the painting that parallels the position Bin Laden occupies in regard to the spectacle of the assault. If, once the spectator becomes aware of this skull they cannot view the picture in the same way, so, in the light of Bin Laden's video appearance, the intended focus of the spectator's attention is diverted from the spectacle of the assault, by the presence of Bin Laden – a presence that will come to haunt the occupation of Afghanistan (and the failure to bring about his capture) and the War on Terror more broadly.

The US government's response to Bin Laden's video was to ask broadcasters in the United States not to broadcast any portion of it, for fear, it was claimed, that it would be used for propaganda purposes and that it may contain coded messages. Such measures reveal a certain futile desperation on the part of the administration though, with anyone wishing to access the footage able to via the Internet, or from satellite channels located outside the United States. (Al Jazeera, the first channel to broadcast the video at this point had some one hundred and fifty thousand subscribers in the United States).[9]

To take the attempt to suppress this broadcast in these terms is perhaps to miss the point of this gesture though. Rather, this constituted the first significant attempt by the United States' government, in the wake of the September 11 attacks, to foreclose opposing perspectives on the War on Terror, and in so doing to attempt to assert their domination of the Imaginary. The lengths the Bush administration was willing to go to achieve this is evident in its subsequent dealings with Al Jazeera – in the aftermath of Bin Laden's first video appearance the US government requested that the channel do not broadcast any further recordings of Bin Laden, a request that was denied. A few weeks later a US missile destroyed Al Jazeera's office in Kabul, an 'accident' that was repeated in April 2003 with a missile hitting the channel's Baghdad offices, killing the journalist Tarek Ayoub – the playing out of a logic of censorship that faced with an uncontrollable Imaginary is instead directed towards the Real. This was not to prove the end of the affair though. In November 2005 a story began to circulate in the UK press that in April 2004 Bush had been 'talked out of' launching a strike against the station's headquarters in Doha, Qatar, by Tony Blair,[10] a story that (especially in the light of Doha constituting the operational headquarters for the US military during the Iraq War) is suggestive of the measures the Bush administration was willing to take to cancel out conflicting voices. And yet, despite these measures, Al Jazeera has continued to constitute a principal outlet for Bin Laden's video appearances. As will be examined in greater detail in the following chapter, a ghost of this nature is not exorcised that easily.

Disappearances

Early December 2001 saw the fall of the last major Taliban stronghold in Khandahar and the establishment of Hamid Karzai as the head of a new regime in Kabul. Despite the presence of the United States and its allies' forces, at no point have Karzai and his backers been able to establish effective control over all of Afghanistan – with the Taliban constituting a renewed threat to the regime.

In the period since the installation of Karzai's regime, doubts have repeatedly been raised about the West's commitment to securing the long-term future of Afghanistan – with significantly less resources and personnel committed to the country than to Iraq, and with resources being diverted from Afghanistan to the latter.[11] While the attention the assault generated provided a platform for Bin Laden's first video appearance since the September 11 attacks, so the form the assault took can be seen to have raised a series of problems for the longer-term status and security of Afghanistan.

In one respect, as Patrick Cockburn has asserted, 'The ease of victory in Afghanistan was to have a fatal impact on Washington and in London', giving rise to 'a mood of extraordinary imperial arrogance'[12] – and the presumption that the occupation and reconstruction of the country would prove relatively unproblematic (a hubris that carried over into the invasion of Iraq). The apparent success of the assault, in appearing to play a decisive role in the defeat of the Taliban, encouraged the idea that what was to follow would be as straightforward. Such an outlook was, Cockburn argues, illusory: 'The Taliban appeared to have deliberately decided to disappear in order to fight another day'. In another respect, in contrast to the spectacular acting out afforded by the aerial assault upon the country, the occupation has necessitated instead the slow, unspectacular challenges and complexities of reconstruction – with the latter task something the US military was little equipped to deal with – a situation exacerbated by Donald Rumsfeld's desire as Secretary of State for Defense (from January 2001) to transform the military into an increasingly hi-tech, low manpower fighting force (what has been referred to as 'the Rumsfeld doctrine').[13] Writing in 2002, Bob Kuklick (2002: 562) questioned whether as much effort would go into the reconstruction of Afghanistan as went into Germany and Japan after World War II. This has not been the case, and rather than commit substantial ground forces to Afghanistan, the United States and its allies have to a great extent relied upon air power to wage war against the Taliban, a result of which has been the steady accumulation of civilian casualties – a significant and mounting source of resentment in Afghanistan that has contributed to support for the Taliban.[14]

The Taliban's temporary disappearance constituted but one of a series of disappearances that in the immediate aftermath of the assault served to undermine and destabilise the prospects for the country's future. A second disappearance was that of the evidence of the assault's destructive impact upon Afghanistan. While the assault provided a spectacular display of military strength to audiences across the globe, its impact has remained largely unseen in the West. Notably few images of the destruction appeared in the western media, few certainly in comparison with the saturation coverage of the aftermath of the September 11 attacks. This invisibility contrasted markedly with the attention focused upon the military hardware deployed in the assault. As Justin Lewis (2003: 331) has argued in regard to the 1991 Gulf War, it was likely that 'most [or, at least more] people could name some of the sophisticated "smart" high-tech weapons … on display, but they had little idea of the numbers of people being killed by those weapons'. So few images were available, in fact, that an appeal for Afghanistan by the Disasters Emergency Committee in the UK had to be postponed for fear that there was insufficient footage to persuade the public to respond.[15]

As a series of journalists made clear, the United States and its allies were anxious to restrict media coverage of the bombardment.[16] Commenting on the absence of coverage in the US media, Robertson noted how

> This silence was matched by the effort on the part of the military to control access to the theater of war, and especially to images of the destructive consequences of American air power. … American bombs tried to put the Al-Jazeera television studio in Kabul out of business. The major television networks in the United States did not seek to know the civilian casualty counts, and the Pentagon was not interested in offering them.
>
> (2003: 427)

In fact, the United States' government was to spend several million dollars buying up civilian satellite imagery of the effect of the bombardment, so as to limit its dissemination.[17]

The absence of imagery of the destruction produced by the assault can be seen to have created a blind spot in western perceptions of Afghanistan, at once serving to cover up the destruction wrought by the assault, and the scale of the reconstruction effort needed – not simply in the wake of the assault, but in response to the decades of war that have scarred the country. (The practical consequences of this absence are apparent in the example of the Disasters Emergency Committee's appeal.) Indeed, the fear that Afghanistan has been overshadowed by other aspects of the War on Terror, including the invasion and occupation of Iraq, has come to constitute an ongoing theme of assessments of the country's instability and the lack of progress made in its reconstruction since the fall of the Taliban.[18]

The third disappearance takes the form of the 'spiriting away' of the first prisoners from Afghanistan to Guantanamo Bay, that occurred in the wake of the arrival of US forces in the country in the aftermath of the assault – and which served to constitute the first stage in the United States' seizure and transport of suspects around the globe, which has emerged as such a notorious feature of the War on Terror. Gordon (1997: 63–135) writes of the 'disappeared' ('desaparecido') of 1970s and 1980s Latin America (and in particular in her discussion Argentina) in terms of ghostly presences that continue to haunt these countries. A similar scenario has developed in Afghanistan (and indeed not only here – the process of 'extraordinary rendition' has extended it across the world – a theme that will be returned to in Chapter 8), creating a succession of ghosts whose absence will, if the experience of Argentina can be taken as a precedent, at some point in the future to be accounted for.

Gordon quotes from an Amnesty International study from 1981 to describe the process of the Argentinian disappearances, a description that can be applied verbatim to those which occurred in Afghanistan:

> Secret arrest, transportation under cover of darkness, the refusal to give information 'as to [the prisoners'] whereabouts or their fate,' and the belief that 'deterring' resistance could best be accomplished by people vanishing 'without leaving a trace' are the elements that prefigure the system of repression known as disappearance.
>
> (ibid.: 72)

And yet it has not only been the case that suspects have been taken from Afghanistan. At the same time Afghanistan has itself become the destination for the 'ghost detainees' (as they are termed) transported there by the United States via the CIA's 'extraordinary rendition' programme (examined in Chapter 8) – with the detention unit at Bagram airbase constituting a key site for the holding and interrogation of suspects.

In considering the Argentine 'disappeared', Gordon (1997: 64) writes of those moments 'when entire societies become haunted by terrible deeds'. In the case of the disappeared of Afghanistan this haunting has taken on a double quality: Afghanistan is haunted by the absence of these figures, and the United States by what has been carried out in its name. In regard to the latter this haunting can be seen to entail the multiplying in number of those who seek revenge against the United States for what has happened to them (as extraordinary rendition more broadly has been seen as doing) – with Gordon emphasising the capacity of ghosts, despite the obstacles that might lie in the way, to return to haunt those who created them.[19] At the same time such practises have served to undermine the moral claims made by the Bush administration for the War on Terror (a theme to be returned to in subsequent chapters). While the aerial assault on Afghanistan can then be configured as raising its own problems for the future of the country, at the same time, at the very commencement of the War on Terror, these seizures and disappearances served to raise broader doubts about precisely the nature of the conflict that had been embarked upon.

3
The Bin Laden Tapes

If in the position he assumed in relation to the spectacle of the assault on Afghanistan Bin Laden can be conceived as constituting an 'anamorphic ghost', as will become evident across the course of this chapter, the conception of Bin Laden as a type of ghostly presence reveals much about the role he has continued to play in the War on Terror in the midst of a hunt for him claimed to be the largest ever undertaken for an individual.

This chapter takes as its focus Bin Laden's video appearances since the September 11 attacks (while also discussing aspects of the audio material from this period that purports to feature him)[1] – to scrutinise both the means by which these appearances have allowed Bin Laden to continue to intervene in the War on Terror and the terms in which they have served to shape perceptions in the West of the nature of the enemy faced in this conflict.

To be seen, to remain unseen

These video appearances can be understood as emanating above all from the desire of Bin Laden to, in the midst of the War on Terror, sustain a visible presence for both his opponents and supporters. As Clifford Geertz (1977) has argued, such a presence has figured as crucial to the authority of diverse types of leader across history, proving of particular significance to the version of a charismatic leader – delineated by Max Weber ([1922] 1978: 241–5) – Bin Laden exemplifies. As Terry Smith, writing in 2003 in the *Critical Quarterly*, has contended:

> Bin Laden remains the spiritual guru and strategic guide for many thousands of Muslim militants around the world; every time

he demonstrates that he is alive and can still make a forceful presentation on tape, he can be assured of more recruits to his cause of global jihad.

(2003: 22)

In western media coverage the content of Bin Laden's verbal statements in these video (and audio) recordings has been accorded comparatively limited attention,[2] with interest focused instead on Bin Laden's visibility – the fact that he has reappeared and been seen again (or, in the case of the audio recordings that his voice might have been heard again[3]).

These video appearances have provided a means by which Bin Laden has sought to issue a reminder of the threat he continues to present to his opponents, with the visibility he achieves in these recordings presenting a further instance of the technique of intimidation outlined in discussing the September 11 attacks, in terms of the 'over-valuation' the subject tries to attain at the Imaginary over and above the threat they constitute at the Real. In the case of these video appearances it is Bin Laden's own visible profile that functions in such terms, presenting to his opponents the image of their most wanted adversary accusing, threatening, and goading them, having harmed them already and declaring he will do so again, and having resisted the attempt to capture and destroy him. At the same time though, such has been the degree of attention focused upon Bin Laden as the head of Al Qaeda – in part thanks to these very video appearances – that he has come to function as a metonym for Al Qaeda and the enemy more broadly in the War on Terror, as charismatic leaders in general have a tendency to do for the groups they lead.

While maintaining a visual presence has been crucial to Bin Laden in his attempts to continue to play a role in the War on Terror (and to maintain his position as the recognised head of Al Qaeda), the issue of his visibility possesses another, quite different dimension – lying at the heart of the attempts to hunt him down and capture or destroy him. In an era of weapons technology in which the sighting of a target is intimately linked to the capacity to strike at it, where, as Paul Virilio (1989: 4) states, 'once you can see the target, you can expect to destroy it', and in which, 'winning is keeping the target in constant sight' (ibid.: 2), the technology deployed to identify and assassinate Bin Laden relies crucially upon making a successful sighting of him. This is evident in previous attempts to strike at him. On 20 August 1998, in response to the bombing of United States' embassies in Kenya and Tanzania, the United States launched 60 Tomahawk Cruise missiles at a suspected chemical weapons factory in Khartoum and a training camp in Khost, Afghanistan. Bin Laden was identified as being in the latter only an hour before the missiles landed, and yet managed to escape, thanks, it is thought, to a tip-off (Mayer 2003: 32). In February 2002, an unmanned Predator drone equipped with sophisticated observation technology able to provide high-quality, live video surveillance monitoring fired on a group of 15 to 20 individuals moving between the border of Afghanistan and Pakistan that appeared as if they were Al Qaeda fighters and might contain Bin Laden. However, DNA samples from the dead suggested that the party did not contain Bin Laden or any senior Al Qaeda figures (ibid.: 33–4). Events such as these serve to emphasise that until a verifiable sighting is made of Bin Laden, he is unlikely to be captured or killed. In an acknowledgment of this, in the spring of 2004 the US military augmented a system of 24-hour 'constant surveillance' of the region Bin Laden was suspected to be hiding out in – on the Afghanistan–Pakistan border – combining U-2 spy planes, Predators, and ground sensors, linked by satellite transmissions:[4] measures which have failed (to date) to yield a sighting of him.

In the context of this hunt Bin Laden's visibility evokes the linkages Sartre ([1943] 1957: 578–80) outlines in *Being and Nothingness* between the desire for knowledge, seeing (in this instance seeing Bin Laden and knowing where he is), and devouring (in this sense destroying) him. In the face of this hunt Bin Laden's video appearances acquire an added aura of defiance, demonstrating that despite the measures taken to achieve a sighting of him, he can persist in making himself seen across the globe – apparently if and when he so wishes – without being captured or destroyed. While providing Bin Laden with the means of maintaining a presence at the Imaginary, these video appearances present Bin Laden in a disembodied, dematerialised form, allowing him to retain an absence at the hard Real (as a physical, embodied being) – when it is precisely his presence at the latter that constitutes a precondition for his capture or killing.

Ghostliness, haunting, the objet petit a

The dematerialised form Bin Laden assumes in these video appearances accords with the conception of Bin Laden as a type of ghostly presence introduced in the previous chapter. Indeed, the ghostliness of Bin Laden's appearance in portions of this footage has been repeatedly remarked upon,[5] with his typically wan pallor (the result, it has been rumoured, of life-threatening liver problems), combining with the low quality of portions of this footage – that blurs and distorts his appearance – serving to call to mind the association of poor picture quality in television of the 1950s as evidence of phantoms inhabiting the medium (Sconce 2000: 124–66).

While the sense of ontological indeterminacy associated with the ghostly is evocative of the difficulties that underpin the hunt for Bin Laden, at the same time the quality of ghostliness and the sense of indeterminacy associated with it has constituted a key element in the fears and phantasies associated with the threat both he and the enemy more generally are conceived as presenting to the West. Indeed, as will be explored in Chapter 8, the enemy has repeatedly been depicted as constituting a ghostly or spectral presence. The type of fears this ghostliness can give rise to are invoked in Henry James's *The Turn of the Screw* ([1898] 1975) – a work which pivots on the very question of the presence of ghosts. When the narrator responds to Mrs Grose's question about what the being that is haunting them is with the retort, 'What is he? He's a horror'. 'A horror?' comes Mrs Grose's reply, to which the narrator replies, 'He's – God help me if I know *what* he is!' (ibid.: 35).

This sense of the uncertain ontological status of Bin Laden and the attendant sense of not knowing the specific type of threat he might present at any one time (as in not knowing what his present activities are and what he might be plotting or planning) are suggestive of the affinities between the position Bin Laden has come to assume for the United States and its allies and Lacan's notion of 'the Thing' ('Das Ding'), developed in *Seminar VII: The Ethics of Psychoanalysis* ([1959–60] 1992: 43–70). The Thing constitutes the abject locus of the subject's primary incestuous desire – that the subject is at once drawn towards and repelled by – that exists in 'the beyond-of-the-signified' (ibid.: 54) of the Real, and as such remains unknowable and unreachable.[6] (The term is also evocative of the title of certain horror films – there is a 1982 John Carpenter film called *The Thing*. Indeed, Zizek (2000) outlines how the Thing has repeatedly figured as central to narratives of Horror). Yet, it is the notion of 'the objet petit a' – developed out of the notion of the Thing – that provides a further, more nuanced conception of the position Bin Laden has come to assume for his opponents in the wake of the September 11 attacks.

The objet petit a occupies a pivotal position in Lacan's work, denoting the object cause of desire – that which sets desire in motion – much like, in the aftermath of the September 11 attacks, Bin Laden was situated as the force behind the attacks, with his capture or killing coming to constitute a principal objective of the United States and its allies.

And yet, the objet petit a remains elusive – while it may constitute desire's catalyst it can never be possessed, remaining perpetually beyond the subject's grasp – and as such ensuring the sustenance of desire. As such the objet is at once redolent of the inability to seize Bin Laden and the terms in which (as will be discussed in a moment) he can be said to have become 'uncaptureable'. The unobtainability of the object petit a derives in part from its rooting in the Real – a position that at once overlaps with the conception of Bin Laden as a type of ghostly or monstrous presence, according with the position he assumed in regard to the bombardment of Afghanistan as an anamorphic ghost. Indeed, while the object petit a serves to provoke scopic desire, as Lacan (see, for example, 1962–3, 30 January 1963) outlines, it remains beyond the field of the visible, only registering there in the form of the blot – of which the anamorphic ghost presents one version.

As the objet petit a can be located as haunting the subject – constantly present, yet forever out of reach – so the conception of Bin Laden as a type of ghostly presence serves to position him as haunting the West, in a process that is revealing about the type of threat Bin Laden and the enemy more broadly are conceived as presenting. This sense of haunting is eerily evoked in Langlands and Bell's computer-generated projection *The House of Osama bin Laden* (2003).[7] In October 2002 the artists visited Afghanistan and pursued rumours of a house occupied by Bin Laden in the late 1990s. They located the building west of Jalalabad and used the material they gathered there to construct a virtual model of the house and its immediate surroundings that is then projected onto a gallery wall, with a joystick provided for navigation through the virtual abode. The experience of moving through this environment bares close similarity to that of playing a first person shooter game, in which the player moves through an enemy's lair, confronting and destroying them.[8] The process of being able to wander through one of Bin Laden's former abodes as if about to confront him, aware that he had once been there but now remains out of sight, is evocative of the type of threat Bin Laden has come to assume in the midst of the hunt for him.

Haunting, in many of its forms, suggests the capacity of the being that haunts to appear as and when it wants – including at unexpected junctures and moments of particular resonance – and indeed the tactical value of this ability has been exploited by Bin Laden in the timing of his video appearances. As outlined in the previous chapter, the first of these to occur in the wake of the September 11 attacks took place at the same time as opening of the United States' strikes on Afghanistan in October 2001, serving to distract attention away from and disrupt the spectacle of this assault. A similar sense of timing was evident in the footage broadcast days before the 2004 United States presidential election, which was widely perceived as an attempt to intervene in the election. Furthermore, the anniversary of the September 11 attacks have been accompanied by the release of video footage purporting to feature the voice of Bin Laden (in 2002), video footage of Bin Laden himself (2003, 2007), as well as Al Zawahiri (2004, 2005, 2006).

The sense of Bin Laden haunting the West, and the sense of threat associated with this process, carries over into the series of audio recordings purporting to feature his voice that have circulated alongside these video appearances. In these recordings the absence of a visible profile itself comes to constitute a source of anxiety, with Bin Laden assuming a disembodied presence, issuing threats and inciting attacks while remaining out of sight. In so doing the presence Bin Laden assumes in these recordings conforms closely with Zizek's portrayal of the type of threat the enemy more generally in the War on Terror is conceived as presenting to the West, as he outlines in a discussion of Srdjan Dragojevic's Yugoslav civil war film *Pretty Village, Pretty Flame* (1996). In one sequence of the film a group of Serbian troops are trapped inside a tunnel by Bosnian Muslim forces who are heard but remain unseen until the end of the sequence. As Zizek discusses, the presence of the Bosnian troops takes the form of 'vulgar insults or wild half-animal shouting which are not (yet) attributed to particular visually identified individuals, and thus acquire an all-powerful *spectral* dimension' (2002: 38).[9] Zizek notes how such a narrative device has figured as a feature of a number of film genres 'in which a group of sympathetic characters is encircled by an invisible Enemy who is mainly heard and seen only in the guise of fleeting shadows and blurred appearances' (ibid.: 38). This is an analysis that is equally applicable to Bin Laden's video appearances, and in particular those in which the picture quality renders Bin Laden's visual profile somewhat distorted, while at the same time pointing to the position the United States and its allies perceive themselves more broadly to occupy in the War on Terror in regard to the difficulties in achieving a sighting of the enemy.

Applying the analysis Michel Chion develops in *The Voice in Cinema* (1999) to the audio recordings that purport to feature Bin Laden, Bin Laden can be said to constitute a type of 'acousmêtre': a being that speaks but is not seen. In the cinema such a creature has repeatedly figured as a source of fear, having been associated with a series of powerfully malevolent beings, imbued with four principal attributes: the ability to be everywhere, to see all, to know all, and have complete power (ubiquity, panopticism, omniscience, and omnipotence) (ibid.: 24–7). Locating Bin Laden in these terms serves to illuminate the scale of the fears associated with him, in suggesting he is able to enact a form of total or universal haunting from which it is impossible to escape.

The demon, metamorphosis

For many in the West Bin Laden can be seen to have developed into a specific type of ghostly or spectral presence – a demon, the personification of evil that exists in similar forms across a host of cultures, and typically combining an intense capacity for malevolence with the type of shifting ontological profile that characterises the ghost. Indeed, as Marina Warner (2004: 13–14) has observed, historically, in the West at least, the devil – the supreme demon – has been portrayed as 'a mimic, an actor, a performance artist', an illusionist able to play with and reconjure his image and appearance. In his video appearances Bin Laden displays similar powers, assuming the form he wishes to take – be it, at the opening of the assault on Afghanistan, dressed in military fatigues with a Kalashnikov by his side, or, on the eve of the 2004 presidential election, of a statesman seated behind an office desk.

This ability to change appearance draws attention again to the terms in which the type of visual presence Bin Laden assumes in these recordings has contributed to the threat he has come to be perceived as presenting to the West. In responding to Bin Laden's appearance on the eve of the presidential election, one commentator noted that the video 'could prove almost as damaging'[10] as an attack, a reference to the propaganda power of this particular appearance that also serves to suggest the sense in which Bin Laden's image has metamorphosised into a type of weaponry, not unlike that assumed by the video in Hideo Nakata's film *Ringu* (1998),[11] in which whoever views it dies exactly a week later.

Bin Laden's gaze can be located as constituting a particular point of focus for the sense of threat associated with his image. In these video appearances western audiences are not only confronted with Bin Laden's visible presence, they are made aware that he possesses a gaze and that while they can see him, at the same time he possesses the capacity to see them. Such fears build upon the long running notion that – as Walter Benjamin ([1931] 1985: 244) discusses in 'A small history of photography' – the figures that gaze out from images are able to see the spectator. Indeed, the sense in which Bin Laden's gaze constitutes a type of threat echoes the repeated anxieties associated with the Other's gaze – as evident in associations as various as 'the evil eye' (Brennan 1996: 219–21), Sartre's (1957: 259–60) conception of the voyeur, the motif Zizek observes in Hitchcock's films in which 'the Other's gaze ... epitomizes a lethal threat' (1997: 214), and in Michel Haneke's 2004 film *Hidden*. The emphasis placed here, and in Bin Laden's video appearances, on the significance of being seen by the Other, accords with Lacan's (1994: 67–119) formulation of the gaze as constituting not the subject's own point of view, but the subject's awareness of their inhabiting an abstract field of the visible in which they are seen by the Other. (Indeed, in *Seminar X* (1962–3) Lacan locates this as a key domain in which anxiety emerges.) These fears are given added weight by the sense in which Bin Laden constitutes a type of demonic-monstrous presence – that he possesses what Zizek (1997: 256) in discussing Horror films calls 'an absolute gaze', in which, 'what is truly horrifying about a monster is the way it seems to watch us all the time' – a conception of Bin Laden that accords with the panopticism associated with the acousmetre. Indeed, the subject who watches Bin Laden's video appearances can be located in terms of Barbara Creed's (1993: 154) analysis of Horror films and the way in which the spectator repeatedly assumes the 'victim position' in which they identify with 'the masochistic look'.

However, while it is as a type of demonic presence that Bin Laden is most starkly perceived as presenting a threat to the West, at the same time the configuration of Bin Laden in these terms has proved profoundly useful to the proponents of the War on Terror. As Anustup Basu (2003: 12) has noted, nations 'Like Afghanistan, Iraq, Iran and North Korea, and spectacular profiles like that of Osama bin Laden indeed make a reassuring world picture of evil, because evil that cannot be re-presented cannot be governed' – or, it should be added, acted against. And as Zizek (2002a) contends in discussing the predominant conception in the West of the enemy in the War on Terror, 'The enemy is by definition always (up to a point) *invisible:* it cannot be directly recognised because it looks like one of us, which is why the big problem and task of the political struggle is to provide/construct a recognisable *image* of the enemy.'

In the Manichean terms in which the War on Terror has been configured by the Bush administration, the conception of Bin Laden as a type of demon provides a primary justification for the conflict of global dimensions the War on Terror has developed into – by suggesting the United States and its allies face an opponent so monstrously evil that it cannot be reasoned with in any other way than to be hunted down and destroyed. Furthermore, with surveys suggesting that a high proportion

(68 per cent) of the adult population of the United States believe in the existence of the devil,[12] and, with a host of popular preachers seeking to equate Bin Laden and his supporters with this figure – including Pat Robertson, who in March 2006 spoke of radical Islamists as inspired by 'demonic powers'[13] – this is a conception of Bin Laden that should not be considered too far fetched or empirically distant.

Indeed, the configuration of Bin Laden as a type of demonic being can be located as symptomatic of the type of attitude held by both sides that led to the September 11 attacks in the first place. As Alex Schmid cautions in a commentary on the proliferation of Weapons of Mass Destruction written prior to the attacks, that now reads like something of a warning:

> The best defence is not to give offence. Continuous constructive dialogue and pragmatic compromise with actual and potential political opponents at home and abroad must be sought in order to prevent unilateral or mutual demonization and dehumanization which is one of the preconditions for mass murder with a 'clean' conscience. With the given limitations of physical deterrence, there is no effective substitute for conflict prevention.
>
> (1999: 122)

Since the September 11 attacks conflict prevention is something the Bush administration has had little time for, seeking to marginalise it as a strategy of the morally weak. Rather, the fact that a force of evil of Bin Laden's supposed magnitude remains 'out there' has proved of considerable value to the administration and supporters of the War on Terror in contributing to the justifications for the type of global struggle the conflict has developed into. Without a leader of Bin Laden's infamy, the threat posed by the enemy might be perceived as significantly diminished. Indeed, the fact that Bin Laden remains uncaptured, and that this figure of profound evil remains 'at large', has served as a support for the panoply of contentious measures – both at home and abroad – through which the Bush administration has pursued this war. (These measures are discussed in greater detail in Chapter 8.) Such an analysis can be extended to the United States' allies in the War on Terror, who may have their own uses for Bin Laden continuing to evade capture, with, for instance, repeated doubts cast on the desire of the Pakistani authorities to apprehend him (Mayer 2003: 28–31[14]).

As Homi Bhabha (1994: 149) has asserted though, in discussing conceptions of community and otherness, 'paranoid projections "outwards"' hold the capacity to 'return to *haunt* and split the place from which they are made'.[15] Indeed, the type of paranoid imagining that lies behind the conception of Bin Laden as constituting a kind of demonic-spectral being that haunts the West can be understood as having brought about a splitting in western societies in regard to the relationship of Muslim communities to the rest of society – with the potential ramifications of this process evident in the 7 July 2005 attacks on London. Here, one of the bombers, Mohammed Siddique Khan, in a video tape recorded prior to the attacks (that, to extend this chapter's concern with the spectral and the monstrous, Tariq Ali (2005: 52) has described as 'the ghoulish video tape'), declared that the attacks were motivated by disgust at the UK's foreign policy: 'Your democratically elected government continuously perpetuate atrocities against my people and your support of them makes you directly responsible.'[16] In so doing this splitting – born from the perceived need to take on the enemy in the guise of Iraq – can be located as contributing, quite directly, to this attack.

The Uncaptureable ...?

The conception of Bin Laden as a type demonic, spectral presence accords with the United States' failure to have achieved a definite sighting of him – despite the scale of the hunt for him. While in the form of these video appearances Bin Laden is able to continue to assert his presence at the Imaginary, the absence of the hard Real of his physical presence allows him to remain beyond the grasp of his captors. As such Bin Laden accords with the conception of spectre Derrida (1994: 12) offers as existing 'beyond the opposition between presence and non-presence, actuality and inactuality, life and non-life, of thinking the possibility of the specter, the specter as possibility' – with Bin Laden's metamorphosis into a type of ghost having multiplied the possibilities of the role he is able to play in the War on Terror, while remaining beyond his opponent's reach.

On flyers shaped as dollar bills distributed in early 2003 by the US military on the border of Afghanistan and Pakistan there appears three images. In the first Bin Laden is preaching, a finger raised, in the second appears a pile of dollar bills overlaid with an arrow that points to the third image – that of Bin Laden caged behind bars. In relation to the question of visibility, so crucial to Bin Laden's capture, the phantasy laid out in this sequence of images accords with the sense – as Stephen Baker (2000: 129–132) in his study of 'the postmodern animal' asserts – that the cage provides a means of better seeing and monitoring a creature, by restricting its ability to move out of sight. In the case of Bin Laden, once caged he would no longer be able to appear and disappear as and when he wishes, but would instead be rendered perpetually visible as he languishes in his cell.

However, as an interviewee suggests towards the end of *I met Osama Bin Laden* – a documentary screened by the BBC in March 2004[17] – for his admirers and followers Bin Laden is regarded primarily as a spiritual figure (again the spectral allusions of such conception can be noted), and as such imbued with a transcendental relationship to space and time. Such a conception of Bin Laden points to the terms in which he can be said to have assumed the status of the uncaptureable and the unkillable. Even if a successful sighting were made of him that led to his seizure or death, he would continue – for an indefinite time – to present a potentially threatening presence, not least thanks to his video appearances and the means they provide for his supporters to continue to be guided and counselled by him. Aware of such possibilities, as one commentator has suggested, Bin Laden may have already videotaped his will for posterity.[18] In a still more uncanny development – one which I will return to in the final chapter of this book – it may be that Bin Laden has already died, but prior to his passing away stockpiled a selection of video recordings that allow him to continue to appear from time to time to reassert his presence. In either instance Bin Laden's capacity to continue to cast his shadow over the War on Terror is clear.

The 'impossibility' of destroying Bin Laden adds a further dimension to the critique of the United States and its allies for instigating a conflict of the scale of the War on Terror against an adversary of Bin Laden's nature. While ghosts may not be able to be captured or killed, they might, as Derrida contends (1994: 128, 170, 129), be negated, dissipated, or exorcised – processes that entail seeking to remove their presence through addressing the causes of their coming into being. And yet, in the period since the September 11 attacks, addressing the process through which Bin Laden has come to assume the status he has for many in the Muslim world has been accorded far less importance than confronting and destroying him. A more subtle strategy 'would have exorcised the ghost by depriving it ... of any interstice, lodging, or spacing favourable to haunting' (ibid.: 129). Yet, as will be examined in the next chapter, it is the opposite strategy that has been pursued.

4
'Shock & Awe': Iraq, Spring 2003 and since

In the early summer of 2007 Christoph Büchel's *Memorial* (2007) appeared at the Institute of Contemporary Arts in London, as part of a show in which artists presented ideas for a memorial to the Iraq War.[1] Büchel's contribution was to recreate in detail and with uncanny verisimilitude a hospital waiting room and dispensary that the exhibition-goer could walk into – an experience that initially raised the questions: What was going on here? And, what was the connection of this work to the Iraq War? Only with the realisation – as the accompanying exhibition handout outlined – that the drug administration room was for the inhalation of the body ashes of the victims of war, did the unsettling import of Büchel's work become clear.

Both in the difficulties of making sense of what is taking place and in the unfolding sense of horror it conjures up, Büchel's memorial can be located as mirroring the experience of those who have observed developments in Iraq since the invasion of the country in the spring of 2003. While prior to the invasion (despite the US government's claims to the contrary) Saddam Hussein's regime possessed no tangible links to Al Qaeda, since the fall of the regime Iraq has metamorphosised into precisely the type of space – a magnet, breeding ground, and site of export – for those seeking to wage war against the United States and its allies that Derrida counsels against allowing the spectre to inhabit. From the initial intention of toppling Saddam Hussein's regime and installing a democratically elected and pro-western government, the rapid growth of the insurgency led to a shift in focus to defeating (and when this became impossible, limiting) the insurgency and the presence of Al Qaeda in the country (under the banner 'Al Qaeda in Iraq' or 'Mesopotomia'), while at the same time seeking to ensure the survival of the Coalition-backed regime.

If the invasion of Iraq commenced with a Shock and Awe assault – the spectacularity of which constituted both a focus of media attention from around the globe, and was located as integral to the impact the assault was intended to achieve – post-invasion Iraq has served to emphasise the significance of questions of seeing and visibility in regard not only to the condition of the country, but to the War on Terror more broadly.

'Some some sort of aurora'

In the months leading up to the war the US military trailed the strategy for the invasion of Iraq as taking the form of a 'Shock and Awe' operation[2] of the type developed by Harlan Ullman and James Wade in their assessment of the need to revise US military strategy in the aftermath of the Cold War – *Shock and Awe: Achieving Rapid Dominance* (1996) (a document identified as having had a significant influence on Rumsfeld's conception of a transformed US military) – in which:

> In the post Cold War world, America's military power might be made more effective if it principally were concentrated on affecting, influencing and, ultimately, controlling the will and perception of an adversary rather than exclusively destroying or attriting enemy capabilities as envisaged under the currently prevailing doctrine of employing 'decisive force'.
>
> (Ullman and Wade 1998: v)[3]

Such a conception of military power can be conceived as prioritising the Imaginary over and above the Real (the realm of 'decisive force'), as the order to which attention should be accorded in the new type of conflicts faced by the United States. (Again here then there are echoes of the technique of intimidation discussed in regard to the September 11 attacks and Bin Laden's video appearances.)

In media coverage of the Iraq War the label 'Shock and Awe' was applied primarily to the spectacular aerial assault on the country that commenced on 19 March 2003 and constituted the war's first stage. The bombardment of Baghdad figured as a focus of this coverage,[4] with pictures of blasts in the capital – rendered particularly visible at night, when most of these attacks took place – having become established among the defining images of the war.[5]

The spectacular dimension of the assault can be seen to closely parallel Phyllis Greenacre's conception of experiences of 'awe' in childhood (1987),[6] in which the subject, in a description that bares comparison with the spectacle of the strikes on Baghdad:

Receives a stunning psychic blow, usually an overwhelming visual experience which has the effect of dazing and bewildering it. There is generally the sensation of lights, flashes of lightning, bright colours, or some sort of aurora.

(ibid.: 122)

The aetiology of such experiences are elaborated upon by Greenacre (1956) elsewhere in her work, in terms that make explicit the links between the intended effects of a Shock and Awe assault and the attempted assertion of dominance that underpins it:

It is evident too that the awe, extreme wonder or terror has come in response to experiences involving the show of masculine strength, power, glory, virility, or the phallus itself.

(ibid.: 19)

Indeed, in associating these experiences with childhood, and in locating them as a response to 'masculine' power, Greenacre suggests a further dimension of the assault: the terms in which it reproduced an Orientalist conception of the Iraqi populace as assuming the position of the child in the face of the United States' 'masculine' power – with the former located as passive, submissive, and acted upon. While in regard to the assault itself such an analysis might be questioned in terms of – how else is a population likely to respond to such a display of military power? – this infantilising conception of the Iraqi populace acquires greater clarity in the idea that the invading forces would be greeted with joy by the local population, and that the version of democracy implemented by the United States and its allies would be gladly taken up by the Iraqis. Indeed, as Badiou (2004: 233) observes (in a series of lectures presented around the time of the invasion of Iraq), it was expected that 'the terror of unlimited [US] power, should have transformed' the Iraqis 'into an amorphous mass waving tiny stars and stripes, awaiting their liberators'. One outcome of the insurgency has been to shatter these infantilising projections, while replacing them with others: that Iraqis are not 'ready', or politically 'mature' enough, for democracy, or to realise what 'we' (the United States and its allies) have done for them.

As Mark Danner (2006) has outlined, Rumsfeld's conception of the US military transformed into a hi-tech, comparatively low manpower,

fighting force (of which the Shock and Awe assault offered one manifestation) provided a template for the invasion of Iraq – in which victory over the Iraqi military and the establishment of a new regime was
envisaged as requiring only twenty-five thousand US troops to still be in
the country by August 2003 (six months after the invasion) (ibid.: 88).
Danner makes explicit the problems this limited vision of the invasion
produced in generating 'not one war but two' (ibid.: 82). The first war,
which was regarded by the Bush administration as 'the Real Iraq War'
(but more closely resembled a war of the Imaginary, in terms of its
concern with how the invasion was imagined and initially appeared
to have worked out), entailed defeating the Iraqi military and toppling
Saddam Hussein's regime. This ran closely to plan and was achieved
with relative speed. The second war, 'the postwar phase' that followed
this 'victory', has stretched on until the present day, and was never
envisaged or effectively prepared for, remaining, 'something unnamed,
unconceptualized – unplanned' (ibid.: 82).[7] Clear parallels can be drawn
here with Afghanistan, pointing to an ongoing narcissism on the part
of the Bush administration, obsessed with the spectacularity of its own
military power at the expense of according sufficient attention to the
state of both countries following a successful invasion.

Indeed, Danner suggests that, as with the assault on Afghanistan, the
shape the Iraq War took can be traced back to the September 11 attacks,
in which, headed by a Shock and Awe assault, 'victory was to be decisive,
overwhelming, evincing a terrible power – enough to wipe out the disgrace
of September 11 and remake a threatening world' (ibid.: 82). While it
would be an oversimplification to reduce the invasion to a simple response
to the September 11 attacks, the terms in which the September 11 attacks
contributed to the invasion are worth pursuing further. The desire to erase
the disgrace of the attacks was highlighted by Henry Kissinger in an interview in Bob Woodward's *State of Denial* (2006). (Kissinger had emerged as
a key White House adviser in the lead up to the Iraq War.) Asked why he
had supported the Iraq War Kissinger replied:

> 'Because Afghanistan wasn't enough' … In the conflict with radical
> Islam, he said, they want to humiliate us. 'And we need to humiliate
> them'. The American response to 9/11 had essentially to be more than
> proportionate – on a larger scale than simply invading Afghanistan and
> overthrowing the Taliban. Something else was essential. The Iraq war
> was essential to send a larger message, 'in order to make the point that
> we're not going to live in the world that they want for us'.
>
> (ibid.:408)

This emphasis upon 'humiliation' accords with Badiou's contention (2004: 234) that the invasion of Iraq was born out of 'a culture of vengeance' for which international law was perceived as providing insufficient redress. While the assault on Afghanistan had provided an initial context for the acting out of the anger provoked by the September 11 attacks, the achievements of this undertaking had by now become clear – much of the Al Qaeda hierarchy, including Bin Laden, still remained at large, and, as the attack on Bali in October 2002 demonstrated, the enemy was still capable of staging attacks across the globe. (For a discussion of the expanding conception of the enemy in the War on Terror, see Chapter 8.) Such failures can be understood as fuelling the logic that underpins a process of acting out, in which, in the failure to address the causes of a past trauma, a cycle of repetition occurs in which the subject is drawn back to enact the impact of this past event – in a failed attempt to address what has taken place. After the assault on Afghanistan failed to produce its intended outcomes the Bush administration turned to an adversary that appeared to offer a more straightforward target for its anger, with Iraq – the subject of years of hostility between Saddam Hussein's regime and the United States – constituting a ready candidate for such a role. Indeed, as David Simpson (2006: 145) has asserted, Iraq constituted, 'a simple space-time location at which to claim to fight the war against terror', with 'the panic at imagining terror without a definite profile', presented by Al Qaeda, 'assuaged by calling it Iraq'. This is an assessment echoed by Jeremy Black: 'In 2003, the USA focused on Iraq – a definite and defiant target with regular armed forces – rather than on the more intangible struggle with terrorism, which challenged Western conventions of war-making' (2004: 165).[8]

More broadly though, Danner identifies the humiliation wrought by the attacks as providing the opportunity to 'remake a threatening world' promoted by the neo-conservatives linked to the Bush administration, in which Iraq – given its geopolitical status and weakened by years of UN sanctions – was accorded a central role.[9] As stated in a letter, signed by 41 prominent neo-conservatives, sent to President Bush days after the September 11 attacks:

> It may be that the Iraqi government provided assistance in some form to the recent attack on the United States. But even if evidence does not link Iraq directly to the attack, any strategy aiming at the eradication of terrorism and its sponsors must include a determined effort to remove Saddam Hussein from power in Iraq. Failure to undertake such an effort will constitute an early and perhaps decisive surrender in the war on international terrorism'.[10]

The absence of evidence pointing to Saddam Hussein's regime possessing links to 'international terrorism' has served to underline how the invasion of Iraq reached beyond these concerns, presenting the first stage in the attempt to remake the Middle East by removing Saddam Hussein from power.

And yet, while prior to the invasion Iraq may have seemed to offer a suitable opponent for the United States, this has not proved to be the case. Indeed, the condition of post-invasion Iraq has come to raise questions about the whole progress of the War on Terror, while at the same time serving to highlight the centrality of questions of seeing to this conflict.

Plumes of black smoke, legions of the dead, 'Alive in Baghdad'

While western media coverage of the invasion initially focused upon the Shock and Awe assault on Baghdad, with the passing of this stage of the war attention shifted to the approach of ground forces on the capital. Footage from 'embedded' journalists (utilising developments in technology, including satellite camera phones) seemed to provide the viewer with an unprecedented degree of intimacy with the combat zone. As Zizek has observed:

> In contrast to the Gulf War of 1991, epitomized by the camera shot of a computer-guided projectile hitting its target, thereby depicting war as an abstract computer game (there were no battlefield reports during the war; the blackout was complete), the Iraqi war of 2003 was well characterized by the 'embedded reporters' – reporters staying with the troops, providing live coverage of their day-to-day life and the battles themselves, thus contributing the 'human touch' and generating an instant identification of the spectator's perspective with that of the soldier.
>
> (2005: 3)

And yet, as Zizek goes on to conclude, this sense of identificatory intimacy between the spectator and 'the troops' has to be regarded as significantly limited. Indeed, the terms in which this identification takes place raises the question of the type of knowledge produced by the process of seeing that underpins it. As Lacan contends, visuality is generative of 'Imaginary knowledge' – knowledge that is confined to the Imaginary as the order of appearances, and as such is prey to the lures, misrecognitions, and phantasies that pervade it (see, for example, *Seminar X* (1962–3, 22 May 1963)). Not only is this form of knowledge limited to this domain, Lacan positions it as serving to hinder or divert attention from 'Symbolic knowledge' – knowledge of the Symbolic and the terms in which, as the linguistic dimension of the social order, it serves to structure the social and the subject's position within it.[11] (Here Sontag's ([1977] 2002: 23, 108–9) elaboration of the terms in which language serves to determine the 'meaning' of an image is pertinent in regard to the role played by titles, captions, and commentaries in framing the content of an image, with their absence rendering it difficult to determine what is witnessed there.)

The significance of the relationship between seeing and knowledge to both the invasion and occupation of Iraq, and the War on Terror more broadly, is suggested by a particular image of the invasion: a NASA satellite photograph taken on 2 April 2003 (a week before the fall of the Iraqi capital) that shows oil wells burning close to Baghdad, the black plumes of which obscure the view of the city below (Figure 4.1).[12] A primary purpose of aerial surveillance is to accord a privileged viewpoint from which to observe a location (offering a version of the 'god shot' – to use the term applied to the point of view in Hitchcock's *The Birds* (1963) from above Beluga Bay, as the town starts to burn). In the case of this smoke-obscured NASA image, the black plumes that rise from the burning oil wells can be positioned as constituting a version of the blot, with their presence serving to foreground the question of what can and cannot be seen here. (In so doing this image serves as a reminder that whatever the technology employed, and the sense of being able to see 'more than ever' it might seem to engender, the scope of vision always remains limited – a theme returned to in Chapter 9.[13])

In foregrounding questions of the seen and the unseen this NASA image draws attention to the way in which two particularly significant dimensions of the invasion and occupation of Iraq have been configured in visual terms. The first is that of the dead and wounded and their large-scale absence from western media coverage of the conflict. In one respect this includes western casualties – which have remained all but entirely absent from media coverage of the conflict[14] – a situation that conforms to the broader injunction against showing the western dead delineated by John Taylor (1998). At the same time though, Iraqi casualties have to a great extent also remained absent (or 'at best' only fitfully present), in so much western media coverage of the invasion and occupation.[15]

Figure 4.1   Aerial shot of Baghdad, 2 April 2003, NASA satellite image

Indeed, not only have the latter remained largely unseen, the vast majority have not even registered (or been made 'visible) in the most minimal of bureaucratic terms – that of being counted – a situation that has resulted in extensive debate around the number of Iraqis killed or wounded since the invasion. This question was foregrounded by the publication in October 2006 by the John Hopkins Bloomberg School of Health, of research which claimed the death toll in Iraq since the invasion had exceeded 655,000 people. This figure was contested,[16] yet the very fact that such a debate – with such differing figures suggested – could take place, draws attention to the extent to which Iraqi casualties have been rendered invisible. Such a situation points towards the sense in which the Iraqi populace have come to assume the status of what Donna Harraway has designated the 'killable' (2006) – who acquire such status because they are regarded as possessing 'no history'. The latter formulation takes us back to the neo-Orientalist conception of Iraqis underpinning the imagined ease with which Iraq would be transformed into the type of country desired by the Bush administration.

At the same time this notion of the killable points towards the vulnerability of Iraqis to being killed. Since the invasion Baghdad has become established as the violent death capital of the world, with the city coming to resemble a 'necropolis'[17] in which as Danner adumbrates:

> As Iraqis do their shopping or say their prayers they are blown to pieces by suicide bombers. As they drive through the cities in broad daylight they are pulled from their cars by armed men at roadblocks who behead them or shoot them in the back of the neck. As they sit at home at night they are kidnapped by men in police or army uniforms who load them in the trunks of their cars and carry them off to secret places to be tortured and executed, their bound and headless bodies to be found during the following days in fields or dumps or by the roadside.
>
> (2006: 84).

This evocation of life in Baghdad conjures up a sense of the horror that permeates the quotidian. This is emphasised (to cite one piece of evidence among many others) in an interview on the 'Alive in Baghdad' website' with 'Wissam' – a resident of the city who spends most of his time at home playing on his Playstation because 'There's no option to go outside. If I go outside what am I going to do there? There's just killing and blood and a lot of military patrolling there. So you can't go anytime and anywhere ...'[18] – an assessment that points to the sense of horror that has come to permeate the temporal and spatial dimensions of the Iraqi capital.

In emphasising the pervasiveness of this sense of horror such accounts serve to raise the question how, given the wide-scale absence of media coverage of life beyond the Green Zone – itself a product of the violence subsuming the country – it is possible for non-Iraqis, including western publics, to gain some sense of what it means to live under these conditions on a day-to-day basis? One such source has been provided by those documentaries that have sought to depict the lives of Iraqis since the invasion, including Andrew Berends's *Blood of my Brother* (2005), Laura Poitras's *My Country, My Country* (2006), and James Longley's *Iraq in Fragments* (2006). And yet, these films remain limited in their scope and scale – necessarily so it might be argued, given the conditions they were produced under. The collaborative project *Voices of Iraq* (2004), which gathered together footage shot by ordinary Iraqis, has provided a broader portrait of the country since the invasion – although, in terms of the impact it has made upon western audiences, its limited distribution has to be noted. At the same time, while a number of feature films have taken the US experience in Iraq as their focus, they have accorded little attention to the plight of Iraqis. An exception here is Brian De Palma's *Redacted* (2007), that, in taking as its focus the killing by US troops of a family in Al Mahmudiyah, has conjured up something of the horror of life in the country. (De Palma's film has faced problems with distribution, in part due its controversial subject matter.) As a supplement to these depictions, I want to suggest that narratives of Horror, in their fascination with the threatening, abject Thing (which Lacan (1992: 104–5) links quite directly to the experience of conflict in the guise of nuclear war), provide a source for visualising or imagining life in Iraq since the invasion. In so doing these narratives provide an approach to conceiving of the legions of the dead from Iraq, as they join the ranks of the ghosts that are gathering across these chapters.[19]

If the dead and the wounded have remained largely absent from western media coverage, they have appeared elsewhere though – on for example the award winning 'Alive in Baghdad' website referred to a moment ago (that provides a platform for Iraqi film-makers to present coverage of otherwise overlooked aspects of life in post-invasion Iraq). Indeed, as a piece on wounded car bomb survivors from the site emphasises, 'It's nearly impossible to find accounts of the victims' (of the violence that has engulfed the country since the invasion).[20] Evident here is an initial instance of a notion that will be turned to at various stages across the following chapters – that I want to call 'the minor gaze'. This concept is adapted from Deleuze and Guattari's (1986) conception of Kafka's work as presenting a 'minor literature', that while written in a dominant, 'major language' (in regard to Kafka German, in regard to Iraq the domain of institutional media coverage), emanates from a marginalised or minority standpoint, and in so doing offers a perspective which works to challenge the supremacy of those 'major' voices or gazes which seek to define the cultural-political order.

The insurgency, the travelling enemy

The second key dimension I want to emphasise of the terms in which the occupation of Iraq has served to foreground the significance of questions of seeing to the War on Terror, is the extent to which the insurgency and its protagonists have remained invisible – both in media coverage of the occupation and also to the Coalition forces. While Virilio has emphasised the need for a successful sighting to be made of an enemy before it can be acted against, a crucial obstacle in combating the insurgency has been the difficulty in seeing and hence identifying insurgents. Such is the occupying forces' superior weaponry and firepower that this relative invisibility has constituted a necessary precondition for insurgents to operate, with the principal tactics employed by insurgents – suicide bombings, car bombs, roadside ambushes and sniper attacks – relying upon the perpetrators not being seen until at the very least an attack is underway. The invisibility of insurgent activity is highlighted in a report on the growing use of sniper attacks from November 2006.[21] Here the unseen status of the snipers – described as constituting a type of 'ghost' – constitutes a precondition for them to operate, with at the same time these snipers relying upon the visibility of Coalition forces (as the insurgency does more generally) to provide their target. In this respect the insurgents display a version of the 'visor effect' Derrida (1994: 7) locates as a chief characteristic of the spectre, in the form of the latter's capacity to see while remaining unseen.

In another respect western media coverage of the scale of the fighting that has taken place since the invasion has remained significantly limited. There have been exceptions to this, such as in the United States, *Discovery Times* channel's documentary series *Off to War*, that follows members of a National Guard unit from Arkansas on their tour of Iraq,[22] and in contributions to image sharing sites such as *YouTube* – which includes a channel set up by the Multi-National Force Iraq (the official name of the Coalition forces).[23] However, much of this fighting has remained all but unseen. Very little coverage was forthcoming, for example, of Operation Phantom Fury, the US military's November 2004 assault on Fallujah intended to clear insurgents from the city, in which 60 per cent of the city's buildings were destroyed. In addition, as Tom Engelhardt has highlighted, the numerous daily air strikes conducted in Iraq (and Afghanistan) by the United States have remained all but absent from media coverage.[24] The latter constitutes a reversal of the focus accorded to the spectacular use of air power in the Shock and Awe assault on the country (and the aerial assault on Afghanistan). In part this can be explained in terms of these operations lacking the lustre of imminent victory associated with the Shock and Awe assault – rather, they have provided a means of keeping at bay an enemy that should already have been defeated.

This condition of invisibility carries over into the movements and processes of travelling undertaken by insurgents as they have crossed into Iraq.[25] Foreign fighters have been estimated as making up 10 per cent of the overall numbers of insurgents, a figure that at first glance might appear quite low, until one considers the high proportion of members of Al Qaeda in Iraq who come from outside the country. Indeed, the group was headed by the Jordanian Abu Musab al-Zarqawi until his death in June 2006, when he was replaced by the Egyptian Abu-Hamzah al-Muhajir. At the same time a significant proportion of those who have carried out suicide bombings in Iraq have been identified as arriving from Saudi Arabia (Cockburn 2005: 48). In part, as Danner (2006: 95) suggests, these processes of travelling reflect the failure of Coalition forces to provide enough troops to guard Iraq's borders – which have since the invasion never been secured. More broadly though, this sense of mobility can be situated as symptomatic of the status of the enemy more broadly in the War on Terror – as evident in the September 11 attacks; the growing presence of foreign fighters among the ranks of the Taliban in Afghanistan[26]; the movement between the UK and Pakistan of those responsible for the 7 July 2005 attacks on London; and the broader presence of individuals in Europe and North America who have attended training camps in Afghanistan and Pakistan.[27] These patterns of movement attest to the way in which, as Renata Salecl (2004: 11) suggests, in an era of globalisation 'the enemy' has come to take 'the form of a wandering terrorist'.

The convergence of fighters upon Iraq has contributed to the transformation of the country into a key theatre in the War on Terror. Not only have groups claiming affiliation with Al Qaeda emerged in Iraq (where previously their presence was negligible), but for periods of time at least these groups have taken control of portions of the country – most noticeably in the vast western province of Anbar. In so doing the United States has been drawn into precisely the type of large-scale counter-insurgency campaign that, since the Vietnam War, it has sought to avoid. Indeed, the sense in which the continuing presence of the US military in Iraq has played into the hands of the enemy is evident in the May 2007 declaration from Al Zawahiri that the US has been caught in an 'historic trap', with Zawahiri urging the United States to remain in Iraq until 200,000–300,000 US personnel had been killed.[28]

One of the Bush administration's responses to the establishment of Iraq as a new theatre in the War on Terror has been to attempt to blame this development upon Al Qaeda. As President Bush declared towards the end of 2006:

Success in Iraq is vital for our own security. If we were not to succeed in Iraq the enemy, the extremists, the radicals would have safe haven from which to launch further attacks. They would be emboldened, they would be in a position to threaten the United States of America. This is an important part of the War on Terror'.[29]

While it may now be true that Iraq has come to constitute a type of haven for Al Qaeda – with the withdrawal of Coalition forces from Iraq allowing Al Qaeda to continue to utilise the country in this fashion – this contention serves to overlook the obvious fact that without the invasion no such haven would have existed. Indeed, a similar logic has provided the basis for a series of further, equally contestable claims. The presence of Al Qaeda in Iraq has allowed the Bush administration to in turn blame Al Qaeda for the violent chaos the country has descended into, with Bush declaring in November of the same year, 'There's a lot of sectarian violence taking place, fomented, in my opinion, because of these attacks by al-Qaida, causing people to seek reprisals'.[30] At the same time it has been argued that the invasion and occupation have served to draw supporters of Al Qaeda to Iraq in place of their targeting the United States. As Scott McClellan, the White House Press Secretary, has asserted, 'That's why we're fighting them in Iraq, and we're not fighting them here at home. We're fighting them in Iraq so that we can defeat them abroad, so we don't have to fight them here at home.'[31] This contention serves in one respect to overlook the fact that to an overwhelming extent it is far easier for supporters of Al Qaeda to travel to Iraq (with its porous borders and lack of administrative infrastructure) than to the United States. At the same time it serves to occlude the terms in which the occupation has increased support for Al Qaeda in neighbouring countries (and beyond). What this argument does serve to reveal though is the persistence of the phantasy of being able to draw the enemy into a definite territory where it can be located and destroyed – that has, as noted above, been identified as contributing to the invasion of Iraq in the first instance.

It is not only the case that Iraq has become a magnet and breeding ground for insurgents though. As the duration of the occupation has worn on, so Iraq has begun 'to export fighters and the tactics they have honed in the insurgency to neighbouring countries and beyond'.[32] This is evident in the case of the bomb-maker and co-ordinator of a planned suicide attack on Queen Alia airport in Amman, Jordan, Youssef al-Abidi, who was able to move freely from Iraq to Syria and Jordan, crossing national boundaries, that officials concede they cannot control'. Similarly, the summer of 2007 saw the Lebanese army engaged in a major operation against the Fatah al Islam group – believed to include around 50 veterans from Iraq – holed up in a refugee camp near Tripoli. At the same time it is not only personnel who have come to participate in these processes of travelling. Iraq has also become 'a laboratory for urban guerilla tactics' (more so than Afghanistan, where urban fighting has been much more limited), and an exporter of instructional material (including videos and newsletters) as evident as far apart as Somalia, Algeria, Afghanistan, and the United Kingdom.[33] In the latter instance, techniques developed in Iraq are purported to have been used in the failed car bomb attacks on London in June 2007. These intended attacks, along with those that occurred days later at Glasgow airport, also bear witness to the movement of personnel from Iraq, with Bilal Abdullah, identified as the instigator of both attacks, qualifying as a medical doctor in Baghdad in 2004, before registering as a doctor in the UK.[34]

The Green Zone, Crusader fortresses, imperial decline ...?

With the exception of the northern Kurdish dominated part of Iraq, since the invasion of the country, the limits of the Coalition forces and Iraqi government's stable control have been limited largely to 'the Green Zone' – the seven square miles of central Baghdad in which the Iraqi government and Coalition agencies are based. Yet even this portion of the capital has never been completely secured – as evinced in the attack in April 2007 on the Iraqi parliament that killed one of its members, and with the infiltration of Iraqi security services having resulted in a situation in which, as one observer noted in June 2007, 'no one walks anywhere in the Green Zone for fear of being snatched off the street'.[35]

Writing in the spring of 2005 Robert Fisk compared the Green Zone to a Crusader fortress from which the occupying forces attempt to look out from a position of protection upon a territory they purport to control, but which remains profoundly unstable[36] – with these fortresses turning into prisons for those who inhabit them, much as the Green Zone has been spoken of as becoming, 'walled off, literally and psychologically, from the rest of Iraq'.[37] Indeed, as Mary Kaldor (2004: 29) has asserted, 'people in the Green Zone do not have much of a clue about what is happening in the Red Zone [the rest of Iraq]' (ibid.: 28).[38] In discussing future US strategy in Iraq, Engelhardt has drawn attention to the plan for US forces to withdraw to a series of 'super-bases', including the vast new US embassy in Baghdad.[39] Engelhardt identifies such bases – which more clearly still bare comparison with Crusader fortresses – as providing a model for policing and garrisoning the United States' model of empire (with such bases long established in Germany, South Korea, and Japan). And indeed, in a speech in August 2007, George Bush compared the withdrawal of US troops from Iraq 'too soon' as leaving the country to the same fate as Vietnam in 1975, contrasting the latter with the 'successes' of South Korea and Japan – where the US has maintained its bases.[40]

Such discussions invoke the question of the position the invasion and occupation of Iraq has come to assume in the trajectory of US power and the progress of the War on Terror – with numerous commentators identifying Iraq as precipitating a commencement of a decline in US power.[41] These assertions have been contested, with the Retort collective (2006: 89), in counselling against such interpretations, locating Iraq as part of the 'ordinary (unforgivable) chaos of imperialism'. And yet what the situation in Iraq has served to throw into stark relief is the limits of a specific aspect of US power – its military variant – that might be said to constitute the 'ultimate' Real basis of US supremacy. Badiou (2004: 228) in his comments on the invasion of Iraq invokes the 'absolute ... military superiority' of US military power, and the desire to maintain this unparalleled supremacy prevalent among US politicians (both Democrats and Republicans). And while this may for the present appear true – at the least at the level of technological sophistication[42] – Iraq has served to demonstrate the limitations of this form of power. While in Iraq the US has possessed vast supremacy in firepower and total air dominance, the US military has still found itself embroiled in a counter-insurgency campaign that it appears it cannot win. While a surge in troop numbers in the summer of 2007 might have done something to reduce the scale of violence in the country, without a resolution of the political stalemate in Iraq the prospect of an end to sectarian and anti-Coalition violence remains limited.[43] Indeed, the situation in Iraq is widely regarded as having left the US military severely overstretched, with this troop surge itself constrained by a lack of available personnel, and with insufficient troops available to serve elsewhere – including in Afghanistan. As former Chairman of the Joint Chiefs of Staff and

Secretary of State Colin Powell declared in December 2006, 'the active army is about broken'.[44]

As such, the terms in which Immanuel Wallerstein (2006) locates the invasion and occupation of Iraq within the period of 'accelerating decline' in US power he surveys as running from 2001–25, acquires greater clarity. Militarily the United States has now reached its limit point, with the country unable to engage in a significant intervention elsewhere around the globe. (At the same point it has become clear that a nuclear capability ensures a country can remain beyond the reach of the US military – an issue that lies at the heart of the simmering tension over Iran's nuclear programme.)

To return then to the Shock and Awe assault that marked the commencement of the invasion, the question might again be raised of who precisely it was that was overwhelmed by the spectacle generated by it – the Iraqi populace, or the Bush administration itself?

5
Hostage Videos: 'scenes of slaughter'

The footage is grainy and the colours are bled half-dry. It shows a man's head face on and in close-up. He's blindfolded and his mouth is covered by tape. The sounds are uncertain and it's difficult to make out where they're coming from or what they mean. It's not clear what's about to happen, but a sense of menace hangs over the scene that makes you wonder whether you should be watching it at all.

Zawahiri's letter

As Badiou (2004: 230) suggests, 'nondemonstration' – not allowing publics to witness certain aspects of a conflict – has come to figure as integral to the terms in which wars are waged. In light of the absence of depictions of casualties, and particularly of Western casualties in Iraq and the War on Terror more broadly, videos of Western hostages held captive and pleading for their release – that culminate in the most infamous cases in these hostages being beheaded – have acquired a particular notoriety: as reflected in the media attention accorded to this footage. Indeed, in regard to questions of the visibility of post-invasion Iraq, these videos have constituted a particular point of focus for Western audiences. At the same time though, as I will be exploring in the second half of this chapter, these videos have served to raise significant questions about the condition of contemporary politics in the West, and the relationship of publics to the War on Terror.

While the majority of videos of Western hostages seized since the September 11 attacks have emanated from Iraq,[1] videos of Western hostages captured in Pakistan (in the case of the execution of the US journalist Daniel Pearl in Karachi in February 2002), Afghanistan, Saudi Arabia, and Gaza have also appeared in this period.[2] In the case of Iraq the appearance of these videos focused upon a particular period – the spring of 2004 to the latter half of 2005 – with the reduction in these videos having been linked to a letter from Al Zawahiri to Al Zarqawi, warning that footage showing the execution of Western hostages risked alienating potential sympathisers from across the Muslim world.[3]

While it would be an oversimplification to identify this letter by itself resulting in a decline in the number of Western hostages – with the reduction in foreign workers in Iraq, in part due to the fear aroused by the numbers kidnapped, contributing to this. Zawahiri's letter is at the same time revealing in the attitude it displays to the content of these videos. (Indeed, the withdrawal of foreign contractors and non-governmental groups from Iraq has been identified as a key objective of these videos.[4]) In a section of the letter titled 'Scenes of slaughter', Zawahiri argues that what 'the Muslim populace will never find palatable ... are the scenes of slaughtering the hostages'. While Zawahiri identifies the killing of hostages as a justified response to the death and destruction wrought by the United States and its allies in Iraq (and more broadly in the War on Terror), he points to the sense in which the audience's response to these videos has been shaped by 'the malicious, perfidious, and fallacious campaign by the deceptive and fabricated media'.[5] And he adds that by bringing an end to the dissemination of these videos 'we would spare the people from the effect of questions about the usefulness of our actions in the hearts and minds of the general opinion that is essentially sympathetic to us'.

In seeking to bring a halt to the distribution of these videos, Zawahiri's letter suggests a divergence in strategy between the hostage takers (including the Tawid and Jihad group, that came to form the nucleus of Al Qaeda in Iraq, and which was responsible for a number of the most infamous hostage executions) and the 'formal' or 'core' Al Qaeda hierarchy. While the hostage takers might appear little concerned about cultivating a 'positive' media profile, for the Al Qaeda hierarchy the development of a profile intended to enhance its support among Muslims around the globe has figured as a key dimension of its broader strategy.[6] Indeed, as a commentary on Bin Laden's September 2007 video appearance highlights, Bin Laden, 'has always shown a keen interest in the global media', having, from 1996–2001, made himself available to Western journalists, and having used his video appearances to seek to sway Western public opinion – in, for example, urging the US public to embrace Islam and to bring a halt to the occupation of Iraq.[7] Such an approach is contrasted with 'the more psychopathic adherents of al-Qaeda' and the disregard they have displayed for public opinion. Indeed, in the context of post-invasion Iraq, cultivating a 'positive' media profile can be seen of little practical value to the insurgents in their struggle against the Coalition forces, with, by the time of the appearance of these videos, the brutal reality of the insurgency already apparent on a day-to-day basis.[8] Instead, the suffering and violence on display in these videos can be understood as serving to demonstrate the commitment of the insurgents to their struggle against the Coalition forces. (At the same time it might be argued that the impact registered by these videos in the West has been enhanced by the very disregard they display for the desire to cultivate just such a positive media profile.)

At one level the appearance of these videos might appear relatively straightforward – with the hostage takers presenting a series of demands for the release of the hostages – focused upon the freeing of prisoners held in Iraq and the withdrawal of foreign troops from the country. At times certain of these demands have been met. In July 2004 the Philippines government agreed to withdraw their troops from Iraq in return for the release of Angelo de la Cruz. Furthermore, the financial gains to be made from seizing hostages has become apparent, with the French, German, Italian, and Canadian governments all rumoured to have struck deals for the release of their nationals.[9] It can be argued that in serving to increase the pressure upon Western governments, and in rendering visible what will happen to the hostages if their captors' demands are not met, these videos have assumed an important role in this logic of exchange. And yet the impact these videos have registered around the world and the position they have come to assume in the War on Terror extends far beyond this.

In their gaze ...

Western publics have rarely encountered depictions of the enemy's gaze while a conflict is taking place.[10] While in the Vietnam War – the first conflict in which media coverage can be said to have played a critical role (in both senses of the term) – certain images, such as Mai Nam's 1966 photograph of an United States F-105 pilot ejecting after his plane had been hit, did achieve a profile in the West, Western publics were confronted with comparatively few images of the conflict as seen from a North Vietnamese standpoint. Instead, deliberate efforts have been made to foreclose the awareness of the enemy's gaze, in acknowledgement both of the fears its recognition might generate – fears of a nature that will be elaborated on in a moment – and its possible value as an instrument of propaganda. In the invasion and occupation of Iraq (as in other conflicts) Western publics have had the greatest chance of encountering the enemy's gaze if it depicts the enemy as victim (just as it is as victim that Western publics are most likely to encounter representations of the enemy). In both the 1991 Gulf War and the Iraq War, for example, images of these conflicts seen from an Iraqi perspective were largely restricted to brief excerpts of Saddam Hussein and his ministers (taken from Iraqi television) – the exception being footage of Iraqis lying wounded and dying in hospitals and medical centres, of which repeated excerpts were shown (often gleaned from Iraqi television).

Where these hostage videos differ is in serving to locate the enemy as aggressor.[11] This footage establishes not only that this enemy does indeed possess a gaze – and as such serves to confirm the awareness of the existence of the enemy, in the sense that as Sartre (1957: 256) contends, 'my fundamental connection with the Other-as-subject must be able to be referred back to my permanent possibility of being seen by the Other' – but that what this enemy sees (what appears in its field of vision) makes clear its ability to capture and kill its opponents. In so doing these videos reach beyond the broad anxieties associated with an awareness of the Other's gaze – as adumbrated in Chapter 3 – to something more specific and terrifying. Joan Copjec's (2002: 189) analysis of Lacan's conception of the gaze, in regard to the terms in which the shape or structure of the field of vision resembles a 'torus', is suggestive in regard to this issue – 'If the space of the painting is not flat, it is because it is shaped, rather, like a torus or an envelope that folds the eye of the observer back in the field it observes' – an analysis that serves to emphasise the sense in which these videos threaten to drag the spectator into the scene they witness. Indeed, the spectator who encounters these videos can be located in a similar position to that which Sartre (1957: 259–60) identifies with the voyeur at the moment they realise that they themselves might be being watched – the realisation, Miran Bozovic (1997: 170) delineates in a discussion of Hitchcock's *Rear Window* (1954), that 'What I have been doing to other people they can do to me – as a voyeur I myself can be seen.'

In the context of the enemy having 'infiltrated' and come to 'exist within' Western societies – as evident in, for example, the September 11 attacks and the subsequent strikes on Madrid (March 2004) and London (July 2005) – these fears have moved from the realm of the abstract to taking on a locatable reality. These attacks have served to foreground the awareness that the enemy's gaze can indeed be trained upon the spectator, 'Right here, where they are', provoking the realisation that the suffering Western audiences witnesses in these videos could come to be inflicted upon them as they go about their everyday lives.

'Scenes of slaughter'

The hostages that appear in these videos have come to constitute a source of fascination, a lure, or trap for the gaze of audiences in the West, as manifest in the media coverage accorded to these videos, as well as the myriad of websites that have played host to them.

In October 2004 the BBC asked users of its news site for their reasons for watching these videos.[12] Prominent among the responses was the contention these videos provided a means of 'better understanding' what was taking place in Iraq. As one respondent (Edward Hammerbeck) asserted, 'Sure, they say on the news that twelve were killed here, five were killed there, but as they say, a picture is worth a thousand words.' Such an attitude echoes a long running belief in the capacity of the visual to take one closer to the reality of conflict than the written word. As the photographer of the US Civil War, Alex Gardner declared in his 1866 *Photographic Sketchbook of the War* (the Civil War was one of the first conflicts to be photographed): 'verbal representations' of places and events 'may or may not have the merit of accuracy; but photographic presentations of them will be accepted by posterity with an undoubting faith' (quoted in Huppauf 1995: 97). This distrust in the Symbolic can also be read in a comment, quoted in the BBC report, from Douglas Hagmann, the director of the *Northeast Intelligence Network*, whose website has provided access to the hostage videos:

> The American people need to know the tactics of our enemy ... All too frequently, we hear the mainstream news talk about a hostage being 'beheaded' by 'militants', 'insurgents' or other innocuous sounding descriptive terms ... These are acts of pure evil and savagery that must not be minimised by such references in the press.[13]

Evident across these contentions is a valorisation of the Imaginary as a source of knowledge over and above the Symbolic (that Lacan seeks to reverse in his prioritising Symbolic over Imaginary knowledge), that, as surveyed in the previous chapter, attests to the significance accorded to questions of visuality in understanding what is happening in Iraq and the War on Terror more broadly. And yet beyond the claim that the desire to watch these videos emanates from the aim of better understanding what is happening in Iraq can be located another, further desire. In the context of the relative absence of Western casualties in media coverage of the War on Terror, these videos offer the opportunity to see death, in a culture in which – while fictive depictions of death proliferate (in cinema, photography, and film), pointing to the desire to witness death – real deaths are rarely seen.

At the same time, the desire to watch these videos can be located in terms of the attempt to make sense of the position Western publics have come to assume in the War on Terror. Since the September 11 attacks these publics have repeatedly been reminded of the vulnerability of their position in this conflict, via the further attacks that have taken place, but also through repeated warnings about the prospect – and 'inevitability'[14] – of forthcoming attacks (explored in greater detail in the following chapter). At the same time though these publics have been presented with comparatively few figures with which to identify with in this position of vulnerability. The casualties of those attacks that have occurred in the West constitute one such type of figure – and yet, such is the Western media's injunction against showing Western casualties, the instances in which they are seen are comparatively rare. At the same time, in temporal terms, these casualties assume their significance in regard to an event that has already occurred – rather than, as in the case of the hostages (with the exception of the footage showing their execution), those who await their fate. In so doing the hostage videos accord with the position occupied by Western publics as they await the prospect of a forthcoming attack, providing, albeit in dramatically condensed form, a version of Western publics' own experience of waiting in the War on Terror (the subject of the next chapter).

The sense in which the hostages function as figures of identification is enhanced by these videos' mise en scène. The hostage typically appears alone in these videos, facing the camera and in close-up, encouraging the spectator to identify with them as a discrete individual – with the face the supreme marker (in Western culture at least) of individuality, and with the close-up, in the words of Jacques Aumont (1997: 103), bringing 'the spectator to extreme psychic proximity or intimacy' with the filmed. (Such aspects of this mise en scène have typically been absent in coverage of the September 11, London, and Madrid attacks.) Indeed, these videos can be understood as working with an awareness of the capacity of the camera to permit the spectator both to encounter aspects of the world that would not otherwise possible and to see in a level of detail often denied to a live observer. In so doing, as Susan Sontag (2002: 168–9) asserts in regard to the depiction of suffering, these acts are rendered more terrible at a visual level than they would otherwise appear to a spectator who might never encounter them at first hand.

And yet if the hostages that appear in these videos can be located as presenting significant figures of identification, such a status is rooted in the terms in which the position they occupy accords with the position of vulnerability Western publics have come to assume in the War on Terror – with the most notorious and widely disseminated of these videos culminating in the hostage's death by decapitation. As Elaine Scarry documents in *The Body in Pain* (1985: 63–81), while typically elided in writing on the theory and practice of war, the body constitutes the ultimate target and last-line of violent conflict, comprising the point which the enemy's actions are finally directed towards and which either side seeks to defend against the other.[15] Indeed, the body in its raw physicality, its status as flesh, muscle and bone, tissue and interior, can be said to constitute the most intimate realm of the hard Real, precisely the realm these videos depict destroyed in such brutal fashion. Indeed, at first glance these videos might appear to accord with Philip Brophy's (1986: 8) analysis of 'Slasher' films and realist Horror from the early 1980s – and the argument that these films play not so much upon the audiences' fear of death, as anxieties around, 'the destruction of the Body'. While the two cannot be simply separated, with death underpinning the anxieties associated with the destruction of the body, Brophy's analysis points towards a significant issue: that of death's visibility and the terms in which it might be seen, of how a process that occurs at the Real can be represented in visual terms, and the sense that, as Vivian Sobchak (1984: 287) asserts, 'death confounds all codes ... we do not see death on the screen'.

Indeed, the emphasis placed in these videos upon the spectacular destruction of the body can be understood as stemming from the desire to overcome or work around the problem of depicting death at a visual level, and to do so in terms that will prove profoundly shocking to the spectator – through recourse to an act of violence similar to that repeatedly employed in fictive cinema with the precise intention, Sobchak (ibid.: 287–9) asserts, of making death visible. In so doing these videos can be understood as attempting to displace death from the Real, where it cannot be seen, to the Imaginary, where it might be. Indeed such is the brutality of what is shown in these videos that the viewer can be said to be taken as 'close' to the hard Real of the body and its destruction as is possible via the Imaginary – as close to an encounter with the Real that Lacan (1994: 53) designates 'the tuché', that underpins the sense of shock experienced by viewers of these videos.

Abu Ghraib, the Real is not enough, the fake

In their concern to create a spectacle of suffering and death these videos find a mirror in the scenes of US service personnel torturing and humiliating prisoners detained at Abu Ghraib, that appeared in May 2004[16] (which has given rise to a repeated questioning about how to make sense of this material).

In similar terms to the hostage videos, this baroque body of images of torture and brutalisation can be positioned as reflecting the desire to create a spectacle of humiliation, degradation, and pain that derives from the attempt to depict psychological-emotional conditions that cannot be identified at a visual level with any degree of certainty.[17] For, as with death – and as Scarry (1985: 3–11) has asserted, as with physical pain – the ability to see with any certainty an individual's experience of these and other 'interior' states is highly problematic. (How do we see shame or love in another? How can we, with any degree of certainty, be sure when we see these states? Thousands of fictions and narratives touch upon or take as their focus precisely these questions.) As with the hostage videos and their attempt to make death visible, the multiple spectacles of torture and humiliation depicted in these images can be understood as deriving from the desire to make evident at the Imaginary that the victim has been subject to these degrees of humiliation and degradation – to leave whoever sees these images in no doubt that this has indeed been achieved.

Furthermore, both the hostage videos and the images from Abu Ghraib can be tied to the act of exhibitionism as it is conceived in psychoanalytic terms. At the kernel of the various psychoanalytic accounts of this act lies the subject's aggressive attempt to assert their power – and specifically their sexual power – in defiance of a sense of powerlessness (Lucas 1990). (And, it should be remembered that images of a sexual nature form a leitmotif of the Abu Ghraib material, with the affinities between this material and pornography having been repeatedly commented on – see, for example, Simpson (2006: 107)). The same desire and sense of inadequacy can be detected in both the hostage videos and Abu Ghraib images. Both emanate from groups who inhabit positions of relative powerlessness. For the hostage takers this stems from their being faced with the might of the US military. For the low-ranking US military personnel at Abu Ghraib this entailed being caught up in an occupation that had gone horribly wrong, with these images appearing against the backdrop of the rise of the insurgency in Iraq.[18] Indeed, the hostage videos and images from Abu Ghraib (and more broadly of detainees at Guantanamo Bay) can be located in dialogue with one another, with each seeking to present a spectacle of humiliation and degradation that exceeds the other. This is apparent at one level in the footage of hostages (such as Nic Berg, Paul Johnson, and Eugene Armstrong) dressed in orange jumpsuits similar to those worn by detainees at Guantanamo Bay.

In both instances as well though can be detected the sense that carrying out these acts themselves without photographing them, and without the images being disseminated is not enough, and that alongside this desire to make visible the Real is the sense that the Real by itself is 'insufficient' or of secondary importance (a basic trope of 'the postmodern'). As Sontag (2004) has suggested in regard to the Abu Ghraib images, only once these images have undergone this process of dissemination, and have acquired a profile at the level of the Imaginary, do they assume sufficient status to confirm the validity of the acts they depict. Such a logic takes us back to the original problematic underpinning the hostage videos: how to put on display at a visual level experiences (of pain and death) that cannot be seen. The unresolvable nature of this paradox is evident in the case of Benjamin Vanderford, a US citizen living in San Francisco, who in 2004 produced a fake execution video that found its way onto a number of Islamic militant websites, where it was taken as showing an actual execution.[19]

The Dead Christ, the crisis of democracy

This question of seeing death lies at the heart of Julia Kristeva's discussion in her study of depression and melancholia, *Black Sun* (1989), of Holbein's *The Dead Christ in the tomb* (1522) (Figure 5.1), a painting that as Jonathan Jones contends, 'has haunted European culture'[20] and has figured as a repeated focus for analyses of the visual depiction of pain and death.[21] As Kristeva (1989: 138) asserts, while death obsesses us and we hold a deep desire to witness it, seeing death remains highly problematic: 'death is not visible in Freud's unconscious. It is imprinted

Figure 5.1 Hans Holbein, *The body of the dead Christ in the tomb* (1521), Oil on wood, Offentliche Kunstsammlung, Basel

there, however ... by spacings, blanks, discontinuities, or destruction of representation.' As she argues, the power of Holbein's painting stems from it presenting such an uncompromising vision of the dead Christ that appears to bring us so close to seeing death.

Kristeva's analysis of Holbein's painting raises a number of issues around the depiction of suffering and death in the hostage videos and the position they have come to assume in the War on Terror. In delineating the responses generated by the painting Kristeva draws attention to a character's (Ippolit) comment from Dostoyevsky's *The Idiot* on seeing Holbein's work[22]:

> The people surrounding the dead man, none of whom is shown in the picture, must have been overwhelmed by a feeling of terrible anguish and dismay on that evening which had shattered all their hopes and almost all their beliefs in one fell blow.
>
> (ibid.: 109)

This response to Holbein's painting can, I want to suggest, be reconfigured to illuminate the position the hostage videos have come to assume in relation to the War on Terror.[23]

While certain governments have come to an agreement with the hostage takers for the release of their nationals, the UK and US governments have refused to negotiate with the hostage takers. This has given rise to a situation in which audiences have witnessed a sequence of videos showing the hostages pleading for their release that have culminated in a video showing, or news of, the hostage's execution. In such terms the videos showing US and UK citizens as hostages can be configured as symptomatic of the position publics in these countries (and to a lesser extent elsewhere in the West) have come to assume in the War on Terror. While in the case of Holbein's painting it is the question of religious belief that is thrown into doubt by this work, it is the realm of the political that the hostage videos cast their shadow over – in serving to make visible the inability of publics in the UK and US to alter not only the hostages' predicament, but at the same time their own position in the War on Terror and the course this conflict has taken.

The invasion and occupation of Iraq has been identified as providing a particular focus for this sense of impotence. Tariq Ali (2005) reads the Blair government's decision to go to war with Iraq as symptomatic of a broader crisis in democracy in the United Kingdom, as evident in the contrast between the scale of the opposition to the invasion – with the war producing 'Britain's biggest demonstration against anything ever'[24] – and a level of electoral support for the Blair government that was the lowest for any government in the European Union (with 22 per cent of the electorate voting for Labour at the 2005 general election (ibid.: 16)).[25] In the United States, despite mounting opposition to the invasion and the presence of US troops in Iraq,[26] the US public has been presented with little means of altering or halting the occupation. As Alexander Cockburn (2007) emphasises, despite controlling Congress since November 2006, the Democratic Party has consistently refused to act to limit the Bush administration's actions in Iraq, resulting, as Cockburn contends, in a situation in which 'the war in Iraq' has become 'a bipartisan enterprise' (ibid.: 33). Underpinning the attention accorded to the lack of public support for the invasion of Iraq can be traced the sense that there is something particularly traumatic about democracies asking their citizens to die in wars which are not supported by the public. (Vietnam – with which Iraq has repeatedly been compared – again constitutes a key reference point here.) Not only then has Iraq assumed the status of the Thing in relation to the violence that has engulfed the country, at the same time, the situation in Iraq and the presence of Coalition forces there has taken on the dimensions of the unreachable Thing, in it occupying a position beyond the capacity of Western publics to influence or alter.

While Iraq might have provided a particular focus for a questioning of the condition of politics in the West, the case of Iraq reflects a broader diagnoses of the state of contemporary politics, and the sense in which a pervasive process of depoliticisation in Western societies has given rise to a condition of 'post-politics'.[27] In *Black Sun* Kristeva (1989: 33–68) stresses the sense in which depression typically entails the subject's loss of belief in the signifying capacity of language, that in turn leads to a curtailing of the desire to speak. A process akin to this can be identified as having occurred in Western democracies, as evident most literally in low rates of voter turnout (with voting constituting a, or the, principle act of democratic enunciation). The latter has been accompanied by what Peter Mair (2006: 25) identifies as a broader 'hollowing of western democracy', as evinced in the decline in membership of political parties and unions, falling levels of political activism, and at an ideological level, the rise of a managerialist 'non' or 'anti-politics'. Taken together these developments suggest a retreat from and loss of faith in the political, underpinned by doubts about the value of politics as a means of engaging with the world. (At one level such an outlook is reinforced by those politicians who declare that there is no other choice than to comply with the logic of neo-liberalism and the economics of globalisation).

In such terms Western societies have become afflicted by what I want to call a condition of 'political depression'. In the context of the War on Terror this serves to encourage the belief that nothing can be done to alter the course this conflict has taken, or the position publics have come to assume within this conflict.

Indeed, it can be argued that even those movements that have emerged in opposition to the invasion and occupation of Iraq indicate a decline in the political vigour of Western societies. As Cockburn discusses in regard to the United States, the anti-war movement has lacked the scope and vigour of previous movements, most obviously that against the Vietnam War but also that opposing the Reagan administration's interventions in Central America. And in the UK, while initial demonstrations against the war were on an unprecedented scale – with between 750,000 and two million people gathering in London in February 2003 – the movement has lacked durability, with, by 2005, organisers struggling to attract 10,000 protestors.[28]

Doubts about the condition and conception of politics in the West can at the same time be traced in the attempt to 'export' democracy around the globe, that up until the failure to effectively implement democracy in Iraq was identified as a significant corollary of the War on Terror. The attempt to introduce multi-party democracy in Afghanistan and Iraq has failed to bring stability to either country – with in both cases questions raised about the validity of the elections that have occurred.[29] Furthermore, the promotion of democracy by the United States and its allies has come to be associated with a duplicity of motives – as foregrounded in the January 2006 election of Hamas to the Palestinian government and the subsequent refusal of Western governments to accept Hamas' legitimacy – with, it seems, only those governments that conform to the West's desire for the type of regimes it wants to see achieving recognition. Indeed, the version of democracy promoted by the Bush administration and its allies has appeared to take the form of 'The right to chose to be like us ...'. At the same time, other regimes – such as Pervez Musharraf's in Pakistan, that in 1999 came to power in a coup against a democratically elected government – have assumed the status of key allies in the War on Terror. In another respect, the existence of Guantanamo Bay, the practice of 'extraordinary rendition', and the use of torture have served to raise recurring doubts about the values purportedly embodied by the version of liberal democracy promoted by the Bush administration (as discussed in greater detail in Chapter 8). Of still broader significance though is the contribution such developments have made to the sense in which democracy as a political system in general has come to be regarded as little more than a means by which the West seeks to impose its will on others.[30]

To return to Holbein's painting, this is a work that is directly concerned with the religious (rather than the political). As such, in the context of this discussion, it functions as a reminder of the way in which religion has been foregrounded by both sides (Al Qaeda and the Bush administration) as a guiding principal of the War on Terror. This process can itself be located in the broader context of the way in which religion has come to figure as an increasingly significant referent for politics in general in the West. This has most obviously been the case in the United States, but it is apparent in Western Europe as well – as evinced at one level in the multiple controversies around the construction of mosques and minarets, themselves fuelled by the very anxieties foregrounded by the War on Terror.[31] And yet Holbein's painting, in the challenge to belief it has been conceived as presenting, has served to cast doubt on the capacity of religion to offer any more positive vision of the world than that presented by politics. Indeed, such a sense of despair or loss of hope in the religious can be understood as enhanced by the purposes religion has been utilised for by both sides in the War on Terror.[32]

Goya, 'We cannot look at this'

Despite the sense of Holbein's painting providing a vision of Christ in a state of isolation and decay, the figure depicted in Holbein's work is still a body that is intended to be venerated, and as such it differs markedly from the bodies of the hostages. Indeed, in these terms the hostage videos come closer to another key depiction of the suffering body in Western art – that presented by Francisco Goya in his later sketches and prints, including *The Disasters of War* (1810–20) series, produced in response to another experience of occupation – that of Spain during the Napoleonic wars.

The sense in which Goya's depiction of the body in this late work challenges the conception of the idealised, classical body, and the template it has offered for the way the body 'should' appear in Western art is evident in etching 37 of *The Disasters of War*, titled 'This is worse' (c. 1812–15). This portrays a mutilated figure, based as Victor Stoichita and Anna Marie Coderch (1999: 95) suggest in their study of Goya's later works, on *The Belvedere Torso*, but with its anus pierced on the branch of a tree. In so doing Goya is positioned as offering a vision of the classical body subject to what Stoichita and Coderch term 'a rhetoric of degradation and denigration' (ibid.: 95). It is this version of the body that is encountered in the hostage videos – most graphically in those showing the hostage's execution. Indeed, these videos present a depiction of the body so far removed from the template of the classical body, that they serve to reinforce the sense – as Scarry (1999: 279–80) suggests in tracing the ties between bodily security and the social contract – that

Figure 5.2 Francisco Goya, 'We cannot look at this' (1814–24) Drawing C101, *Sketchbook Journal*, 1814–24, India ink wash on paper, Museo del Prado, Madrid

the body exposed to harm constitutes a failure of the social contract as the guarantor of 'bodily inviolability' (ibid.: 279). (This is an assessment echoed by Kristeva (1982: 102) in her contention, 'The body ... must be clean and proper in order to be fully symbolic', with its wounding constituting, 'the sign of belonging to the impure, the non-separate, the non-symbolic'.) Configured in such a way the hostages videos can be viewed as emblematic of the sense that the War on Terror has itself contributed to the threats faced by Western publics – as evinced in the links between the Madrid bombings and the presence of Spanish forces in Iraq, and in the ties declared by Mohammed Siddique Khan (outlined in Chapter 3) between the 2005 attacks on London and the UK's role in the invasion and occupation of the country.

In his *Sketchbook-Journal* (1814–24) Goya offers another image titled, 'We cannot look at this' (Figure 5.2) that depicts the figure of an old man bound and hanging upside down from an instrument of torture. As Stoichita and Coderch suggest in commenting on this sketch, 'the unbearable nature of the image is heightened by the fact that the torture victim ... is still imploring the heavens. But ... finds no salvation' (1999: 90) – a position that echoes that which the hostages find themselves in as they plead for assistance from their governments and yet receive none. And yet the title of Goya's work is doubly suggestive. In one sense it points towards the terms in which the pain experienced by this figure remains invisible at the Imaginary. In another (the meaning probably intended by Goya) it alludes to the difficulties encountered by the spectator in looking at such a scene, and the inability to intervene in or alter what is seen it conjures up. This sense of passivity constitutes a central concern of the next chapter, in terms of the position Western publics have found themselves in as they await the prospect of a forthcoming attack – while seemingly little able to alter the position of vulnerability they have come to assume in this conflict.

6
Endless Waiting

In June 2007 video footage purportedly shot that month appeared in the world's media showing a graduation ceremony for would-be suicide bombers, presided over by the Taliban's military commander Mansoor Dadullah, on the border of Pakistan–Afghanistan. The graduates had purportedly come from around the globe to attend the training camp and were to return to their countries – which included the US, the UK, Germany, and Canada – to carry out their missions. (The footage included excerpts of graduates speaking in the languages of the countries they had supposedly arrived from about their planned operations.)[1]

The aspect of this footage of principal concern to this chapter is the sense in which it sets in motion a process of waiting, in regard to Western publics waiting to see if these bombers would 'successfully' carry out their missions. Indeed, the initiating of precisely such a process of waiting and the anxiety it generates can be understood as the purpose lying behind the release of this footage in the first place. In so doing this footage serves to foreground the relationship between waiting and questions of seeing. While this footage initiated a process of waiting, the disappearance of the would-be suicide bombers out of sight, and their ability to inhabit the realm of the unseen, is vital if they are to remain uncaptured and to travel to their target destinations to carry out their missions. In turn the 'success' of these missions will result in their presence being rendered visible again – in the form of the spectacle of the attacks they have carried out.

This graduation ceremony presents just one instance though of the terms in which waiting has come to figure as a key dynamic in the War on Terror. Zulaika and Douglass (1996: 26–30) have noted how 'Waiting for Terror' has constituted 'the most typical mode of terrorism discourse in the United States'. And yet beyond Zulaika and Douglass's brief analysis there has been little assessment of how waiting figures as an experience of conflicts, let alone of how waiting has constituted a feature of the War on Terror. These absences mirror the fact that waiting as a process in general has been the subject of scant scholarly attention, reflecting the sense in which, as Terry Eagleton (2006: 72–3) asks in interrogating the political in Samuel Beckett's work: 'Is waiting doing something, or the suspension of it?'. As Zulaika and Douglass's analysis suggests, experiences of waiting in conflict situations have not been confined to the War on Terror. In the case of the Cold War, for example, awaiting the prospect of a nuclear confrontation between the superpowers and their allies constituted a focal point of the experience of this conflict for publics around the globe. And yet, as suggested in the Introduction, where the experience of waiting in the War on Terror differs from the latter is in regard to the degree of uncertainty that has pervaded this process – as outlined in a moment.

The concern of this chapter is with the form waiting has come to take for Western publics in the War on Terror – in regard above all to the experience of awaiting a forthcoming attack – and what this process serves to reveal about the terms in which conflict has been fought, and the position Western publics have come to assume within it.

Waiting, Horror

Waiting can be located as constituting a pivotal dynamic in narratives of Horror, in regard to both the internal dynamics of these narratives but also the spectator-reader's experience of their unfolding. Crucial to the majority of Horror narratives is a two stage process: of waiting for the horror or the source of the horror to appear, followed by waiting for this horror to be expunged or dealt with, with the first of these stages serving to create a sense of imminent or impending threat on which the tension or suspense of the narrative is founded. In so doing these narratives serve to foreground the capacity of waiting to constitute a source of anxiety – a feature associated more broadly with waiting, as emphasised by Barthes ([1977] 1990) in his commentary on waiting in a somewhat different context – the anxious wait for a lover's arrival.

Since the September 11 attacks the subjecting of Western publics to a process of awaiting a forthcoming attack has constituted one of the principal means through which Al Qaeda has waged war on the United States and its allies (as evident in the graduation ceremony footage). And yet, the deployment of this 'weaponry' has not been entirely intentional. Rather, it has emerged as a corollary of the series of 'successful', as well as planned, failed, and foiled attacks carried out by Al Qaeda since 11 September 2001 (and prior to this date). While the attacks that have occurred during this period have constituted the clearest reminders of the enemy's ability to strike at Western societies, those attacks which were intended to take place but did not occur have served to add to the sense of threat the enemy is perceived as presenting to the United States and its allies.[2] As was noted in the wake of the arrests on 10 August 2006 in the UK of suspects linked to a plot to blow up a series of passenger aircraft:

> Even when their operations are thwarted as they were last week, they achieve a kind of victory in defeat, because we allow our imaginations to colour in the empty spaces of what might have been. We know what might have been, because variations of it have already happened: in Nairobi, in New York, in Bali, in Madrid, in London, in Mumbai. And we know, too, that it will happen again, because we are warned continuously, even as we go about our daily business and try to forget.[3]

The anxieties invoked here around this process of waiting have been intensified by the uncertainties surrounding it, in regard to when the next attack will take place, where it will occur, the form it will take, and who (and how many people) will be harmed – variants on the fundamentals of the process of waiting identified by Maurice Blanchot (1995: 272) in his 1959 essay on waiting: 'What was he waiting for, why was he waiting, what is awaited in waiting?'. This sense of uncertainty can be located as emanating in part from the shifting, indeterminate ontological profile of the enemy in the War on Terror, and the way in which this enemy has been configured in reference to the ghostly. The experience of waiting constitutes a corollary to that of being haunted,[4] with the haunting undertaken by the enemy in the War on Terror at once serving to exploit and enhance the anxieties associated with the experience of awaiting an attack. And yet, while the form a future attack could take might be shrouded in uncertainty, the very anticipation of such an attack occurring can be understood as serving to heighten the sense of anxiety surrounding it. In discussing cinema, poetics, and terrorism, Sven Lutticken (2006: 95–6) notes how Hitchcock – in taking the example of a bomb on a bus – acknowledged the greater fear generated in audiences by suspense: knowing something is going to or might happen and therefore awaiting its occurrence, than surprise: in which the audience is given no sense of what is about to occur.

In a piece that appeared in the autumn of 2005, Jonathan Raban adumbrated the effects the experience of awaiting a forthcoming attack can inflict upon the individual subject, in a sketch that is worth quoting at some length for the detail in which it evokes this process of waiting:

> Waking from an unpleasant dream before 5 a.m., not by first light finding a crack in the drapes, for it's 15 minutes or so too early for that, the roused sleeper's hand moves on an instinctive tour of the bedside table. This is familiar terrain, even in thick darkness: the easily upsettable plastic bottles of pills – aspirin, diazepam, B-blockers, C-blockers, melatonin.
>
> The experienced hand knows every one, and slides stealthily between them. It weaves its way around the half-empty tumbler of grapefruit juice, and over the face-down paperback copy of The Last Chronicle of Barset until it reaches what it was searching for: the knurled volume knob of the elderly, tinny transistor radio whose broken antenna was long ago replaced with a wire coat hanger.
>
> [...] This is how mornings begin now, with the vague, routine apprehension of atrocity that almost never happens, but happens frequently enough to justify the hand's habitual excursion across the bedside table. Pacific Standard Time is partly to blame; the worst things tend to take place while the west coast is sleeping. Baghdad, Cairo, Rome, Madrid, London, have survived the conventional hours of atrocity by 5 a.m. PST; New York is about to enter them.
>
> Many dead in Baghdad, Judge Roberts, New Orleans ... The hand embarks on its return journey to the radio and the sleeper goes back to the difficult business of sleeping. No atrocity – at least none of the anticipated kind – today, so far. Hours later, he'll click on the BBC website at frequent intervals, to make sure that it (and he has a very indistinct notion of what it is) hasn't yet taken place. In daylight, he'll jeer at this behaviour as symptomatic of a neurosis he needs to take in hand, and a feckless excuse for goofing off from work. But he still does it, and dates these unhealthy habits back to September 11 2001 – four years' worth of broken sleep and lost threads in his professional life.
>
> [...] There's a certain perverse appetite that prompts the groping hand as it feels its way to the radio. As we get increasingly caught up in asymmetric warfare, one of whose central definitions is that it blurs the distinction between military and civilian to the point of non-existence, we may perhaps be beginning to acquire some of that

dangerous thirst for adrenaline that keeps soldiers being soldiers. A friend's brother – an American lieutenant colonel in the reserves, just back from a year's stint in Iraq – reports that some of the jolliest moments in the Green Zone occurred when the American embassy came under attack from rocket-propelled grenades. Office staff and soldiers would be sent sprawling, everyone turning white with falling debris from Saddam's palatial baroque stucco ceilings. Then would come the inevitable remark, spoken in a tone of enormous satisfaction, 'That was a big one!'

Big ones – when you survive them – feed the addiction that makes war tolerable, and, more than that, exciting, for the warriors. They keep the adrenaline running through the veins. So, as the disembodied hand snakes past the pill bottles, some truant synapse in the brain anticipates the rush only the baddest of bad news can bring. It is, one might say, just one more of those post-9/11 things, this insidious and corrupting mental adjustment, this disconnect between mind and motor response, this guilty, secret hunger for catastrophe.[5]

Beyond acknowledging the resonance of Raban's evocation of the experience of waiting in the midst of the War on Terror, two particular aspects of Raban's commentary are worth drawing further attention to. Firstly, Raban highlights the sense in which this process of waiting can constitute a process of becoming, of how this process is transformative, how it holds the capacity to reposition and remake the individual subject as the 'waiting subject' whose life is lived in anticipation of a potentially catastrophic future event. In such terms the waiting subject comes to occupy a position that accords with that which Blanchot in *The Writing of the Disaster* (1986: xi) designates 'the interim': that period after one disaster has occurred and another is awaited. Blanchot's notion serves to cast light on the sense in which lives lived in the midst of disaster – or, what one UK newspaper described, in the wake of the arrests in the UK in August 2006 of those suspects linked to a plot to blow up a series of transatlantic flights, 'the calendar of terror' come to acquire a 'provisional' and 'temporary' quality.

Secondly, Raban points to the sense in which this experience of waiting is shadowed by an 'appetite' or 'hunger' for catastrophe – invoking the mixture of the individual subjects' aggressive projections, phantasies, and masochistic desires, that, as Freud ([1915] 1973: 280) suggests in 'Thoughts for the times on war and death' (written in the midst of World War I), come to achieve a particular resonance with public discourses in times of conflict. Present in this desire for catastrophe can be traced the sense of release that the occurrence of whatever is feared can bring – by foreshortening the experience of having to suffer the anxieties that pervade the process of waiting, and by lessening the uncertainties surrounding the next attack. In his 1945 essay 'Logical time and the assertion of anticipated certainty', Lacan (2006: 161–75) identifies three moments that serve to illuminate the process of waiting set in motion by the footage of the suicide bomber graduation ceremony. First comes 'the instant of the glance', and the recognition of what is taking place – as in the case of seeing this footage. Second comes the 'time for comprehending', and the attempt to ascertain what is going to take place from what has been seen. This is the moment Western publics inhabit in regard to this footage – the time of waiting to see what the outcome of their encounter with this footage will be. The latter is directed towards the third moment – 'the moment of concluding' and the resolution of this process. In the War on Terror it is this second moment which publics have come to inhabit in awaiting a forthcoming attack, with, as Lacan suggests, this moment giving rise to a 'temporal tension' born from a 'haste' to arrive at a condition of 'anticipated certainty', that will suggest a resolution to this waiting.

This desire to establish some sense of the form a future attack might take can be traced in the myriad phantasies of catastrophe evident in popular culture since the Second World War,[7] and the attempt they constitute to make present at the Imaginary the threat of imminent catastrophe and at once define and limit it, see it overcome, and maintain it at as external to the spectator. Such depictions constitute a version of what Barthes (1990: 37) identifies as the 'scenography of waiting', that in turn serves to shape the experience of waiting – with, as Adrian Rifkin (2003:337) contends, those who wait particularly attentive to what they see, as they seek a sign of what is to happen to them. Since the September 11 attacks a particularly prominent version of this scenography has taken the form of those television dramas – most notably perhaps *24*, *Spooks* and *Sleeper Cell*[8] – that have taken the struggle against terrorism as their focus, with central to each a process of waiting to see whether a forthcoming attack will take place or be averted. And yet, while, emphasising the successful prevention of attacks, these narratives are marked by a notable, and in the context of this discussion, telling absence in regard to the depiction of publics' experience of awaiting a forthcoming attack – that remains at best only marginal to these dramas. In one respect such an absence serves to avoid identifying Western publics as victims of the experience of awaiting a forthcoming attack. And yet, the other side of this absence is that audiences are provided with little sense of how they might conceive of or imagine their own position as waiting subjects in the War on Terror.

It might be argued that this absence, and its eclipse by an emphasis upon the spectacle of 'fighting terrorism', derives from the problems of rendering waiting as dramatic material – as suggested in Eagleton's question as to whether waiting is 'doing something' or the 'suspension' of it. And yet it is possible to point to an antecedent from a relatively recent conflict situation that demonstrates not only how experiences of waiting can constitute a focus for portrayals of a conflict, but the capacity of culture to engage with the politico-historical circumstances in which this waiting occurs: Susan Sontag's 1993 production of Beckett's *Waiting for Godot* (the twentieth century's emblematic work on waiting), with the Youth Theatre of a besieged Sarajevo. Sontag received a certain amount of criticism for her role in this production that focused upon the perceived 'triviality' or 'superficiality' of undertaking such a project in the midst of the siege of the city, in contrast, as one commentator suggested, to Walt Whitman's bandaging the wounds of dying soldiers during the American Civil War.[9] Yet such criticisms failed to acknowledge the significance of what Zizek (2001: 85) conceives of as 'a defying symbolic gesture' – that provides a rallying point for a struggle to go on when other aspects of the struggle are under threat or have become impossible to sustain. Indeed, in the context of a conflict in which media coverage was judged to have played a pivotal role in influencing US policy (Robinson 2002), Sontag's production and the international media attention it generated served to emphasise how an intervention in the scenography of waiting might contribute to a transformation in the political context in which this process of waiting occurs. While it would be wrong to overemphasise the similiarities between Sarajevo in 1993 and the War on Terror, the 1993 production of *Godot*, while serving to highlight the absence of a similar engagement with the experience of waiting in the War on Terror, at the same time raises the broader question of the politics of waiting, and the terms in which the awaiting of a forthcoming attack intersects with the political underpinnings of the War on Terror.

Waiting, politics

Such a question takes us back to the issue discussed in the previous chapter of the depressed state of contemporary politics in the West. Indeed, the depressive condition invokes the passivity and sense of impotence repeatedly associated with waiting – with, as Freud ([1917] 1991a) conceives it, melancholia constituting an indefinite process of waiting for the work of mourning to take place, which will allow the absence of the lost object to be properly come to terms with. At the same time waiting has been associated with a sense of powerlessness, in that those who wait must do so because they are unable to act in such a way as bring about what they desire. Indeed, the other side of Barthes's (1990: 40) formulation, '*To make someone wait:* the constant prerogative of all power', is that being made to wait constitutes a form of powerlessness.

In the context of the War on Terror the attempts made by Western governments to manage the experience of waiting can be positioned as having contributed to the anxiety associated with this process. In one respect this has derived from the nature of the warnings issued about possible forthcoming attacks. These have perhaps taken their most dramatic tone in the United Kingdom, where the certainty or unavoidability of future attacks has been repeatedly iterated – in March 2004, John Stevens, the then head of the UK Metropolitan Police called an attack upon London 'inevitable',[10] a diagnosis echoed by the head of Scotland Yard's Anti-Terrorist Branch, Peter Clarke, in September 2006 and April 2007.[11] Such declarations have acquired an additional historical-comparative dimension by assertions, such as that made in August 2006 by the Home Secretary, John Reid, that 'We are probably in the most sustained period of severe threat since the end of World War II'. This is a statement that, while intriguing in its attitude to the Cold War, at the same time, in company with Stevens and Clarke's claims, implies that despite the attention accorded to security since the September 11 attacks, publics must still await the inevitable (and as such might raise the question: what has been the ultimate point of the myriad security measures introduced since the September 11 attacks?).

In another respect the permanence of certain forms of warning have also contributed to the anxiety associated with this process of waiting. This is evident in the United States in the Department of Homeland Security's 'security advisory system', with its colour-coded threat scale constantly accessible via the department's website.[12] Michael Moore's *Fahrenheit 911* (2004) includes an interview with Democrat Congressman Jim McDermott, who draws particular attention to this system in accusing the Bush administration of having, since the September 11 attacks, created 'an aura of endless threat':

> They played us like an organ. They raised the [level] ... to orange then up to red, then back to orange ... It's not going to go down to green or blue – it's never going to get there. There clearly is no way that anyone can live constantly on edge like that.

Here even the lower threat levels – blue ('general risk of terrorist attacks') and green ('low risk of terrorist attacks') – provide no respite from the prospect of attack, with the (lowest) green level assessment containing a series of 'recommended actions for citizens', directed towards practical preparations for the prospect of a raising of the threat level.[13] If in one respect such a device serves to reinforce the sense that the awaiting of a forthcoming attack is always ongoing, at the same time it serves to create a situation in which the anxiety associated with waiting comes to be manipulable via changes in the threat assessment level.

The issue of manipulability raises the question of how, since the September 11 attacks, governments have sought to utilise the threat of forthcoming attacks as a means of extending their control and surveillance of publics – a focus of considerable academic attention.[14] And yet while such measures are at one level argued for in their making publics feel safer, at the same time, via a process that Oliver Kessler and Christopher Daase (2006) term 'the paradox of security', they have produced the inverse effect. In foregrounding security as a field of concern publics have been rendered more acutely sensitive to the threats that they face, resulting in a heightened sense of insecurity. Indeed, the logic underpinning such a paradox can be understood as supporting an upward spiral in 'securitization', with the heightened sense of insecurity resulting from the pursuit of security generating (and justifying) a demand for further security measures (that in turn results in a heightened sense of insecurity, that in turn ...). Here a comparison with the Cold War is illuminating. As James Fallows (2006a) has noted in discussing alternative strategies for winning the War on Terror, 'The Cold War went on for decades, but not with the open-ended emergency approach to spending, civil liberties, and executive power that have applied in this case [the War on Terror]'. Where then, and when, might the endpoint in this process come? Under what circumstances will security ever come to be regarded as tight enough? The logic of the paradox of security suggests that such a situation can never be attained, with a state of 'absolute security' that would put an end to the awaiting of a forthcoming attack, not only practically unrealisable, but undermined by the anxiety such a state would produce.

At the same time as giving rise to an anxiety directed towards the prospect of forthcoming attacks, this process can be seen to be generative of another form of anxiety, that which Janet Flower MacCannell (2006: 209), in discussing the Vietnam War, labels 'political anxiety' – the anxiety this conflict produced in the United States in the functioning of politics. In her discussion MacCannell alludes to the contribution made by the seemingly interminable nature of the Vietnam War to this variant of anxiety – an issue I want to focus upon for a moment in regard to the apparently limitless waiting for the conflict to be over this produced. Not only can the latter be positioned as having figured as a source of anxiety for the US public in the functioning of the political system, at the same time it constituted a source of anxiety within the political system itself, in regard to how to 'manage' this conflict. (Evident here again is the sense in which war assumes the contours of the unmanageable Thing.) The latter can be seen to be closely paralleled in the War on Terror, with the seemingly interminable process of waiting this conflict has given rise to, contributing to an anxiety among politicians in regard to how to deal with the threat that is faced, and their fear of being held culpable for future attacks because not enough was done (or was seen to be done) to attempt to stop them. (Such accusations were levelled at the Bush and Clinton administrations in regard to the September 11 attacks). Indeed, beyond the desire to extend their control and surveillance of publics, this anxiety adds a further dimension to the significance accorded to security since the September 11 attacks.

And yet, while a focus of waiting and the anxieties associated with it has been directed towards the defensive aspects of the War on Terror (a concern with homeland security), questions of waiting also weave their way through the aggressive dimensions of this conflict – 'fighting terror' around the globe. In one respect such anxieties derive from the question of the progress made in Afghanistan and Iraq, and the sense in which each has come to take the form of endless conflicts – as *The Economist* asked on the front page of its 15 December 2007 issue, 'Must these be wars without end?'.[15] In another respect, this dimension to waiting raises the question of how Other, distant, faraway places are conceived of from a Western standpoint (the focus of the next chapter). Barthes in his account of waiting points to the perception that 'the other never waits' (1990: 39), suggesting both the difficulties in imagining the other engaged in a process which might, as Eagleton's question suggests, be difficult to perceive – but also, that a focus upon one's own experience of waiting and the anxieties this can generate, is conducive of a myopia that serves to curtail the sense of others' engaged in such a process. And yet waiting can be understood as having figured as central to non-Western publics' experiences of the War on Terror, as in, for example, waiting for the United States' led assaults on Afghanistan (that began in October 2001) and Iraq (in March 2003) to commence (the parallel perhaps of Western publics' awaiting forthcoming attacks), but also in the form of waiting for some measure of peace and stability to emerge in the aftermath of these assaults and the invasions and occupations that followed them. The difficulties Barthes points to in conceiving of the Other waiting serves to highlight the difficulty Western publics are faced with in relating their experiences of waiting to the Other's experiences – a situation that serves to obscure the intersecting nature of these processes of waiting and the fact that they cannot be understood without reference to one another.

'Waiting is a delirium'

In his account of waiting Barthes (1990: 39) contends that 'waiting is a delirium' – in its combining the anticipation of whatever is awaited with the delay (perhaps endless delay) of having to await it. And indeed, the notion of delirium serves to illuminate Western public's experience of waiting in the War on Terror. Here these publics have found themselves surrounded by the spectacle of a war configured as, inter alia, a clash of apocalyptic dimensions – a war that they are little able to alter the course of, and in which they are haunted by a shadowy, spectral enemy, their vulnerability to which they are repeatedly reminded of. This sense of delirium is all too apparent in Raban's sketch, in its evocation of the 'apprehension of atrocity', the 'perverse appetite' for news of catastrophe, and the awareness of war's capacity to take the form of an 'addiction'. Indeed, the extended process of waiting Western publics have been subject to in the War on Terror can be seen to constitute a type of prolonged, slow panic – punctuated by sharper spikes of fear – in which, as Pascal Bonitzer (1997: 28) argues in discussing 'Hitchcockian suspense', 'the paradoxical use of slowed-down time in suspense' serves to enhance 'the prolonged necessarily disturbing undecidability of an event'.

In turn this sense of delirium can be understood as serving to render the experience of waiting increasingly obscured – as manifest in one respect in the difficulty in recognising or acknowledging that one is awaiting a forthcoming attack – a disavowal in the face of the repeated warnings that this is what is taking place. And yet such a disavowal can be seen to constitute a key 'coping strategy' – at least in regard to how the individual subject conducts their day-to-day affairs – when faced with the prospect of a forthcoming attack. In part such an attitude can be seen to stem from the degree of 'place-fixity' that structures the majority of lives in contemporary Western societies, in regard to the practical difficulties encountered in moving somewhere that is considered less at risk from attack (and in likelihood more 'remote').

Faced with such obstacles most people have seemingly little option but to, in the words of Cowley cited above, 'go about our daily business and try to forget'. (A similar *modus vivendi* can be identified with those publics that during the Cold War were faced with the prospect of nuclear confrontation between the superpowers and their allies.)

The terms in which waiting and the anxieties associated with it are generative of a sense of delirium are repeatedly evident in narratives of Horror – as in, to take one notable example, George Romero's landmark film *Night of the Living Dead* (1968). Here the characters assemble in an abandoned house as they await the attack upon them by 'the living dead' to begin, a situation that replicates the position Western publics have found themselves assuming in the War on Terror. In Romero's film the very process of waiting for the monstrous enemy (taking the form of zombies[16]) to attack produces a state of panic among the assembled characters – so much so that they come to fight among themselves – as they become aware of the helplessness of their situation. Indeed, if phantasies of the different forms a threat can take are central to Horror, in the War on Terror this condition of delirious waiting has provided fertile ground for the promulgation of phantasies about not only the form the next attack might take, but the nature of the enemy responsible for it. Barthes adds to the sense of delirium he associates with waiting, that those who wait are prey to, 'hallucinating' (1990: 39), and imagining that 'the being I am waiting for is not real', an assessment that accords with the series of projections about the type of enemy that is faced in the War on Terror, as not only presenting some kind of ghostly or spectral presence, but as monstrous and/or demonic – as most clearly evident in the case of Bin Laden.

Beyond the depiction of the enemy, these delusory tendencies can be traced in the attitude to potential forthcoming attacks and the affinities these possess with the type of perceptual over-sensitivities and misrecognitions Freud delineates in *The Psychopathology of Everyday Life* ([1901] 1975: 317–18), where the paranoid is described as seeing in the minutiae of others' appearance and behaviour evidence of threats to their selves. In the UK a result of the proliferation of a similar way of seeing can be traced in the series of arrests made under anti-terrorism legislation which have perceived a terrorist threat where the grounds for such fears have ranged from the non-existent to the quite bizarre.[17] At the same time similar tendencies can be detected in fears held by the public, as in the instance – in the wake of the arrests on 10 August 2006 of individuals suspected of plotting to blow up a series of transatlantic flights – of fellow passengers insisting that two men be removed from a passenger flight from Malaga to Manchester on the basis of their being Asian or Middle Eastern in appearance and 'wearing heavy clothes and speaking a language claimed to be Arabic'[18] (but which was Urdu). Perhaps the most dramatic example to date though of the rise of this way of seeing and the delusions it is prone to occurred with the police shooting of Juan Charles de Menezes in London in July 2005. Here similar details of personal appearance to those Freud identifies with the paranoid's fears – the clothing worn by Menezes – figured as a crucial factor in his killing. A number of eyewitnesses and police officers identified Menezes as wearing a 'padded jacket' of a type that could conceal an explosive device. It subsequently transpired that Menezes was wearing no such a garment, but a lighter jacket unsuitable for such a purpose.[19]

In another respect this condition of delirium can be traced in the profusion of rumours about attacks, which have been provided with a new impetus by the Internet and the opportunities it has presented for their dissemination. Such rumours include (as encountered by the author): an attempted suicide bomb attack in 2002 on a McDonald's restaurant in central London that was subsequently covered up by the police, and a blast having occurred at Liverpool Street Station, London, on the morning of the first anniversary of the 7 July 2005 attacks on the city. Such rumours about attacks taking place have been accompanied by a myriad of related hoaxes, conspiracy theories, and urban myths. In the case of the July 2005 attacks on London,[20] these included the claim that dialling 112 (the international emergency number) on a mobile phone even when the phone is not receiving a signal (because it is underground) would connect you with an emergency call centre,[21] and that the UK government and security services were behind the attacks. The latter claim is a leitmotif of conspiracy theories, as evident in the mass of such theories about the September 11 attacks that has given rise to the '9/11 Truth Movement'.[22] In one respect the claim that governments were behind the London and September 11 attacks can be understood as a response to the uncertain ontological profile of the enemy in the War on Terror, with these claims serving to provide the source of the threats faced in this conflict with an identifiable and locatable form. At the same time though these claims can be read as suggesting a lack of trust in the role played by governments in the War on Terror, fuelled by incidents such as the build-up to the invasion of Iraq, and the false assertions made by the UK and US governments about Saddam Hussein's regime possessing WMDs.

These stories, myths, and theories can be located on a spectrum reaching from rumour (as suggesting the possibilities of something having happened) to hallucination (in which the subject experiences an event as real which has not occurred). Freud ([1911] 2001a: 219) identifies hallucination as a response to unsatisfied desires and the attempt to 'make real' that which is awaited, with phantasy playing a similar function, albeit in a less definitely expressed form. Indeed, the imagining of forthcoming attacks can (as suggested above) be configured as providing a means of attempting to come to terms with, or lessen, the 'disturbing undecidability' (in Bonitzer's words) surrounding the prospect of an attack. In so doing this imagining seeks to address what Adam Phillips (1994: 79) in discussing boredom and waiting terms, 'the agonies of waiting indefinitely', and the indefinite delirium this gives rise to.

Endlessness

The anxiety and delirium emanating from the process of waiting Western publics have experienced in the War on Terror has been provided with an added dimension by the sense in which there appears to be no end in sight to this conflict. In August 2004 George Bush admitted that the War on Terror could never be won, an admission that was interpreted as implying that United States had embarked upon a conflict without end.[23] (Estimates of the duration of the conflict were given a slightly different complexion by the State Department's announcement in February 2006 of the conflict constituting a 'Long War', that would last at least as long as the Cold War[24] – an assessment that has all but faded from view since its appearance.) In positioning Western publics as subject to 'the agonies of waiting indefinitely', such a claim can be understood as contributing to the sense of delirium associated with this conflict, suggesting that this process of waiting is a permanent state which will not disappear or pass by and which cannot be escaped from. Indeed, the notion of a limitless process of waiting suggests a scenario for a Horror film in which the Thing cannot ever be escaped from or reached beyond. This conception of the conflict as endless serves to position publics – in the terms Lacan discusses in his 'Logical time' essay – as forever denied the 'anticipated certainty' they seek and that is promised by 'the moment of concluding'. And yet, at the same time, this conception of the endlessness of the conflict points to the process of 'retroaction' (a reworking of Freud's 'nachträglichkeit') Lacan also presents in this essay – whereby only over time do the ramifications of the September 11 attacks and the process of endless waiting they have set in motion become clear.

At a somewhat different level, as Fallows (2006) has warned, the conception of a 'long' or limitless war renders this conflict more dangerous for the United States and its allies, in inviting the enemy to partake in a confrontation that cannot in the near future be won. As Fallows (ibid.: 72) declares: 'an open ended war is an open-ended invitation to defeat'. In such terms the logic of Blanchot's assertion, 'Whatever the importance of the object of waiting, it is always infinitely surpassed by the movement of waiting' becomes clear. In a condition of permanent waiting, with no visible end in sight, the actual experience of waiting acquires a significance that serves to eclipse the event which is awaited – the situation Western publics have come to experience in the War on Terror.

7
Imagining Kabul

The waiting subject is a subject that is prey then to visions and imaginings as they attempt to ascertain what is to happen to them. How in the case of Western publics does the waiting subject imagine, conceive of, and comprehend the 'distant places' which have figured as pivotal sites in the War on Terror – of which Afghanistan and Iraq present perhaps the most high-profile examples? Or, to put it another way, how do these publics come to conceive of the relationship – identified by David Simpson (2006: 44) as so crucial to perceptions of the War on Terror – between 'the homeland' and 'the faraway place'? And in turn, how do these publics come to comprehend the terms in which these faraway places have come to constitute a source of the threats they await? Such questions point in the direction of a further aspect of the relationship between seeing and travelling – the terms in which imagery of these distant places travels back to the West, and the ways in which these depictions are received back here.

The significance and strangeness of these distant places was emphasised in Tony Blair's comment, in a speech to British troops serving in Helmand province, Afghanistan, from November 2006, that 'Here in this extraordinary piece of desert is where the future of world security in the early 21st Century is going to be played out'[1] – a statement that at once points to the importance attributed to these distant places and the sense of otherness that defines them: in the Western imagination the desert constitutes an exemplar of 'elsewhere' (or indeed 'nowhere' – which a dimly perceived elsewhere stands constantly on the verge of disappearing into). The nature of Western publics' perception of these places has come to constitute a particular focus of attention, in terms of the gap between the experiences of Western military personnel 'out there' and publics' limited comprehension of these experiences, as highlighted by Lawrence Kaplan in regard to the US military and Iraq,[2] and by the head of the British Army, General Richard Dannatt, in regard to the role played by UK forces in Afghanistan and Iraq.[3] Indeed, to relate for a moment this sense of division to questions of seeing, an awareness of this gap lay behind the agreement of Davey Mcmahon, father of Private Davey Graham, of the 1st Battalion the Worcestershire and Sherwood Foresters Regiment, to allow photos from the same day (14 August 2007) of his son serving in Helmand – firstly relaxing and smiling, and later in agony after having been shot in the abdomen – to appear in the news, with Davey's father citing his approval for the publication of these images in terms of, 'The public are not seeing pictures like this at the moment ... I don't think anyone is seeing the real story.'[4]

This chapter takes Kabul as an exemplar of a distant place, to scrutinise the differing standpoints from which the city has been portrayed – primarily at a visual level (although the connections between the Imaginary and the Symbolic will also be examined) – to survey the differing possibilities for Western publics to imagine Kabul presented by the differing terms in which the city has been depicted. In so doing this chapter foregrounds the question of how processes of imagining have figured as a means by which Western publics have perceived and comprehended the War on Terror – a question foregrounded by the centrality accorded to imagery in this conflict. The act of imagining is associated above all with the realm of images (as derived from the Latin 'imaginare' – form an image of, and 'imaginari' – picture of oneself). And yet, as Elkins (1996: 101–3) contends, it would be an oversimplification to draw a clear line between the work of the imagination and other cognitive processes. Indeed, as Elkins asserts, the imagination plays a fundamental role in the dimensions of a subject's thinking: 'few people spend time thinking about things they cannot see' (ibid.: 101) (as in the sense of visualise or imagine), to the extent that he wonders, 'Is it possible to think of something we want to see but cannot visualise?' (ibid.:103). In taking as its focus these questions of the imagination, this chapter returns to the issue raised by Duras (cited in discussing the September 11 attacks), of the terms in which cinema serves to hinder the imaginative capacities of the spectator – 'the cinema stops the text and kills its offspring: the imagination'. Here though this question is addressed in regard to a broader range of visual material, and the terms in which this can both constitute a source for and serve to limit the work of the imagination. While the imagination can be understood as coming into play at the point at which a depiction halts – in the realm beyond that which is directly seen (hence Duras's contention) – at the same time, without some type of source material to provide a catalyst for the imagination, it becomes difficult to conceive of particular events, places, and people at all – an issue highlighted by Simpson (2006: 103–19) (and David Campbell (2004)) in regard to the lack of awareness among Western publics of those conflicts and catastrophes which have received minimal media coverage.

In addressing 'the difficulty of imagining other persons' Scarry (1999: 277) stresses the particular problems involved in imagining culturally 'foreign' Others – an issue rendered more complex still when this takes the form of multiple Others (ibid.: 284), as in the context of a city the size of Kabul (with a population of circa three million). In the case of Kabul though a still further demand is placed upon the imagination in regard to imagining the appearance and material structure of the city this population inhabits. Scarry identifies the ability to imagine the Other as constituting a bar to the capacity to harm the Other (1999: 281) – 'The difficulty of imagining others is both the cause of, and the problem displayed by, the action of injuring', asserting that (ibid.: 282) 'if they stood visible to us, the infliction of that injury would be impossible'. This is a contention that is at once problematic and revealing. In one respect it occludes the terms in which processes of imagining can constitute a source of the aggressivity directed towards the Other (as evident in regard to both sides' conception of one another in the War on Terror). In another it serves to ignore Virilio's analysis (1989) – foregrounded in discussing the hunt for Bin Laden – in which a condition of visibility constitutes precisely the precondition for the enemy to be targeted and attacked. Rather than focusing here upon the question Scarry takes as her focus – of whether the Other is or is not imagined at all – I want to delineate the type of imagining of the city and its populace offered by the differing standpoints from which Kabul has been depicted. Such an issue points in the direction of a further concern addressed towards the end of this chapter: how the imagination can come to constitute anything other than a process interior to the individual subject, and how it might figure as a spur to engagement with the political – in the immediate context, in relation to the terms in which the War on Terror has been fought.

News, mastery, boredom

For Western publics perhaps the most obvious and widely disseminated depictions of Kabul have come from the body of media coverage – in particular, given the size of its audience, television news, and current affairs output – that has featured the Afghan capital. The portrayal of the city offered in this coverage has followed a broad trajectory – from the fall of the Taliban and the liberation of the city; to the city as a site of reconstruction and of a nascent democratic society (as foregrounded in the election of the national assembly in September 2005); to, since the summer of 2006, the city having become increasingly insecure and subject to attacks.

While the content of this coverage has passed through this broad series of moments, the terms in which Kabul is positioned as an object of this output (has figured as a 'news object') has altered comparatively little – with coverage of the city conforming with the more general standpoint television news offers on the world. At the basis of the latter lies the terms in which news seeks to declare 'how the world is ...', as Justin Lewis (2003: 336) identifies it, the belief that news possesses 'the power ... to define the world'. This is the form the majority of news coverage of Kabul has assumed, with declarations of fact (and where 'the facts' are unclear, the desire to establish them) dominating this output – as apparent across the BBC and CNN's video archives of reports on the city.[5] (Indeed, the core function of news can be said to constitute the relaying of facts about the world.) Underpinning such a standpoint can be traced the desire to sustain an aura of certainty and definitude, upon which the 'authority' of new broadcasts are typically regarded (at least by their producers) as based. In so doing news can be understood as seeking to assume a position of mastery over the objects it surveys – with the knowledge it produces of the world at once emanating from and working to confirm this relationship.

In regard to the visual dimensions of television news, the position Kabul assumes here can be seen to accord with the phantasy[6] of mastery or omniscience outlined in Dziga Vertov's (1984: 16–17) 1923 'Kinoks: a revolution' manifesto: 'I am a mechanical eye. I, a machine, show you the world as only I can see it ... I put together any given points in the universe no matter where I've recorded them' – a standpoint made visible in Vertov's *Man with a movie camera* (1929), in the image of a giant camera that straddles the city (Moscow). In so doing news asserts its capacity to seemingly 'define' or 'put together' the world at the order of the Imaginary. And yet, both in terms of the broad standpoint it offers on the world and in regard to the specifically visual dimensions of this output, a feature of news coverage is the extent to which it is characterised by processes of repetition.[7] As David Marash (1995) contends, news broadcasts can be understood as marked by a pervasiveness of coding in the form of 'story types' (hurricane, election, famine, and so on) based on their utilising 'familiar pictures and familiar texts' for each code. This result is a high degree of repetition, not just in regard to a particular channel's output, but across channels, in terms of the narratives and images they present. Indeed, as Barthes ([1980] 2000: 41) observes, 'news photographs are very often unary' – an assessment which can be applied to the moving images news uses as well – in the sense of their conforming to predetermined templates and formulas, which, for Barthes, serves to render much of this imagery 'banal'.

In one respect the extent to which this coverage is marked by repetition can be seen to emanate from the very position of mastery news seeks to assume over its objects, and the sense in which the world can be made to conform to the categories it constructs to do this. While it might be argued that the use of such codes in news broadcasting occurs for 'practical reasons', in this respect too though a will to mastery can be detected at work – in terms of this desire for mastery resulting in the practical 'demands' of news production coming to be prioritised over a rethinking of how the stories news seeks to cover might be presented differently. In terms of this coverage functioning as a catalyst for the imagination, the degree of repetition that marks this output serves to limit the source it presents for the audience to imagine Kabul, presenting, as evident in the BBC and CNN's coverage, a narrow conception of the city that reduces Kabul to a series of thematics: as for example newly liberated, or, increasingly subject to car bombs and suicide attacks. In so doing this coverage serves to occlude the city's complexity and diversity, while positioning the city as familiar and known about in a way that serves to divert or hinder further questions or speculation about it. Indeed, the extent to which news output is marked by a high degree of repetition can be located as a significant source of the boredom Lewis (1993) identifies as a feature of audience responses to news coverage. In this respect too, this output can be understood as serving to limit the function of the imagination, in its serving to dull rather than stimulate the interest of its audience (as Lewis et al. (1991) scrutinise at greater length in their study of the 1991 Gulf War). Indeed, one definition of boredom might be said to be a failure or deficit of the imagination.

In another respect the conception of Kabul offered in Western news coverage of the city conforms to the terms in which this coverage reproduces a neo-Orientalist, neo-imperial conception of Kabul. As Bhabha (1994: 66–84) elucidates, the stereotype – itself a function of a process of repetition – presents a means to fix an unknown Other in place, in the attempt to render the Other a seemingly stable and knowable presence. In regard to news coverage of Kabul, the vast majority of coverage of the city encountered by Western audiences has not been produced by Afghans (who might have played some role in its production – as translators, or 'fixers'[8]), but by Western news teams. In this respect this coverage conforms to the terms in which the non-Western Other assumes the position of the seen and the subject of knowledge, as opposed to the one who sees and the source this knowledge emanates from. (Indeed, the challenge to this relationship is central to the significance of the rise of non-Western news channels such as Al Jazeera.) In so doing this coverage raises the question of who it is that produces the material for imagining the city – an issue returned to in a moment.

Not only though does this coverage serve to constrain the source it offers for the spectator to imagine the city, at the same time it points to a failure of the imagination on the part of its producers. And yet as Marash contends, television news need not be like this. Indeed, when it dispenses with its desire to master its subject matter – Marash cites the silence that overcame CNN's coverage of the ceremony in April 1995 to mark the victims of the Oklahoma City bombing – and is willing to reflect upon the limitations of its procedures, it can achieve something more subtle, innovative, and potentially generative of the imagination of its audience. This is a contention echoed by Terence Wright (2004: 106–7) in contrasting news coverage of Afghan refugees from 2001 with the Norwegian artist Andrea Lange's 1998 video work with refugees from the Middle East – in so doing drawing attention to the imaginative possibilities of the minor gaze, to which I now want to turn.

The balloon seller, ruins, aestheticisation

A significant version of this minor gaze is presented by those independent Western photographers who have documented Kabul and Afghanistan in the period since the September 11 attacks – most prominently in the work of Simon Norfolk, in his collection *Afghanistan: Chronotopia* (2002), shot in the immediate aftermath of the fall of the Taliban; Paul Seawright in *Hidden* (2002); Riccardo Venturi in *Afghanistan: il nodo del tempo* ('the knot of time') (2005); and in the work of Steve McCurry (collected in *Shadow of the Mountains* (2007)[9]). This work has achieved a notable profile, with Norfolk winning prizes for *Afghanistan: chronotopia*, Seawright commissioned by the Imperial War Museum to work in Afghanistan, and McCurry and Venturi both photographers of international renown.

In a number of respects this body of work can be seen to present a richer resource for imaging Kabul than news coverage of the city. In contrast to the latter, the images presented in this work appear less prescriptive – and hence less concerned to master what is depicted – in so doing opening up the terms in which this work might function as a catalyst for the spectator's imagination. In part this is due to the absence of a narrative to order and direct them, with the attempt to tie them to the Symbolic limited, in the main (beyond subsequent commentaries on this work), to titles, dates and in certain cases, brief details about the content of individual photographs. Indeed, Marash's praise for those moments of 'silence' in news coverage can be seen to stem from the terms in which in these moments the use of a narrative to direct how the imagery presented is thought about are dispensed with.[10] In another respect the content of this body of work can be seen to be less obviously marked by a process of repetition, with this work of a type – what might be called 'art photography' – that is premised upon the production of images whose distinctiveness figures as central to their claims to the status of art. Indeed, this work can be said to constitute an exemplar of the minor gaze, that in contrast to television news emanates from outside of an institutional media context, and that rather than seeking to 'put together' the world in visual terms foregrounds the subjective dimensions and partiality of the depiction it offers of Kabul. Here the spectator encounters the city's quiet backstreets, its cemeteries and bazaars (in the work of Venturi); its wrecked suburbs, airport, and open-air cinema (Norfolk); and street-life and traders (McCurry). In so doing this work provides a greater room for the play of the spectator's imagination, in foregrounding the sense in which it offers an incomplete vision of Kabul that leaves so many aspects of the city only partly depicted, and the rest to be imagined.

And yet, at another level this body of work can be seen to display its own conservative tendencies, that raise questions about the type of source it presents for imagining the city. They centre on it conforming to a historically established pattern in which the culturally foreign Other – both in the sense of Other-as-person and Other-as-place or locale – figures as the object of the Western photographer's gaze.

In regard to the Other-as-person such a tendency is, to take one prominent example, foregrounded in Norfolk's images from Kabul of a balloon seller and a man with a caged bird (used for fighting). (Aspects of McCurry and Venturi's work could also be cited here[11]). Each stand in full profile facing the camera accompanied by a ruined backdrop (in the case of the former the frame of a teahouse and the latter a wrecked biplane at an exhibition site). In one respect these images raise the question of why these particular figures have been selected? Why not an electrician, or a mechanic? As it is these figures resonate with a sense of exoticism and Orientalism – albeit filtered through a contemporary aesthetic on the part of portrait photography for a blankness or bathos on the part of the subject's facial expressions. At the same time, in presenting the two men standing, facing the camera in full profile, these images echo the mise en scène of anthropological cataloguing from the nineteenth and early twentieth century.

A similar tendency can be traced in the depiction this body of work offers of the Other-as-place. The photographing of Other, distant places – to record and show what 'elsewhere' looks like – has figured as a persistent desire in the history of photography, as evident from the earliest era of the medium: as Benjamin ([1927–40] 2002: 684–5) documents, 'voyages photographiques' figured prominently among the work on display at the 1859 Salon de Photographie. (Roger Fenton's images from the Crimean War (1853–6) constitute an exemplar of this desire in regard to a conflict situation.) At the same time, evident across this body of work is a desire to aestheticise that, in the context of Afghanistan's recent history, raises the issue of whether a place as traumatised by decades of war as Kabul should be subject to such a process, and in turn, the terms in which this work serves to provide a source of visual pleasure for Western audiences. (Such concerns invoke again the issue raised in discussing the September 11 attacks, of the tensions between scopic desire and questions of morality). While the desire to aestheticise is evident across this body of work – underpinning its status as art photography – (as evident, at one level, in Venturi's use of black and white) this issue is foregrounded in the extent to which ruins and the detritus of war figure repeatedly as a focus of this work: to the greatest extent in Norfolk and Seawright's output. (Indeed Norfolk's work is explicitly concerned to document the ruined state of Afghanistan.) In so doing this work conforms to the sense in which ruins have not only constituted a prominent feature of Western art, but to the terms in which the depiction of 'the east'-in-ruins conforms to an Orientalist conception of Afghanistan as trapped within a pre-modern past (an issue returned to in a moment). While it might be contended that given the condition of Afghanistan it is impossible to avoid depicting Kabul in ruins, the extent to which ruins constitute a focus of this is work is worth highlighting. (Indeed, as a contrast it would be interesting for a photographer to focus upon the redevelopments and new buildings which have appeared in Kabul since the fall of the Taliban – and to devote a book to this aspect of the city.) Taken together, these aspects of the depiction of the Other as person and place raise questions about the type of source this work presents for imagining Kabul, and the extent to which it serves to reinforce a conception of the city and its populace marked by a reworking of historical stereotypes and formulas.

This issue is provided with an added dimension by a further, some-what earlier instance of the encounter of a Western photographer with Kabul, reproduced in *The Guardian* at the time of the US led assault on Afghanistan. On 10 October 2001, a few days after the start of the assault, the paper published a selection of photographs taken by Annemarie Schwarzenbach, a German traveller to Afghanistan at the end of the 1930s, that included photographs of Kabul's street-life along with a guide who led Schwarzenbach and her companion to the buddhas of Bamiyan (destroyed by the Taliban in February 2001).[12] The accompanying commentary, titled 'The land that time forgot', emphasised how these images 'are remarkably similar to those we see in the press today'. As the United States and its allies unleashed their military power on Afghanistan, the paper chose to offer an Orientalist take on the country, framed in terms of a 'timelessness' that worked to position Afghanistan outside history and beyond comprehension in politico-historical terms. This condition of incomprehensibility was further reinforced by the absence of images of the destruction wrought by the assault – a situation in part brought about the actions of the United States and its allies to restrict media coverage of the bombard-ment outlined in Chapter 2. Indeed, the absence of images depicting the effects of the bombardment raises key questions about the terms in which Western publics might imagine the destruction inflicted upon Afghanistan and the difficulties faced for the reconstruction of the country after decades of war. (It is worth distinguishing here between images that depict Kabul in ruins, without explaining the cause of the destruction that produced them, and images which seek to document the causes of this destruction. In this respect the Symbolic plays a key role in explicating what is depicted.)

The Other sees, *Kabul jan*, the democratic gaze

What has rarely been encountered in the West is Kabul photographed or filmed from an Afghan standpoint. This is an issue that reaches to the heart of the terms in which Kabul and its populace might be imagined as anything other than a distant Other, as seen but never seeing, and subjects rather than objects.

The series of feature films set in Afghanistan that have appeared since the fall of the Taliban present one such potential source. And yet, in terms of seeing from an Afghan standpoint, their value is limited. A number of the most prominent of these films have been made by non-Afghan directors, Samira Makhmalbaf (from Iran) in the case of *At Five in the Afternoon* (2003)[13] and the German Marc Forster (whose career developed in the United States) for *The Kite Runner* (2007). Exceptions are Siddiq Barmak's *Osama* (2003) and Horace Ahmad Sanshab's *Zolykha's Secret* (2006). The former does offer an Afghan standpoint on Kabul, yet it is set prior to the September 11 attacks. The latter, while set in part after the attacks, rather than portraying the Afghan capital, has a rural setting.

While images of the city as seen from an Afghan standpoint have emerged since the fall of the Taliban – whose injunction against visual imagery extended as far as defacing and altering street and shop signs and museum exhibits so that they did not show a human figure[14] – for Western audiences these have largely been limited to more 'marginal' (at least in terms of audience sizes and profile) forms of dissemination: primarily image-sharing websites and blogs. And yet it is worth reiterating that developments in digital technology and the Internet have opened up the possibilities for the dissemination of this material in ways that would not previously have been possible.

To take a particularly suggestive example from YouTube, the seven-minute and-forty-seven-second-long film *Kabul jan*[15] mixes still and moving images of Kabul since 1868 to the present, to offer a very different conception of the city to that which predominates in Western portrayals of Kabul. Striking here is the inclusion – and juxtaposition with the city's present state of comparative hardship – of images of the city from its period of relative prosperity and stability in the 1960s and 1970s (pre-bellum Afghanistan), which have largely been occluded in conceptions of the city in the Western imagination.[16] At the same time, blogs (including the award winning 'Afghan Lord',[17] and 'Sanjar'[18] and 'Kabuli'[19] blogs), as well as the photo galleries of sites such as *Afghansite. com*[20] and *Afghanistan Online*,[21] and contributions to photo-sharing sites such as *Flickr*[22] (Figure 7.1), have all presented examples of Kabul seen from an Afghan standpoint. While it would be misleading to overgeneralise about the type of vision these images present of the city, it is worth pointing to three basic contrasts between this work and that offered by the previous two standpoints on the city, in terms of the variety of its content, the relative absence of 'exoticised' portrayals of the city, and a less obvious desire to aestheticise that which is depicted.

More broadly though this work raises the question of the development of visual culture in Afghanistan, and the difficulties this has faced after years of continuous war, the poverty this has engendered, and the Taliban's injunctions against visual imagery. (Thomas Dworzak's

Figure 7.1 'Kabul', Nasim Fekrat, 9 August 2006

(2004) discovery of a stash of Taliban portraits in Khandahar after the Taliban fled the city reveals though a very different attitude to photography – with its repression finding a return in the Taliban's desire to be photographed, often in costume and heavily made up.) In the context of the hopes for the development of a democratic society in Afghanistan such obstacles raise the question of the relationship between visual culture and democracy, and in particular photography and democracy. This latter relationship has been the subject of long running – yet underanalysed – associations, with Baudelaire in 1859 identifying (albeit derogatorily) 'the multitude' as photography's 'natural ally' (as quoted in Benjamin (2002: 691)), an assessment echoed in the *here is new york* project (discussed in the final chapter), that documented the September 11 attacks and their aftermath, and was subtitled 'a democracy of photographs'. The introduction to the book that came out of this project identified the medium as 'democratic by its very nature' (Shulan 2002[23]). Not only might a popular, open visual-photographic culture be located as a marker of a democratic way of seeing or proliferation of a democratic gaze in the country. At the same time photography can function as a means by which the process of democratisation is supported and reinforced. This is a theme addressed in *At Five in the Afternoon* in the scenes in which the principal character is photographed for election posters to support her political ambitions – her participation in a mock presidential election at school, and her dreams of running for president of Afghanistan. Indeed the terms in which photography might contribute to the (increasingly precarious) development of democracy in Afghanistan – in so doing taking the form of what might be called a 'democratizing gaze' – is evident, for example, in Bilal Sarwary's photographs from September 2006 of voters registering and discussing their hopes for the first election of a national assembly since the fall of the Taliban.[24]

The development of a democratic visual culture possesses ramifications not only for the internal political culture of Afghanistan, but for the terms in which the country is conceived of and imagined by the rest of the world – including Western publics – and the capacity of Afghanistan to come to constitute a 'there' (or someone else's 'here') rather than an 'elsewhere' or 'nowhere'. Indeed, without the rise of such a way of seeing, Afghanistan may be condemned to face the condition of other 'developing' countries, of the type Benjamin Stora identifies in his comments on Algeria: 'The absence of images robs Algeria of its reality. It constructs a fantasy country that doesn't exist' (quoted in Armes 2005: 69[25]) – a statement that inverts the sense in which images function as a source of phantasy and imagining, to locate a condition of phantasy-without-images as the purveyor of a false sense of Algeria. Following Stora's assessment, the development of a democratic gaze in Afghanistan is needed precisely for the country to avoid a situation in which democracy and the development of a civil society – and the possibilities they hold for the country's reconstruction after years of war – remain only a phantasy. Indeed without the development of such a culture, the development of democracy in Afghanistan will remain significantly limited. As Lacan (see in particular *Seminar XXII* 1974–5) explores at length in his later work, the orders of the Imaginary, the Symbolic, and the Real are fundamentally interconnected, existing in a relationship that Lacan visualises as taking the form of three inter-secting rings linked in a 'Borromean knot' in which when one ring is severed all three become separated ([1972–3] 1999: 124). Without the development of a democratic Imaginary – or in Christian Metz's (1983: 61–3) terms, a democratic scopic regime – one ring has been lost, jeopardising the overall status and structure of the form democracy assumes in the country, and raising doubts about whether it is possible to talk of democracy existing in Afghanistan at all, except in its most narrow Symbolic form – by name, in voting, and in the existence of a 'parliament'. (And, in asserting, as I am here, the need for democracy to develop in Afghanistan, it should be made clear that this version of democracy needs to be without the compromises and duplicities that has riven the conception of democracy promoted by the Bush administration since the September 11 attacks.)[26]

The limits of the imagining, political engagement, the future

In foregrounding the ties between the Imaginary, the Symbolic, and the Real, this latter issue – while emphasising the significance of the Imaginary as a dimension of the political – also raises the question of the capacity of imagining to reach beyond the Imaginary, and to constitute a source of engagement with the Symbolic and Real dimensions of the terms in which the War on Terror has been waged.

In one respect such an issue takes us back to the type of knowledge generated by images, and the doubts Lacan raises about the value of Imaginary knowledge for making sense of the War on Terror. Lacan's analysis finds an echo – albeit in a different context – in regard to conceptions of the value of different mediums as catalysts of the imagination, as evident in Duras's locating the text as the 'offspring' of the imagination, with cinema serving to 'kill' the spectator's imaginative capacities. Duras's assessment might be read as echoed by Scarry (1999: 285) in the emphasis she places upon literature as providing a resource for imagining the Other. For, while Scarry alludes to the possibilities of film playing such a role, in contrast to literature she offers no analysis of the terms in which it might do so.

And yet even if the spectator is encouraged to engage in 'imaginative labour', as Scarry terms it (1999: 284), by the images they encounter, there remains the question of the type of actual engagement with, and practical, tangible difference to the terms in which the War on Terror is waged, that this imagining might engender. The capacity to imagine, in constituting, as Elkins suggests, a key dimension of the capacity for thinking, rethinking, and providing the sense that things might indeed be another way, constitutes a catalyst – even precondition – for engagement with the political. And yet there exist significant obstacles to the imagination coming to assume such a role. This is highlighted in Jean Luc Godard's *Two or three things I know about her ...* (1967), at the point at which the main character, Juliette, speaks over photographs of the casualties of the Vietnam War:

> It's strange that a person in Europe on 17th August, 1966 can be thinking of a person in Asia. Thinking, meaning to say are not activities like writing, running or eating. They're inside you ... I can

think of someone absent, imagine him, or find him evoked by a remark, even if he is dead ... Now I understand the thought process, it's substituting an effort of the imagination for an examination of real objects.

Foregrounded here is the gap Kristeva (1982: 109) delineates, in regard to the sense in which that which remains interior to the subject (and uncommunicated to an Other) stems from an attitude of 'refusing to meet the Other'. Indeed, a prominent feature of depression is that the subject comes to 'withdraw into themselves' and become lost in their own thoughts and imaginings, with the terms in which a condition of melancholia is productive of imagining evinced in the ties between art and melancholy delineated by Kristeva in *Black Sun*.[27] These questions return us again to the conception of politics in the West having come to inhabit its own depressive state, in which the subject has come to be dislocated from the political as a sphere of action. Indeed, the sense in which – in becoming lost inside themselves, or lost in their imagination and rendered unable to act – the depressive has assumed the status of a symptomal figure of modernity is evinced in one of modernity's archetypal figures: Hamlet.

And yet, putting aside for a moment the hindrances to an engagement with the political presented by the depressed state of contemporary politics – how might imagining function as a catalyst for a move beyond the realm of the Imaginary to an engagement with the Symbolic and Real dimensions of the political? In Lacanian terms, in functioning as the legal-linguistic dimension of the social order, the Symbolic constitutes 'the law' – in constituting both the domain of legal rulings and judgements, but also in the role language plays in structuring social relations. As Scarry (1999: 277–8) notes, while emphasising the benefits of imagining the Other, without recourse to the law this imagining is limited in its capacity to make a practical difference to the terms in which this Other is treated. And yet, while the law might be significant in determining how the Other is acted towards, at the same time – as discussed in the next chapter – the Bush administration's capacity since the September 11 attacks to bend and manipulate the law to its own desires has emphasised the limits of the law in ensuring the 'proper' treatment of the Other. As in the case of the development of democracy in Afghanistan, what is needed is for the Imaginary, Symbolic, and Real dimensions of the political to be engaged with – with the Real constituting here the order at which changes in the conception of the Other at the Imaginary and Symbolic come to register in how the Other as physical, embodied subject is treated materially.

And yet, this move beyond the Imaginary faces a further obstacle in regard to Lacan's (1994: 101, 109) assessment of the pacifying effects of images and the 'trap for the gaze' they present. In this respect, the very proliferation of and centrality accorded to images in the War on Terror – while presenting a source for imagining this conflict – can at the same time be configured as limiting the capacity of this imagining to constitute a catalyst for a move beyond the Imaginary: a contention supported by Scarry (1993) in her analysis of US audiences and the 1991 Gulf War.[28] Here it is worth pointing to the contribution made by the temporal dimension of images to their pacifying function – a dimension of the image not discussed by Lacan. The spectator who encounters an image is faced with a scene that has already occurred, rendering whatever is seen unable to be intervened in or altered (the exception is when images are live – and even then what is depicted is in the process of taking place and will soon be over). This issue is taken up by Scarry (1999: 282) in distinguishing between the 'retrospective' and 'prospective' imagining of harm. The former, Scarry argues, is far easier to imagine than the latter, in part because of the absence of images of the future – giving rise to a situation in which, 'we are as a population almost empty of ethical worry about the future'.[29] (Perhaps what is required then is for a contemporary artist to undertake a project which addresses the future casualties of war – and yet the speculative status of such a project is likely to limit its impact). As Scarry emphasises though, the irony is that while the past cannot be changed, the future might be – an irony that is imbued with added resonance by the configuring of the War on Terror as a conflict without end.

8
Phantoms and Jails

The conception of the enemy as constituting a type of spectral presence has been suggested at various points across the preceding chapters. It is worth reiterating the extent to which, since the September 11 attacks, this enemy has been invoked via reference to a lexicon of the ghostly. To take just a scattering of examples: insurgents in Iraq are described as 'ghosts of death';[1] in Baquba, Iraq, for the US military, 'The enemy was a phantom who never showed his face';[2] weeks after the September 11 attacks, US forces, as they embark for Afghanistan, are described as sailing 'against a ghost enemy';[3] in the UK the terrorist threat conjured up by the government is dismissed as a 'phantom menace';[4] and, as outlined in discussing Bin Laden's video appearances, Bin Laden has repeatedly been described as presenting a type of ghostly, phantomic presence, as in his guise as 'Al Qaeda's spectral anchorman'.[5] The depiction of the enemy-as-spectral at once invokes: the sense in which this enemy has remained only fitfully visible, the uncertainty surrounding its activities and the difficulties of fixing it in place, along with the anxieties and imaginings it has given rise to – all of which have contributed to the conception of the enemy haunting the West.

The sense of uncertainty surrounding this enemy is evident in the contrast between it and that faced by the West in the Cold War. The USSR-Warsaw Pact presented a definite, locatable profile, one that was anxious to assert its visibility – as evident, for example, in the annual Mayday parades. As Renata Salecl (2004: 150) observes in discussing anxiety in the contemporary West, 'When people feel uncertain and afraid they are in search of clear images of their enemies': images which were provided in the Cold War but have repeatedly been denied in the War on Terror. Indeed the relative absence of a visible enemy has resulted in the visible manifestations of the enemy that have emerged taking on a particular significance – as evident in the attention accorded to Bin Laden's video appearances, and in the UK in the media coverage of the 'monstrous' appearance of the (now former) Finsbury Park mosque preacher, Abu Hamza, who possesses prosthetic metal 'hook' hands and has lost an eye – injuries purportedly incurred while clearing landmines in Afghanistan.[6]

There exists a further dimension to the conception of the enemy in the War on Terror as constituting a type of ghostly presence – the sense in which this enemy has the ability to expand or multiply (as ghosts exhibit in their facility to change shape and separate into multiple forms[7]). This is a dimension of the enemy that the United States and its allies have helped to generate. As Stephen Grey outlines (2006: 226–8) in his study of the CIA's secret rendition programme, *Phantom Plane* (the title of which makes explicit the associations between this programme and the ghostly), after the September 11 attacks, 'Islamic militants' in general, as in the case of Hezb'allah in Lebanon, Hamas in Palestine, and in Chechnya – whether or not they possessed any links to Al Qaeda or constituted a direct threat to the West – were located alongside Al Qaeda as targets of the War on Terror. Indeed the tendency to conflate these groups and multiply the scale of the threat perceived to be faced in the War on Terror can be read in the comparison drawn in September 2007 by the UK Defence minister, Des Browne, between the Taliban and Hamas: 'In Afghanistan, at some stage, the Taliban will need to be involved in the peace process because they are not going away any more than I suspect Hamas are going away from Palestine.'[8] Browne's assessment was met with consternation by what one report termed 'an official' in Kabul (seemingly a member of the UK embassy), who contended that 'You can't compare a coherent political organisation like Hamas with a non-unified movement with little grassroots support.'[9] Indeed, Browne's comment points again to the disregard displayed by the United States and its allies for the election of Hamas and the functioning of democracy when it does not conform to the West's desires. At the same time though, this sense of an expanding, multiplying enemy supports the sense in which the War on Terror has come to be configured not just as a war against Al Qaeda, Islamic terrorism, or even terrorism in general, but as Alberto Toscano (2007: 196) identifies it: a war against 'the enemies of humanity *tout court*'. Such an assessment points in the direction of the conflict conceived as a type of apocalyptic global struggle that invokes – as was suggested in discussing the assault on Afghanistan in Chapter 2 – the book of Revelations and the massing of spectres and monstrous beings that occurs there.

This chapter is concerned with another, or further, dimension to the conception of this enemy as constituting a type of ghostly or phantomic presence – the terms in which this conception of the enemy serves to illuminate the attempts to 'deal with' it, as foregrounded in the CIA's 'extraordinary rendition' programme.

A parallel world, to despectralise

The origins of the extraordinary programme extend back to the mid-1990s when the CIA instigated the seizure and transport of suspected Islamic terrorists to foreign states as a means of circumventing US law on the detention of suspects. In the wake of the September 11 attacks, this programme expanded significantly to involve the snatching of suspects from numerous countries (including Canada, Germany, Italy, and Sweden), and their transportation either to US-run facilities outside the United States (notably in Afghanistan), or their turning over to foreign security services for detention and interrogation, in particular Egypt, Jordan, Morocco, Syria, and Uzbekistan – and also, it is alleged, to a number of Eastern European countries, including Poland and Romania.[10] (While there is a degree of overlap here with the transportation to and detention of prisoners at Guantanamo Bay, both the location of the latter and the identity of detainees held there are in the public realm.) Even though the existence of the extraordinary rendition programme has been exposed, the programme purportedly remains ongoing (Grey 2006: 241). Furthermore, the aspects of the programme that have been uncovered raise the question of those features of the programme that have not come to light.

Just as Al Qaeda has utilised a hidden network of global travelling to wage its war against the West, so, via extraordinary rendition, the United States has instigated a parallel (or inverse) system of travelling that also seeks to remain unseen. (It would be revealing to construct a map of both networks to render visible the shape of these movements.) Indeed, extraordinary rendition has relied upon the creation of a form of parallel world for its functioning, utilising – an innocuous and unremarkable, in appearance at least – network of hotel rooms, warehouses, trucks, and aeroplanes. The slightness of the boundary between these two realms, and the speed at which a detainee can be moved from one to the other, is suggested in a scene showing the seizure of a suspect on arrival at Washington Dulles airport in Gavin Hood's *Rendition* (2007) – a film centred on the removal of a suspected terrorist living in the United States to North Africa. In standing in reach of 'normality' – and appearing from the outside as unremarkable – this parallel world invokes the uncanny ('unheimlich' – unhomely) that Freud ([1919] 1995) identifies as emanating from a sense of the familiar made strange. Indeed, a trope of narratives of Horror is the existence of a parallel nightmare world that exists alongside that of the everyday world (as evinced in the films *The Shining* (1980) and *The Exorcist* (1973)). Furthermore, the very capacity for this parallel world to be hidden away, to the extent that the 'network has no visible infrastructure – no prison rolls, visitor rosters, staff lists or complaint procedures' (Grey 2006: 20) – has constituted a precondition of its functioning, with outside observers (human rights groups, the United Nations, political opponents) unable to monitor the programme or gauge the full extent of its operations. This sense of the uncanny is evoked in the terminology the programme has given rise to, with its 'black sites' – those unidentified sites of detention suspects disappear into; the reference to those held as 'ghost detainees'; and in Grey designating the Gulfstream III jet he first identified for transporting detainees a 'ghost plane'. Indeed, the whole system of extraordinary rendition possesses an irreal, shifting quality, constituting a second world in which suspects possess little or no idea where (even on which continent) they are being held (ibid.: 238),[11] and administered by a series of shadowy, unidentified figures – the CIA's 'Rendition Group' – clad in black masks that allow them to utilise the visor effect (to see and yet not be seen) associated with the enemy in the War on Terror.

Two principle objectives have been identified with extraordinary rendition – the rendering inactive of individuals suspected of terrorist activity or links to terrorist groups, and the obtaining of knowledge ('intelligence') about these activities. And yet beyond these goals other processes can be detected at work here.

In one respect, where a defining characteristic of the enemy has been the difficulties in identifying its members, and locating them within a discreet place or series of places, the rendering of suspects to detention centres and holding them there (often for an extended period of time) is suggestive of the desire to fix this enemy in place. Indeed, such is the degree this has been taken – as in the case of 'The Grave' in Damascus, where detainees were held in cells three feet wide and six feet long[12] – that this practice is suggestive of an acting out derived from the frustration at the inability to identify the enemy-in-general in the War on Terror with a distinct locale or territory. And yet this fixing of the enemy in place at the same time suggests a parallel desire – to render the enemy permanently visible. The latter is all too evident in the case of Mohamed Bashmilah, arrested in Jordan in August 2003 and transferred to Afghanistan, where he was held in a US facility until May 2005. Here he was shackled in a ten by thirteen foot cell with two video cameras making him constantly visible to his captors (ibid.: 238). Such is the (extreme) degree of visibility achieved here that it is suggestive of an acting out addressed towards another feature of the enemy faced in the War on Terror – its relative invisibility, and the obstacle this has constituted in the fight against it.

Beyond the co-desires to fix in place and render visible the enemy can be traced to another desire though – confirm that this enemy does indeed possess a physical presence, to give the enemy corporeal form, and in terms of the conception of the enemy as a type of spectre, to 'despectralise' it: to transform the enemy from ghosts into material, fleshly beings. As such this process serves to confirm that this enemy can indeed be fought against, be made to experience pain (an issue that will be returned to in a moment), and be killed. At the same time, such a process can be understood as working against the sense in which the shifting, indeterminate profile of the enemy has given rise to fears about its actual ontology, and the extent to which this enemy is merely a type of projected hallucination – the underlying thesis of Adam Curtis's documentary series *The Power of Nightmares* (initially broadcast by the BBC in the autumn of 2004). (Indeed, *The Power of Nightmares* can be seen to enact its own distorting paranoia – that directed towards the state as using a 'non-existent' enemy to extend its control over its citizenry. While the enemy might well have been used in these terms – it is not the case that this enemy is so non-existent). As Salecl (2004: 16) suggests in regard to Iraq – in an assessment that can be applied more broadly to the War on Terror – a key source of anxiety for the United States and its allies has derived from the very absence of a visible, tangible enemy. As such, as Salecl contends, 'in order to deal with this void, the soldier is hoping to actually find an object he might be afraid of, i.e. a clear adversary' – precisely the absence extraordinary rendition seeks to address.

Taken together, at a strategic level the practice of holding the enemy, not only as ghost detainees but in the myriad of forms this can take – including, for example, in domestic jails in the UK, where the number of inmates held in regard to terrorist offences is expected to rise by tenfold over the next decade[13] – offers a means of confirming that the War on Terror is being effectively waged, that the enemy has been located, is being 'dealt with', and victory is being achieved. And yet such has been the number of wrongly detained suspects and doubts about the value of the intelligence coming out of the extraordinary rendition programme that the faith in this programme can be said to possess a delusional quality. Here, one phantasy – that of seizing and detaining an all too evasive enemy gives rise to yet another – that such a process is worthwhile and implies a degree of progress is being made in the War on Terror that is not justified by the actual value of this programme.

Beyond the law

The use of extraordinary rendition and its associations with torture, as with the accusations levelled at the United States of participating in and condoning torture more broadly, has served to foreground the question of the Bush administration's relationship to the law. Since the September 11 attacks the US government has repeatedly sought to move beyond the law, through the utilisation of a range of what have been termed 'extra-legal' measures and practices. Grey (2006: 33) reads the use of this term 'extra-legal' as serving to obscure the illegality of the administration's activities. And yet this term is illuminating in suggesting the measures employed by the Bush administration have constituted a move into a realm beyond and not governed by the law, rather than simply constituting a breaking with or of it.

At one level the accusation of the use of torture has entailed breaking with the Geneva Conventions against the use of torture (as contained articles 3 and 4 of the convention), along with the United Nations Convention against Torture, article 3 of which prohibits the transfer of a prisoner to a country where there is a substantial risk of them being tortured. In a now infamous memo from the then White House Chief of Counsel, Alberto Gonzales, to President Bush penned in January 2002,[14] Gonzales contended that the 'new paradigm' of the War on Terror, and the type of non-state enemy faced in this conflict, rendered 'obsolete' the Geneva Conventions' 'strict limitations on questioning of enemy prisoners' – an assessment that has provided the administration's de facto approach to the enemy.[15] Such a conception of the enemy has constituted the pretext for the ghost detainees of the extraordinary rendition programme to be located outside the law – both in its orthodox legal form, but also in its Lacanian Symbolic form. In regard to the latter, these detainees can be understood as coming to be positioned beyond the Symbolic – in terms of their loss of their status as recognised, nameable subject-citizens, and the rights that are supposed to follow from this – to assume the status of ghosts, in the sense in which these beings inhabit and emanate from the Real.[16] And yet a paradox is evident here, with the desire to despectralise the enemy evident in the use of torture, based upon the assertion of this enemy's spectral status, in the form of them constituting ghost detainees – as if only once they are confirmed as spectres, can they be despectralised.

The terms in which the Bush administration has sought to move beyond the law is evident not just in regard to its international dimensions, but at a national level too, with extraordinary rendition coming into being as a means of moving detainees beyond the reach and restrictions of US law (itself the raison d'etre of Guantanamo Bay, which as a leased zone of Cuban land stands, the administration has argued, beyond the reach of national law). In another respect this is evident in the 'wiretapping' (rubric for electronic surveillance in the broadest terms) of US citizens by the National Security Agency that came to light in December 2005, and has been the subject of repeated legal wrangling.[17] At both international and national levels though, these moves beyond the law can be understood as born from the logic of vengeance Badiou identifies as underpinning the War on Terror. Here, as Badiou discusses (2004: 234), the law is regarded as insufficient to bring justice, and has to be transgressed if the task of vengeance is to be realised. (At the same time the very transgression of the law might be said to constitute evidence of the commitment to winning this conflict.)

And yet in another sense these moves beyond the law can be understood as constituting a declaration of the exceptional status of the United States. While other states are expected to conform to or be bound by international law – even in its most warped or arbitrary form, as evinced in the legal justifications deployed for the invasion of Iraq in regard to Saddam Hussein regime's possession of WMDs, and its failure to comply with UN resolution 1441 to not possess such weapons[18] (of which none were found) – the United States need not do so. There exists another dimension to the reaching beyond the law enacted in extraordinary rendition though. Namely, the very out-sourcing of torture to a country such as Syria, named as a member of the Axis of Evil[19] – and as such one of the transgressors of the moral variant of the law employed by the United States to differentiate good from evil (and subject to the formal legal rulings and sanctions the administration has brought against these states) – constitutes a perfect site for this out-sourcing.

These moves beyond the law have not been confined to the United States though. A series of European countries have demonstrated their complicity with this disregard for the law, in the support they have given to the extraordinary rendition programme. In a report to the European Parliament (passed by the parliament in February 2007), 14 European states were identified as having cooperated with the CIA in its extraordinary rendition programme, with over one thousand suspect flights identified as taking place in European airspace, and with a number of states accused of refusing to cooperate with the investigations.[20] At the same time the programme has threatened to contravene the laws of other Western states – as evident most clearly in the case of Abu Omar, seized in Milan in February 2003 and transported to Egypt where he was held until 2007. This case has resulted in Italian prosecutors attempting to bring charges against 26 US citizens – an action delayed by the attempts of the Italian government to have these charges dismissed.[21]

Conceived in these terms the law assumes the status of something that can be overcome, ignored, or manipulated to fit the desire of the Bush administration. It would be wrong though to think that the awareness and condemnation of these moves beyond the law has brought them to an end. As Grey suggests, extraordinary rendition appears to continue in some form, while Guantanamo Bay remains open, and the Bush administration continues to argue over the legality of its wiretapping measures. This contempt for the law and contempt for having been found to have broken with it is evocative of the decline Lacan ([1969–70] 2007: 180–93) outlines in *Seminar XVII*,[22] in the experience of shame in late modernity, which he associates with a decline in the notion of honour and the subject's sense of their relationship to the law. This is the position the Bush administration, convinced of the utter rightness – and righteousness – of its cause, can be understood as having assumed. Here, the law is subsumed to the administration's desires, rather than being something the administration need comply with. Indeed, to invoke the administration's sense of righteousness points to the religiosity of the Bush administration's conception of the War on Terror. This is a conception that supports these moves beyond the law, in reinforcing the sense in which the administration, engaged in a conflict of divine significance, can ignore the demands of worldly-secular law. And yet it would be wrong to see the moves beyond the law undertaken by the Bush administration as confined to the past. Rather, they have set in motion an ongoing process, that results in a further weakening of the law, as in the case of the refusal to bring senior Al Qaeda members, including Khalid Sheikh Mohammed to trial, for the fear it would expose the use of torture in their interrogation.[23]

Torture, knowledge ...?

While the Bush administration has consistently denied the use of torture, along with the transporting of suspects to countries suspected of its use, it is as a means of obtaining knowledge from terrorist suspects that torture has been argued for by a body of commentators and legal experts both in the United States and beyond. Indeed, the very conception of the enemy as spectral and/or monstrous – and in some sense less than human or non-human – can be understood as having encouraged the legitimisation of the use of torture against this enemy.

The question of the type of knowledge torture produces needs though to be raised again. As Grey (2006: 236) discusses, torture does typically result in a prisoner 'confessing' to certain acts and providing 'information' – in the sense of replying to the questions posed to them – whatever the validity of these replies may be. In the case of Khalid Sheikh Mohammed (the 'mastermind' of the September 11 attacks) and Abu Zubayah (Al Qaeda's primary military strategist since 2001), the intelligence produced by their interrogation appears to have been of value (ibid.: 219). However, more broadly, as a host of further cases from the War on Terror (and other contexts) indicates, torture repeatedly results in the prisoner confessing and providing 'information' simply as a means of attempting to bring the torture to a halt (ibid.: 219).

In such circumstances – and with typically little immediate means of differentiating valid from invalid 'intelligence' – the value of the knowledge produced by torture is highly dubious. Not only might this knowledge be false, at the same time it is potentially misleading, resulting in a waste of resources and the potential arrest and rendition of other innocents, that in turn sets in place another false trail of investigations and seizures, potentially ad nauseam. Indeed, as Scarry (1985: 33) asserts in *The Body in Pain*, torture places the prisoner in the position in which to talk presents a means of asserting they are still alive and can still function at some level in the face of the intense experience of pain. Conceived in such a way the speech that emerges from torture and the 'knowledge' it offers constitutes little more than the pained eruptions brought into being from out of the terrible jouissance of the tortured.[24] In so doing the speech of the tortured comes closer to Mladen Dolar's (2006: 27) conception of 'the scream' as the 'inarticulate presymbolic manifestation of the voice', that emanates from the Real of the body's experience of pain, rather than constituting a source of Symbolic knowledge.

That the speech of the tortured is regarded as a source of knowledge reveals the extent to which the type of knowledge being dealt in here accords with that which Lacan (1997: 39) designates 'paranoid knowledge': that knowledge which is not concerned with its validity, but with the sense of false mastery it provides the subject with. In the context of the War on Terror, the knowledge produced by torture has served the Bush administration in justifying the means by which this conflict has been pursued. This is foregrounded in the case of Ibn al Shakhal al Libi, captured around the end of 2001 and accused of running an Al Qaeda training camp in Afghanistan – with the information he gave under torture cited by the Bush administration in the months leading up to invasion of Iraq as key evidence of a connection between Saddam Hussein and Al Qaeda.[25] More broadly though, as Susan Willis (2006) discusses in adumbrating the boom in the United States in the security industry since the September 11, rather than seeing the extraction of knowledge from detainees at Guantanamo Bay in terms of its actual usefulness as intelligence, this knowledge has come to function as a symbolic resource in its own right, a commodity the circulation of which (regardless of its validity) serves to feed 'the exponential growth of the American appetite for security' (ibid.: 124). (Willis compares the level of waste in this industry with other industries in their nascent stages). Indeed, as the al Libi case suggests, a use can be found for this knowledge regardless of its validity. This is evident in the claims by John Ashcroft, the US Attorney General, in June 2002, of a plot to detonate a radioactive dirty bomb in the United States. Here, intelligence gleaned from Ethiopian born Binyam Mohammed – who had been held in Morocco and possibly Afghanistan – provided evidence to support Ashcroft's otherwise unsupported claims (Grey 2006: 40). More broadly though, a system has been established whereby the United States supplies suspicions of terrorist activity, while outsourcing the torture of suspects to countries who obtain suitable confessions from suspects, who, in the words of Binyam Mohammed, 'will sign anything; confess to anything' (ibid.: 51). In so doing a seemingly 'perfect' system for the circulation of paranoid knowledge has been established, whereby all suspicions can be found to be justified – a situation that in turn leads to extraordinary rendition and torture coming to be regarded as ever more vital to the War on Terror.

And yet the use of torture extends beyond the question of knowledge production. Not only does extraordinary rendition involve the desire to fix the imagined enemy's body in place, and to confirm that the enemy does indeed possess a physical form that can be rendered supine. The practice of torture extends a stage further than this, to demonstrate that this enemy can indeed be made to experience pain. As such the use of torture can be configured in those terms outlined by Zizek (1996: 105), in which for the sadist, 'by the means of my victim's pain, I make the Other exist'. In this context torture is established as the extended submission of those captured to pain over and above death, with the latter constituting something too final (and too quick) for the torturer, who seeks to sustain the experience of pain undergone by the Other. In terms of the logic of vengeance delineated by Badiou, the use of torture accords then with the sense in which for the enemy to simply die would not be enough – rather an extended process of suffering has to be inflicted upon it. Indeed, as Scarry (1985: 27) asserts, so pervasive are the doubts about the use of torture as a means of knowledge production that the practice of torture must be understood as an acting out intended to demonstrate the capacity of the torturer to assert their power. And yet, as Scarry contends, the very recourse to torture can be taken as revealing the hollowness of the torturer's power – marking its failure in the public sphere and its displacement into the realm of a closed off, acting out of violence (hence the association of torture with regimes that rely upon violent oppression to sustain their position of power). In the context of the War on Terror, the terms in which torture functions as an instance of acting out is all too visible in *Rendition* – reflecting cinema's capacity to focus attention upon the spectacular dimensions of that which it depicts – in which any sense of the extended process of torture depicted in the film producing knowledge of value is eclipsed by the desire on the part of the captors to enact the spectacle of torture.

Here, Lacan's notion of 'the two deaths' developed in *Seminar VII* (1992: 270–283) serves to cast further light on this concern to inflict pain rather than bring death. This formulation of the two deaths is typically ordered in terms of a biological death (death in the Real) constituting a first death, which precedes death in the Symbolic, with the latter presenting the erasure of the subject's presence at the Symbolic from the world – as in the loss of the traces or records of their existence. In the case of extraordinary rendition however, the detainee comes to inhabit 'the zone between two deaths', having died an initial Symbolic death – as Lacan puts it, being 'not yet dead' in the biological sense, but 'eliminated from the world of the living' (ibid.: 280): with their sudden, 'inexplicable' disappearance resulting in the loss of their status as subject-citizens. In so doing the detainees come to inhabit that realm which Lacan identifies with Hamlet's inability to kill Claudius, because 'simply to kill is not enough, he wants him to suffer hell's eternal torture' (ibid.: 251).

'Was it really worth fighting?'

And yet ultimately, despite the purposes torture has been employed for by the Bush administration – namely, victory in the War on Terror (if indeed 'final victory' is what is sought[26]) – the use of torture can be judged self-defeating even in these terms. The matrix 'torture – extraordinary rendition – Guantanamo Bay – Abu Gharib' has served to fatally undermine the values the Bush administration and its allies have sought to identify as directing the War on Terror – serving both to cast doubt on the purposes of this war, along with the claims made for democracy, liberalism and 'freedom' as its guiding stars.[27] This is a situation that has only been worsened by the body of commentators and analysts who have sought to assert the morality of torture – to the extent of casting those who oppose its use as immoral (Grey 2006: 131–3), or, as in the case of Alan Dershowitz, who have argued for a system of 'torture warrants' to imbue its practice with bureaucratic legitimacy.[28] (This latter notion promises to lead us directly into a world of legitimised and more deeply entrenched bureaucratic horror, of which Kafka is the key imaginer). Indeed, such has been the extent to which the raison d'etre of the War on Terror has threatened to be undermined by this terrible matrix that, as Grey (ibid.: 169) suggests, 'If this was the War Terror, many would ask, was it really worth fighting?'

Not only though has the use of torture served to cast doubts on the purpose of the War on Terror, at the same time it has served to increase the number of those around the world who possess a grievance against the United States and its allies, in terms not only of the direct victims of extraordinary rendition, but their families, friends, and more broadly still, the Muslim ummah. Indeed, the practice of torture can be located as a catalyst in the very formulation of Islamic militancy, with Sayyid Qutb – the father-philosopher of militant Islam – penning his principal work during his time (1954–64) inside Cairo's Torah prison where he was tortured. In the period since the September 11 attacks the enemy has been all too aware of the sense in which the accusation of torture by the United States and its allies might be turned to its advantage. As Grey (ibid.: 221) asserts, terrorist groups have long recognised the value of provoking repression – in the recognition that exposing the 'brutality' and 'inhumanity' of the regimes they are pitted against will generate further support for their cause – with Al Qaeda training manuals instructing those captured to insist torture was inflicted upon them (ibid.: 239).

In the face of the corrosive effects torture and this extended matrix of practices have had upon the pursuit of the War on Terror, the desire of the Bush administration to refuse to definitively bring a halt to such practices – quibbling over the precise definition of torture and the status of a variety of extra-legal procedures – emphasises the terms in which the use of torture, rather than possessing any strategic worth, conforms with the acting out of a logic of vengeance. Here, to follow Lacan's conception of acting out, the 'call for interpretation' presented in this act takes the form: 'We will continue to act however we so wish, regardless of how you (the rest of the world) perceive us ...' As such, this demand for vengeance assumes a narcissistic value that serves to not only place it above the law, but above any concern about the way in which the United States is viewed around the world. And yet, as was suggested in discussing the disappeared of Afghanistan, what is occluded and denied in the assumption of this position of calculated defiance is the sense that the United States will at some point have to pay for its actions, and will come to be haunted by what has taken place in its name – that the ghost detainees produced by extraordinary rendition will return in pursuit of redress for what has happened to them: a process already evident in the attempts by former detainees Maher Arar and Khaled al Masri to prosecute those responsible for what has happened to them.[29] In so doing, via the act of haunting, these detainees move from a realm beyond the law into a position where their demands for justice can be heard.

9
The Unseen

If the programme of extraordinary rendition points towards the existence of an aspect of the War on Terror that has deliberately sought to be kept beyond the realm of the seen (at least for anyone not involved directly in the programme), the unseen dimensions of the conflict extend far beyond this programme. Indeed, it is possible to point to two broad dimensions of the unseen that have weaved their way through the War on Terror.

Firstly, there exists what might be called the 'empirical unseen'. Particular attention has been drawn to this dimension of the unseen by those aspects of the conflict which the US government and military have deliberately sought to keep out of the public realm. This is evident in the case of the body of images from Abu Ghraib shown to US senators, but deemed too 'disturbing' to appear elsewhere, which as Simpson (2006: 108) notes, have been kept out of sight by a combination of legal prohibition and 'a conspiracy of silence'.[1] The Bush administration's argument on limiting the disclosure of these images centred on their dissemination damaging US interests, and – in yet another example of the duplicity that has so undermined the moral claims made for the War on Terror – that their disclosure would contravene the Geneva Convention against the humiliation of prisoners, by showing prisoners being treated in such degrading fashion.[2] This aspect of the unseen is evident as well in the case of the CIA's destruction of video tapes of the interrogation of suspected Al Qaeda members from 2002 that came to light in December 2007 in investigations into CIA interrogation practices.[3] While the CIA claimed the tapes were destroyed in order to protect the identity of the interrogators, and because they were no longer of intelligence value, critics pointed to the fear they would reveal the agency's use of torture.

Yet another instance of this attempt to deliberately render aspects of the conflict unseen is evident in the injunction against images showing the coffins of US service personnel returning to the United States from Iraq and Afghanistan. Images of this nature have been subject to a Pentagon ruling dating from 1991 – in the wake of the Gulf War – that prohibits the depiction of 'the movement of remains at any point'[4] of service personnel. This ruling was however seldom applied, until its strict reinforcement in the wake of the Iraq War, as evinced in the action taken against employees of a US cargo contractor in Kuwait whose images of coffins draped in the stars and stripes returning to Dover Air Force base appeared in April 2004 in the *Seattle Times*.[5]

At another level there exists those images which while not subject to deliberate efforts to keep them out of the public domain have been deemed 'unsuitable' for dissemination, through a tacit sense of what is 'inappropriate' to be shown – as already highlighted in the case of images of Western casualties. And yet alongside these categories there stands those aspects of the conflict that have never been seen by anyone beyond those who directly witnessed them. This is due to their having never been photographed or filmed, or if they have, to this material never having been disseminated – either because nobody was on hand with the equipment to record them, or because they were not considered worth capturing and disseminating.

This latter domain of the unseen serves to raise the question though of whether the War on Terror can be delineated in this way at all, of whether it is possible to ascertain precisely where this conflict is present and where it is absent – an issue foregrounded in the creeping securitisation of everyday life in the West that has occurred since the September 11 attacks. Such a conception of the unseen suggests the existence of an imagined total realm of vision – in which the subject locates themselves as seen by the Other – that Lacan (1994: 67–119) designates with his notion of the gaze. (Indeed, it can be argued that an awareness of such a realm is stimulated by the very proliferation of images of the conflict.[6]) Lacan contrasts this realm with another dimension of vision that serves to raise questions about the ontological status of this abstract realm of vision and its applicability to the War on Terror: the terms in which this conflict is seen from the perspective of the individual subject-spectator's point of view – that which in differentiating between 'the eye and the gaze', Lacan (ibid.: 67–78) designates as 'the eye'. The latter suggests another dimension to the unseen, in terms of that domain which surrounds the (and each) individual subject's field of vision – and which serves to emphasise how the existence of a visual field serves to generate its own unseen. The latter highlights that in order to grasp all the terms in which the conflict has and has not been seen would be to grasp all of these points of view, along with their existence over the duration of the conflict.

Beyond these various manifestations of the empirical unseen there exists a second dimension to the unseen, which derives from the limits on seeing as a means of comprehending and providing knowledge of the world: the 'epistemological unseen'. In terms of Lacan's ontological schema this covers those orders that exist 'beyond' the Imaginary (the realm of seeing and surface appearances) – namely, the Symbolic and the Real dimensions of the War on Terror. At the same time this dimension of the unseen points towards the sense in which, as Elkins discusses in *The Object Stares Back* (1996), despite the prevalence of notions to the contrary, vision is a profoundly unstable epistemological device, prey as it is to the fluctuations of desire, misrecognition, and illusion, as well as the panoply of physiological aberrations in the subject's visual capacities, to the extent that Elkins contends, 'no two people will see the same object' (ibid.: 41).[7]

These twin dimensions of the unseen serve to raise questions about the centrality of the significance accorded to imagery in the War on Terror, and the attendant sense in which this conflict has been photographed and filmed to an unprecedented degree. At the same time, these co-dimensions of the unseen problematise the broader notion, pervasive in contemporary culture – as manifest purportedly in 'reality television', and the degree of visual scrutiny accorded to 'celebrity culture' – that we have come to inhabit a world in which we see and hence know more about than ever before. Ignored in such a contention is the way in which every visual field serves to create its own unseen, and the limits of seeing as a means of comprehending the world foregrounded by the notion of the epistemological unseen.

This chapter takes up the question of the unseen in the War on Terror in regard to a specific theme – the field of the image (the form in which publics have encountered so many aspects of the conflict) and its relationship to the unseen – to examine the issues this relationship raises for the terms in which this conflict has been perceived and comprehended by Western publics.

'Blind field', *Taube*, Haditha

Barthes, in his study of photography *Camera Lucida* (2000: 55–7), draws attention to those images which, in seeking to make sense of what he sees before him, provoke him to reach beyond the limits of their frame into what he terms their 'blind field'. For Barthes the majority of images possess no such field, in the sense that they fail to provoke a reflection on the existence of this field, with 'everything which happens within the frame' dying 'absolutely once this frame is passed beyond' (ibid.: 57). And yet, in the context of this discussion, I want to emphasise the sense in which all images possess such a field – while acknowledging the differing extent to which images provoke the spectator into the awareness and consideration of it. Indeed, in regard to the dimensions of the unseen outlined above, the blind field can be understood as made up of both the empirical unseen – that exists beyond the image's frame, and, the epistemological limits of seeing – in terms of that which cannot be comprehended at a visual level.

It is an image from World War I – Christopher Nevinson's painting *A Taube* (1916)[8] (Figure 9.1) – that I want to take as the point of departure for scrutinising the terms in which the relationship between the field of an image and the unseen functions in conflict situations. The painting shows a scene from Dunkirk in which a boy – a trickle of

Figure 9.1 Christopher Nevinson, *A Taube* (1916), Oil on canvas, Imperial War Museum, London

blood running from his head – lies facedown on the ruptured cobbles of a pavement fronting a badly damaged house. This is a picture that foregrounds the question of the relationship between the field of the image and the blind field. While the human casualties and physical destruction wrought by war are, it seems, present in the field of the image, the source of both remain unseen, beyond the image's range. In so doing the painting raises the questions: What has happened here? What has caused this destruction and the condition we see the boy in? To understand what has happened in this painting – and the presence of the blood might be taken as intimating that whatever has happened to the boy has occurred relatively recently – the spectator is drawn beyond the image into the empirical and epistemological unseen. In so doing, and in taking processes which are so fundamental to conflict – a human casualty and the destruction of the physical environment – this image presents a template for thinking about the terms in which the relationship between the seen and the unseen comes to figure as a dynamic in comprehending conflict situations.

And yet, while the questions raised by this painting can be applied to conflicts in general, this painting is rooted in developments associated with a specific historical moment: the emergence in the First World War of air power as a military force, and the terms in which this served to dramatically extend the distance from which opposing sides could wage war against one another – including extending radically the vulnerability of civilian populations to warfare. In so doing Nevinson's painting offers a premonitory image – as the painter recognised in his autobiography, *Paint and Prejudice* (1937: 76): 'Dunkirk was one of the first towns to suffer aerial bombardment, and I was one of the first men to see a child who had been killed by it. There the small boy lay before me, a symbol of all that was to come.'

While Nevinson's painting is addressed towards a specific conflict, the types of issues it raises have taken on a heightened significance since the First World War. The period since that conflict has witnessed the rapid development of military technologies that have made possible the infliction of casualties and the destruction of the physical environment from ever greater distances, with such technologies coming to span the world and reach into space. Indeed, the year 1957 – in which the Soviet Union and the United States staged the first successful ICBM tests – is particularly significant in this respect. One result of this has been that for the spectator those aspects of a conflict which appear within an image (or within moving image footage), or in the spectator's own field of vision, have come to provide an increasingly limited perspective on the overall scale of a conflict – even when the definition of the latter is limited to the actual fighting that takes place. At the same time, the blind field, from which the cause of what has happened in Nevinson's picture emanates, can be understood as having radically expanded in scale and significance. While the significance of this development varies between different types of conflicts, it can be argued that the 1991 Gulf War stands as pivotal to this process – in marking a shift away from the depiction of the conflict via indexical images (photography and film of the conflict taking place), to the use of computer graphics, maps, and diagrams to illustrate the campaign – as evinced at one level in the commonplace description of Operation Desert Storm resembling 'a computer game'. Indeed, this development constitutes one dimension of Baudrillard's ([1991] 2002: 29–30) infamous assertion, 'the Gulf War did not take place'.

In the context of the War on Terror this sense of an expanded blind field raises significant questions for the terms in which publics come to perceive, imagine, and comprehend what is taking place in this conflict of global dimensions.[9] And yet, at the same time, running counter to this development, there stands the twin notions of the centrality of the significance accorded to imagery in the War on Terror, and the sense in which this conflict has been photographed and filmed to an unprecedented degree. This seeming paradox raises the question of which aspects of the conflict are actually seen by Western publics. To take two notable examples (analysed in the preceding chapters), while the aerial bombardment of Afghanistan and the Shock and Awe assault on Iraq may each have been accorded significant media attention, the impact of these assaults, in terms of the casualties they produced and destruction to the physical environment they generated, were accorded comparatively little attention. Indeed, those features of the War on Terror that have provided a focus for media attention can be understood as having served to provide the spectator with the sense that they have indeed seen more than ever before of a conflict, and to limit the sense in which there is 'more' taking place in this conflict 'than meets the eye'. A similar process is evident, as Lewis (2003: 331) suggests in regard to the 1991 Gulf War, in the public awareness of the military technology used generated by the media attention accorded to this technology, in comparison with a lack of knowledge about Iraqi casualties.

While raising significant questions in regard to the empirical unseen, at the same time, Nevinson's painting invokes the epistemological unseen. In one respect this takes the form of the limits of the Imaginary as a source of knowledge, raised by the question, what is happening in this painting? Without recourse to the Symbolic the answer to this question remains indeterminate. The scene depicted in the painting might have been caused by a natural disaster,[10] riot, or some form of internal political unrest. Without reference to the work's accompanying title, date, and commentaries on it – as in Nevinson's own discussion of the work – it is impossible to tell. In such terms, despite the developments made in visual technologies since the First World War, the painting serves to foreground the persistence of the epistemological limits of seeing. This is an issue that has been repeatedly evident in the War on Terror, where it has taken on a particular salience in regard to questions of justice, in which the Symbolic must be applied for judgements about what has taken place to be made – demonstrating how the Symbolic functions as integral to the law. To take two examples from Iraq, this is evident in the case of the Haditha 'massacre' of November 2005 in which 15 Iraqi civilians were purportedly killed by US marines in the western Iraqi city. While images exist of the aftermath of what occurred there – including a photograph taken by lawyer Khaled Salem Rsayef soon after the event of an empty blood splattered bedroom, along with video footage shot by the Hammurabi Human Rights Group and cellphone images taken by a US marine – by themselves these images are insufficient for any conclusions to be arrived at as to what took place, and to constitute a basis for justice to be administered.[11] A similar situation is evident in the case of the May 2004 Mukaradeeb 'wedding party massacre', that occurred near the border with Syria, in which US forces purportedly killed 42 Iraqis celebrating a wedding, believing them to be insurgents. While a video showing a dozen white pick-up trucks escorting a bridal car, from which a bride emerges, have been taken as suggesting that this was indeed a wedding party,[12] without recourse to the Symbolic – including, for example, interviewing eyewitnesses about what they saw take place – little can be established or ascertained. (Again, a similar situation is evident in regard to the September 11 attacks, with the conspiracy theories about the attacks pivoting on the epistemological limits of seeing and the sense in which the 'truth' of what occurred cannot be established at a visual level.)

At the same time as raising the question of the relationship of the Imaginary to the Symbolic, Nevinson's painting serves to foreground the question of the relationship between the Imaginary and the Real, and the terms in which the presence of the latter comes to register in the field of the image. Indeed this painting can be taken as foregrounding this issue – in one respect in terms of the destruction of the physical environment it depicts and the sense of the collapse of the hard Real (as enacted in the collapse of the Twin Towers) this presents, but perhaps more starkly still in the form of the figure of the boy who lies facedown with a trickle of blood from his head, and the question this figure raises in regard to the difficulties around seeing death. Here the boy's body can be understood as taking on the status of Lacan's conception of the blot (as discussed in the opening chapters) – registering the presence of the Real in the image – that in turn takes us beyond the visible field of this painting in the attempt to ascertain what is happening here.

The blot, 'Operation First Casualty', the ghostly

Barthes associates an awareness of the blind field of an image with the presence in the image of a punctum (2000: 55–7) – that unexpected element he finds in certain images which serves to 'prick' or provoke his gaze and constitutes the source of his fascination with them. There are clear parallels between the blot and the punctum, in regard to the capacity of each to disrupt the terms in which the spectator sees the image, in so doing generating a questioning of the nature of seeing, and pointing in the direction of an image's unseen or blind field. Indeed, Barthes alludes to sense in which the punctum invokes the unnameable, unsignifiable Real, in contending that 'What I can name cannot really prick me' (ibid.: 51).

The blot, in constituting the terms in which the Real achieves a presence in the field of the image – and in so doing bringing about a rupture in the Imaginary – raises the question of the limits of seeing, in invoking both the empirical and epistemological dimensions of the unseen: as evident in regard to two examples from the War on Terror.

The first of these is presented in a campaign organised in the United States by the Iraq Veterans against the War, a group formed in July 2004, with the purpose of campaigning for the immediate withdrawal of all foreign forces from Iraq, and improved support for returning US service personnel.[13] The organisation's work has included demonstrations, media campaigns, and confrontations with military recruiters. The aspect of their activities of particular relevance to this chapter though is 'Operation First Casualty' – the re-enactment of combat patrols in a series of cities across the United States, the first of which took place in Washington DC, on 19 March 2007,[14] and was covered by the *Washington Post*:

> 13 Iraq war veterans in full desert camo going on 'patrol' from Union Station to Arlington National Cemetery. They carried imaginary assault rifles, barked commands, roughly 'detained' suspected

hostiles with flex cuffs and hoods – and generally shocked, frightened and delighted tourists and office workers.

They cut a swath across downtown, taking imaginary sniper fire and casualties on the grounds of the Capitol and the Washington Monument, scouting the White House, performing mock arrests at the foot of the Capitol steps and a vehicle search on the Mall. At the Capitol, the veterans almost got detained themselves by civilian peace officers with real guns. The vets brought their act to a military recruiting station on L Street NW and concluded with a memorial ceremony in the cemetery.

As the *Post*'s piece continued:

Outside the Metro station were about eight civilians with white T-shirts over their winter clothes. In real life, they are antiwar activists. On this day they played suspects and bystanders in a war zone patrolled by an edgy occupying army.

Shouts and curses, shoving and arm-twisting, from Reppenhagen and his men: 'Don't move!' 'Get down on the ground!' 'Do I have to shoot you, or are you going to stay still?'

The soldiers twisted on the cuffs and adjusted the hoods, then ordered, 'Get 'em out of here!'

Alongside this Washington action, re-enactments have also been staged in New York (May 2007), Chicago, and Los Angeles (both in June 2007). Underpinning these re-enactments lies the desire to overcome the division in experience between the US homeland and the experience of serving in Iraq – to bridge the gap between the Imaginary semblance of this conflict, as its appears in the media and as it is photographed and filmed, and its Real form. As one participant, Aaron Hughes, a sergeant in a transportation unit that convoyed troops and supplies between Iraq and Kuwait noted, 'When I got home, the hardest thing for me was realizing the war does not exist here.'[15] In so doing these re-enactments can be understood as seeking to bring about a rupture in the everyday life of the cities they were staged in, to bring the Real of the war back to 'the homeland', provoking the tuché of an encounter with this Real that will jolt the US public into reconsidering what is taking place in Iraq, and how much they comprehend of what has happened there. As such these enactments serve not only to assert the continued pertinence of live political actions – in an era in which media and digital technologies are regarded as rendering these actions ever more marginal – but to emphasise the specific role such actions can play in continuing to assert the presence of Real, embodied experience in relation to the political. In so doing these re-enactments can be positioned as working against the pacifying effects of the image delineated by Lacan – at once focusing attention on the Real dimensions of the conflict in Iraq, and constituting a supplement to the imagery publics have encountered of this conflict, in a way that serves to raise questions about the type of access this imagery has provided to the invasion and occupation.

The second dimension to the relationship between the Imaginary and the Real I want to highlight is the conception of the enemy in the War on Terror as a type of ghostly or spectral presence. And here it is worth iterating again the sense in which the ghostly has been located as an emanation of the Real (see, for example, Zizek 1996: 112). In one respect the ghost – in the uncertainties it generates about the relationship between seeing and knowing, in regard to whether a ghost has or has not been (or can or cannot be) seen – serves to cast doubts on the stability of the Imaginary as a source of knowledge, even when the latter takes the form of Imaginary knowledge (the issue taken up more broadly by Elkins (1996)). At the same time, the purported presence of a ghost in an image frequently serves to provoke a questioning as to whether the ghost is 'really there' – a process that, in attempting to establish whether the ghost is present at the Real, serves to configure the ghost as blot. In so doing, in the context of the War on Terror, the ghost raises the question of the correspondence between the form the enemy has assumed at the Imaginary – in terms of how this enemy has been seen, and its presence at the Real – in its material, embodied form. Indeed, the relationship between these two orders raises the issue of how, if the enemy is to be struck at, it is not enough for it to be seen, but – as foregrounded in the case of Bin Laden's video appearances and the hunt for him – for there to be a correspondence between the enemy in its Imaginary and Real forms.

More broadly though, following the links Derrida (1987) draws in *The Truth in Painting* between the frame and the border of an image and how thought is framed, an awareness of the terms in which the enemy has been conceived by the United States and its allies serves to highlight how this conception of the enemy has served to limit the efficacy of the actions taken against it. This was evident, for example, in the immediate aftermath of the attacks, in the desire to reduce Al Qaeda to a locatable territory, in the form of Afghanistan, where it could be bombarded into submission and rounded up and captured. In contrast, the conception of the enemy as a type of ghostly presence – so prevalent in the depiction of the enemy in the Western media since the September 11 attacks – does serve to provide a means of thinking about this enemy in terms which are more attuned to the capacity of the enemy to have slipped away unseen from Afghanistan, to reconfigure itself, and take on new forms: as evident in, for example, the emergence of Al Qaeda in Iraq and in the Maghreb.

At the same time, the ghostly reiterates the sense in which the enemy is positioned as inhabiting and emanating from a realm beyond the field of the visible – the blind field – from which it issues forth to launch its attacks. Indeed, as suggested in preceding chapters, the extent to which the enemy has remained unseen has constituted a key source of the anxiety associated with it. And here it is worth reiterating Freud's ([1926] 1993) contrast between anxiety as lacking an object – as opposed to fear which is directed towards one – and as such being less easy to control and comprehend. Indeed, the terms in which the status of the enemy as unseen contributes to the sense of threat associated with this enemy is illustrated in those narratives of Horror in which the threat is located beyond the domain of the spectator's visual field, and as such is rendered all the more menacing – as evident, in extremis, in *The Blair Witch Project* (1999), in which the monstrous presence is never seen by the audience at all.

As Lacan discusses in *Seminar XI* (1994: 74–97), not only though does the blot constitute the terms in which the Real asserts its presence in the visual field, at the same time it forms the trace or remnant of the objet petit a in this domain. The relationship between the objet petit a (as the object cause of desire) and the visual field raises the issue of scopic desire, prompting a question that hangs over the preceding chapters: what is it the spectator seeks in looking at the myriad of images from the War on Terror? What is it that brings them to watch, perhaps over and again, the two planes hitting the Twin Towers? What is it they seek in seeing Bin Laden's latest video appearance, or videos from Iraq of hostages pleading for their release? And yet, while the objet petit a functions as the object cause of scopic desire, this objet always remains outside the spectator's visual domain, forever out of reach – in so doing serving to provoke the endless play of desire. How then can the objet petit a be configured in regard to the desire to see the imagery the War on Terror has given rise to? This issue was addressed from one angle in discussing the hostage videos to have come out of Iraq, but it is worth raising again as a more general question.

For Lacan the gaze constitutes the subject's awareness of their inhabiting a visual field in which they are seen by the Other. In the context of the War on Terror, the gaze can be configured as taking the form of the spectator's sense of the visual profile they have come to assume in this conflict that serves in one respect to generate an awareness of their existing as a target or victim for the enemy (as delineated in discussing the hostage videos). As Lacan emphasises across his seminar on anxiety (1962–3), anxiety and seeing are intimately bound together, with the visual field constituting a principal domain in which anxiety manifests itself for the subject. Indeed the very significance accorded to imagery in the conflict can be understood as intensifying the spectator's awareness of their potential to be seen by the Other. In looking at these images the spectator strives to situate themselves at the Imaginary in regard to the threats they await in the War on Terror, and to at once ascertain, comprehend, and attempt – at least at a scopic level – to control this sense of threat.

Every image has a silver lining

The unseen constitutes then a realm as complex as that of the seen – while having, for more or less obvious reasons, been accorded considerably less attention. Indeed, the two cannot easily be divided from one another, with each depending on the other for their existence and comprehensibility. And yet, while images might serve to provide the spectator with a sense of their position of vulnerability in the conflict, in another respect the unseen suggests the capacity of this imagery to open onto something more positive and productive.

Barthes (2000: 59), in designating the blind field as the place from which 'I animate' the photograph and 'it animates me', ties this realm to the imaginative capacities of the spectator. And in a certain sense the imagination is always addressed towards the unseen, in terms of imagining constituting a move beyond that which stands before the spectator, into a consideration of what is not immediately there. To return then to the questions raised in Chapter 7: How might the unseen be positioned in regard to the relationship of the imagination to anything beyond the realm of the Imaginary? And in particular, how might it constitute a source of engagement with the political?

In regard to these questions, the unseen can be configured as constituting a realm which extends beyond the pacifying effects of the image, providing an escape from the trap for the gaze images present. This role is emphasised by the type of images Barthes identifies as leading the spectator towards this realm – those which possess a punctum or blot – and that in the disruption their presence renders to the Imaginary results in the spectator coming to question the nature of seeing and their own status as spectators. In terms of the images discussed in this book, the capacity to provoke this questioning has been associated with Inarritu's film on the September 11 attacks, Bin Laden's video appearance at the opening of the US assault on Afghanistan, Nevinson's painting, and the NASA aerial shot of oil wells burning around Baghdad. That all but the latter clearly present an instance of the minor gaze – and it might be argued the NASA image, in emanating from outside of the institutional media does so as well – raises the question of whether the minor gaze constitutes the primary source for these type of images, and the process of questioning they might engender. And, while it would be wrong to assert that this type of image can only emanate from the minor gaze, as Barthes suggests in his critique of news photography (outlined in Chapter 6), for him at least, in this type of institutional media output the presence of a punctum is typically lacking.

It would be an oversimplification though to suggest a deterministic relationship between those images which serve to provoke speculation on the nature of seeing and the imagination coming to constitute a source of engagement with the political dimensions of the War on Terror. While such images might encourage an imagining from which an awareness of these dimensions of the conflict develop, whether these images constitute a source of more substantive political engagement rests on the extent to which the objet petit a around which this scopic desire circulates, is located in relationship to the political – something which the depressed condition of politics in the West and the resulting sense in which the subject comes to locate themselves as divorced from the political, serves to limit.

At its very least then, the unseen constitutes the realm which presents the possibility of not being pacified or trapped by what is encountered in an image, in so doing providing the opportunity to think beyond the Imaginary. At the same time, this realm points in the direction of an alternative past and future to the War on Terror. In regard to the former it suggests an unseen form which the response to the September 11 attacks might have assumed if the Bush administration had not been taken in by the trap for the gaze presented by the September 11 attacks. In regard to the future - that dimension which Scarry locates as so hard to picture - it suggests an approach to dealing with the threat of Islamic terrorism that need not be limited to the type of global scale war without end the War on Terror has developed into.

10
New York: A Return

A lovely morning in New York still brings to mind the cloudless sky on the day aeroplanes crashed into the World Trade Center. Six years on a low-flying plane or a speeding fire truck can still make the heart pound.[1]

As the lines above suggest, since the September 11 attacks New York has found itself haunted by what took place on that late summer morning, as it waits to see if something similar might happen again.[2] (New York can then be said to have experienced a particularly fraught version of Blanchot's notion of 'the interim'.) In New York and elsewhere, this process of post-September 11 waiting has occurred against the backdrop of constant reminders of what happened in September 2001 – reminders that serve to both inform this process of waiting and the terms in which the present state and future course of the War on Terror are thought about.

Lepanto, hierarchies of the dead

The attention accorded to the September 11 attacks stands as a more recent manifestation of the capacity and desire of the West delineated by Davis Hanson (2001: 251–253) in discussing the battle of Lepanto (1571) – to record and commemorate its history, a desire Davis Hanson compares with the relative absence of such a tendency in the non-Western world. As Davis Hanson outlines, in the wake of Lepanto the profusion of Western accounts and commentaries on the battle contrasted sharply with the absence of documentation of the battle on the Ottoman side and elsewhere in 'the east'. (And Davis Hanson stresses that Western accounts of this battle were not simply positive, but also critical and dissenting – with this capacity for self-critique an aspect of Western culture he identifies (ibid.: 389–439) as playing a vital role in the West's historical ascendancy). Davis Hanson extends this analysis – and the terms in which this 'monopoly of commemoration' (ibid.: 251) has promoted the sense in which the West defines 'history'[3] – to the 1991 Gulf War, in contending that 'six billion people on the planet are more likely to read, hear, see accounts of the Gulf War from the American and European vantage points than from the Iraqi' (ibid.: 252). Indeed, the capacity of Al Jazeera (and other non-Western news channels) to challenge a perceived Western hegemony over the recording of history – in the sense that journalism provides 'the first draft of history' – constitutes a further, historically 'deeper' dimension of the hostility felt for the rise of these channels by the Bush administration.

This sense of wanting and needing to record and commemorate the past can be understood as having achieved a kind of apotheosis in the aftermath of the September 11 attacks – underlining the persistence of this desire even in a moment of 'defeat'. The scale and intensity with which the attacks have been commemorated – as evident in the profusion of written material (in various forms: journalism, fiction, poetry, academic analysis), documentaries, feature films, and photographic work devoted to the attacks, along with the attention (within the United States and globally) accorded to the anniversary of the attacks – has outstripped that paid to any other event in recent memory. Indeed, the magnitude and diversity of the ways in which the attacks have been remembered and commemorated has served to suggest that the attacks constituted an event of incomparable significance, a notion reinforced by the attention and status accorded to the victims of the attacks. In one respect this has far exceeded the attention paid to the victims of the other attacks on the Western societies that have take place since September 2001, as in the case of the Madrid and London bombings.[4] And yet the particular significance attributed to the victims of the September 11 attacks has been most clearly evident in comparison with the attitude of the United States and its allies to the non-Western dead from the War on Terror.

The lack of regard for these non-Western dead can be read in General Tommy Franks's oft cited assertion, 'We don't do body counts', a statement that has been repeatedly invoked in regard to the uncertainty surrounding the casualties of the invasion and occupation of Iraq, but was uttered in Franks's role as commander of Operation Anaconda – the March 2002 campaign against Al Qaeda and the Taliban in Eastern Afghanistan.[5] Such a declaration is suggestive of a hierarchy of the dead that has emerged – perhaps most starkly in the United States – since the September 11 attacks. This hierarchy has extended from, at its lowest reaches, the non-Western dead who possess so little value that they are not even deemed worthy of quantification, up to, at its peak the dead from the September 11 attacks. Indeed, the lack of significance attributed to these non-Western dead is reinforced by the sense in which, in a culture obsessed with quantification and metrics, these dead have failed to be counted.[6] At the same time though this refusal can be understood as a further legacy of the Vietnam War, in which, faced with the difficulties in gauging the progress made against the North Vietnamese, body counts were used by the US military as a means of attempting to establish how the war was progressing. The truth of Ho Chi Minh's comment – delivered in the context of the preceding struggle against the French – 'You can kill ten of our men for every one we kill of yours. But even at those odds, you will lose and we will win' – served to emphasise the inadequacies of this procedure, leading to its subsequent abandonment by the US military (as evident in the 1991 Gulf War). And yet, even if this refusal to count the dead is viewed in these instrumental terms, evident here remains the fact that the non-Western dead are accorded secondary significance to this rationale.

This sense of the incomparable value accorded to the September 11 dead has in turn come to the fore in the plans to redevelop the Ground Zero site. The news that the 2007 anniversary would be the last time the victims' families would have access to the Ground Zero 'pit' itself created controversy – not least because human fragments were still being discovered there.[7] Yet such discontent constitutes only a more recent manifestation of a longer opposition to the plans to reconstruct the site. This has included the concern that cultural facilities planned for the redevelopment would detract from the status of the victims of the attacks – as evident in the opposition to an International Freedom Center (shelved in response to the opposition to it). As Michael Burke, a brother of a firefighter killed in the attacks asserted: 'The organizers of the International Freedom Center say that in order to understand 9/11, we must see exhibits about slavery, segregation and genocide and its impact around the world. This is a history that we all should know and learn, but not here - not on sacred ground'.[8] And as Burke went on to add, 'Nobody is coming to this place to learn about Ukraine democracy or to be inspired by the courage of Tibetan monks. They're coming for September 11'. Such statements do possess a certain value in asserting the specificities of place – in a world in which an ever increasing sense of placelessness predominates.[9] And yet, at the same time, evident here is the sense in which the attacks remain incomparable with any other historical event, a claim that serves to locate them somehow outside of or beyond history. Indeed, the narcissism of such a tendency – in serving to occlude an understanding of the causes of the attacks and the politico-historical context in which they occurred – has served to mystify not just the attacks themselves (and as such preserve their exceptional status), but the causes of the War on Terror more broadly. At the same time, opposition to the International Freedom Center extended into criticism of the physical scale of the intended structure, with families of the victims of the attacks contending that the size of exhibition space – planned at roughly double the one hundred thousand square feet intended for an underground memorial to the victims – was too large,[10] a contention that emphasised the significance of the hard Real to the remembrance of an event which had itself witnessed the collapse of this order on such a spectacular scale.

The question of hierarchies of the dead returns us to the realm of the ghostly, and the sense in which – as conceived by Derrida and Gordon – it offers both a source from which redress might be sought for what has happened to the dead, and from which the existence of such a hierarchy might be challenged. In regard to the ghosts that have gathered across the preceding chapters, the ghosts of the non-Western dead can be understood as serving to reassert the value of these dead in the face of the attempt to occlude, ignore, and deny them their significance. In regard to the dead from the September 11 attacks, it might be contended that these dead have already been invoked and called back to the degree that they can raise no new questions. And yet these ghosts can still be conceived of as holding the capacity to play such a role – an issue that will be returned to later in this chapter.

'In the ruins of the future', *here is new york*

The difficulty, invoked at various stages in the preceding chapters, of portraying catastrophe raises the question of how the aftermath of the September 11 attacks have been depicted and documented, and the terms this has provided for considering and reconsidering the attacks over the course of the intervening period.

This is a theme taken up by Don DeLillo in his essay from December 2001 on the attacks: 'In the ruins of the future'.[11] DeLillo contrasts the institutional media's portrayal of the attacks and their aftermath with what he terms 'the counternarrative' – personal narratives and perspectives of the attacks that emanated from beyond the media. DeLillo's notion of the counternarrative possesses obvious affinities (albeit at the Symbolic rather than the Imaginary) with the conception of the minor gaze[12] – an assessment foregrounded in J. Heath Atchley's (2004) reading of DeLillo's essay that asserts the value of those 'minor stories' (ibid.: 351) that make up these counternarratives, and the contrast they offer to those accounts which seek to 'master' what took place on September 11, 2001. (There are clear parallels here with the analysis of news coverage of Kabul presented in Chapter 7.)

In regard to the visual depiction of the September 11 attacks and their aftermath, the *here is new york* project can be located as constituting an exemplar of the minor gaze and its capacity to present a counter-point to media coverage of the attacks. On 25 September 2001 (two weeks after the attacks) *here is new york* opened as a storefront show in Manhattan, made up of New Yorkers' photographs of the September 11 attacks and their immediate aftermath. The show was initially intended to run for three weeks, but continued into 2002, before going on to tour the world.[13] The project included work from some three thousand photographers who submitted more than five thousand photographs, mixing the work of professional photographers with amateurs – all of whom remained anonymous (with prints sold to raise money for the families of those killed in the attacks). The content of the assembled photographs differed widely – from the type of images well known from television news, of the Twin Towers smoking after having been hit, to less familiar scenes such as boxes of lemons covered with the detritus from the attacks, the words 'Nuke them all' finger-painted in dust on a window, and heat-damaged personal artefacts found at Ground Zero.

The subtitle of the *here is new york* project was 'a democracy of photographs', with Michael Shulan (one of the project's organisers) explicitly relating the democratic ideals of *here is new york* as bound to the medium of photography: 'Photography was the perfect medium to express what happened on 9/11, since it is democratic by its very nature and infinitely reproducible' (2002: 8). And indeed it can be argued that *here is new york* was imbued with a distinct democratic ethos, in the openness of the project to submissions from anyone with relevant images, the inclusion of images from such a number of contributors, the anonymity of the images included (one could not tell if a photograph had been taken by a professional or renowned photographer or an amateur), as well as the absence of claims that the project provided some definitive, complete, or authoritative vision of the attacks and their aftermath, rather than a collection of singular perspectives on what had happened. However, if *here is new york* can be said to present an exemplar of the democratic gaze, the project can be contrasted with other approaches to documenting the attacks and the conception of the dead that is offered in them – that raises questions about the existence of a necessary link between photography and democracy (along with the broader question of whether it is possible to locate technology as possessing inherent political affinities). In this respect *here is new york* can be contrasted with *The New York Times'* 'Portraits of grief' series (2002) – that presented a portrait photograph of every (known) victim of the attacks accompanied by a brief account of their life. As Simpson (2006: 21–53) argues, in seeking to offer an homogenising and morally pristine conception of the victims of the attacks, in which every life conformed to a broad template of achievement and civic worth, the series raised questions about precisely the type of democratic values – in regard to questions of individuality and diversity – it sought to communicate. More starkly though the contrast between a project such as *here is new york* and the absence of similar work documenting the death and destruction wrought by the assault on Afghanistan and the invasion and occupation of Iraq highlights the terms in which the democratic gaze presented by the *here is new york* project has been limited to a certain constituency – Western publics – and those groups which are excluded from this. In so doing this project itself comes to figure as a symptom of the terms in which the hierarchy of the dead is made manifest at a visual level.

Unidentified remains, the undead, the lamella

As was the case in examining the September 11 attacks in Chapter 1, I now want to shift from the realm of the Imaginary to the Real, in regard to the unidentified remains of the dead from the attacks and what they might reveal about the terms in which the attacks have been commemorated and comprehended.

A significant number of the victims of the September 11 attacks remain unidentified and unrecovered – with one thousand one hundred victims having never been identified,[14] along with 40 per cent (twelve thousand) of the body parts recovered from Ground Zero.[15] The continuing presence of unrecovered body parts at Ground Zero has figured as central in the ongoing controversies around the redevelopment of the site – including the very attempt to commemorate the attacks and the dead in the form of plans for a memorial museum. One function of the latter is to act as a store for unidentified body parts from the site (identified body parts have been returned to the victims' families), and provide a place where they can be visited by victim's families.[16]

At the same time, efforts have been made to separate these body parts from the remains of the hijackers that have been recovered and identified.[17] This latter concern raises the question of the place the enemy occupies in the hierarchy of the dead, with this enemy assuming a negative value in such a hierarchy – as not simply lacking in status and significance, but, in their 'evil' deemed worthy of anger and disgust.

The use of the memorial museum as a store for the body parts of the victims of the attacks raises the questions of how to think about the remains of the dead and the desire to retain and put on display these body parts – questions that can again be understood as returning us to the domain of horror. (To queries about the need to pursue this line of enquiry, it is worth citing Heath Atchley's assertion, 'Is there not some obligation to pursue insight if not understanding in the face of horror?' (2004: 333)). Here, Lacan's (1994: 197–200) notion of 'the lamella' is illuminating. The lamella constitutes the undead fleshly object-thing that resides in the Real and possesses no presence or status at the Symbolic, in so doing serving to assert the significance of the 'pure' physicality of the body to human experience. Zizek (1995: 208), in discussing David Lynch's oeuvre, conceives of the lamella as that which is located 'under the surface of a beautiful naked body – muscles, glands, veins, etc', which is typically occluded when the body is imagined, with this imagining producing a 'suspension of what lies beneath the surface ... this suspension excludes the real of the life-substance, its palpitation ... the flayed, skinned body, the palpitation of raw, skinless, red flesh'. And yet of course, this typically unseen and unimagined dimension of the body constitutes the 'core' of its capacity to function.

The body parts held in the museum at Ground Zero can be located as closely resembling the lamella, with the desire to preserve and put these body parts on display constituting an attempt to render them undead. In so doing these body parts can be understood as coming to be maintained in the zone between two deaths – between a Real (biological) death and a Symbolic death that would entail the final loss of their status as venerated objects from that September morning. While Black (1993: 180) identifies this zone as the domain of 'the ultimate object of horror', at the same time, as Lacan (1994: 243–87) contends in discussing Sophocles' *Antigone*, this zone constitutes a key locus of tragedy. And yet, a further, third dimension can be added to the zone occupied by these body parts – that of the sacred, as suggested by Kristeva (1982: 90–112) in delineating the ties between the abject (horror) and the sacred – and as evinced in the position Jesus' body assumes after the crucifixion (that points again in the direction of Holbein's painting). This matrix 'horror – tragedy – sacred' delineates the multiple significance these body parts have come to assume in the War on Terror, in terms of their at once constituting object-emblems of the horror and tragedy of the attacks – while at the same time presenting a source from which emanates the conception, promoted by the Bush administration and much of the religious right in the United States, of the War on Terror as a sacred undertaking. As such these body parts can be positioned as constituting the hard Real kernel (or fleshly metonymic emblem-object) of the War on Terror, from which this conflict emanates in all its horrific, tragic, and supposedly sacred dimensions. Located in these terms the preservation of these body parts constitutes a means of holding on, at the level of the hard Real, to the significance of what took place on that September morning in New York: as if to let go of them is to abandon or lose sight of what occurred there. Such an assessment is reinforced by the fact that these body parts have undergone a process of preservation – having been dried and vacuum sealed in the expectancy of a future technology being able to identify who they belonged to.[18] Indeed, this process points in the direction of the lamella these body parts constitute, awaiting its restoration to the Symbolic - in which these body parts will finally come to 'make sense' and confirm again the rightness of the War on Terror.

And yet, as was suggested in discussing the challenge to the hierarchies of the dead presented by the ghosts of the non-Western dead, the ghosts of the dead from which these unidentified body parts come might be configured as playing another, contradictory role – one that has been little commented upon in the pursuit of vengeance for these deaths that has underpinned this conflict. Namely, the ghosts of the victims of the attacks come to ask for their deaths to no longer be called upon as a justification for the War on Terror, and in so doing come to renounce their position in the hierarchy of the dead the conflict has given rise to.

Commemoration fatigue

While the desire to remember the September 11 attacks has been all too apparent, at the same time this process has given rise to a series of questions and doubts about the terms in which the attacks are commemorated – as documented in a *New York Times* piece from the eve of the 2007 anniversary of the attacks.[19]

At a certain level this has manifested itself in a growing sense of fatigue at and weariness with the terms in which the attacks are

commemorated – raising at one level questions about the place occupied by grief and mourning in the contemporary West. As a clinical
psychologist quoted in the *Times'* piece suggests, 'Our society has a very
low tolerance for grief – it's exhausting and unrelenting, we don't want
to hear about it', with a psychiatrist cited in the same piece adding,
'people are unsure about what is expected of them'. Such statements
point to the sense in which death is something that is to be cast out of
sight, avoided, and forgotten in contemporary Western culture, in part
because it constitutes the negation of the injunction to enjoy that Zizek
(2003: 56–7) identifies as having become so central to Western societies. (Here Baudrillard's ([1976] 1993) contention that death constitutes
the only point outside of, or non-co-optable by late capitalism, is also
apposite.) Indeed, this sense of death as disruptive to late capitalism can
be read in Simpson's (2006: 5) comment on local residents' antipathy
to the more sombre plans for the Ground Zero site: 'Many residents
have made it clear that they do not wish to live in a national memorial
emptied of retail, full of tourists by day and deserted at night' – with the
presence of 'retail' here serving as a reminder that the Ground Zero site
occupies one of late capitalism's nodal sites – Lower Manhattan.

In another respect, the expropriation of the commemoration of
the attacks for political purposes has raised questions about the ways
in which the memory of the attacks are used. At one level this has
included questions about the use of the attacks to justify the War on
Terror, and the sense in which the attacks were utilised as a catalyst
for the invasion of Iraq. More specifically it is apparent in the appropriation of images of the attacks in Republican adverts for the 2004
Presidential election.[20] It has been evident too in Rudolf Guiliani, the
mayor of New York at the time of the attacks, having been accused of
using the attacks to further his political career. The latter has been evident in his bid for the 2008 presidency, in which, for example, guests
at a fundraiser party for his campaign were asked to each donate $9.11
to his campaign funds.[21]

At the same time, this sense of commemoration fatigue raises the
question of for how far into the future the attacks will be commemorated for. As the *New York Times* piece makes clear, the dates of numerous 'scarring US tragedies' are no longer commemorated, and seem to
scarcely even be remembered, in the public domain – as in the case of
the attack on Pearl Harbor on 7 December 1941 ('the date to live in
infamy'), the Kent State shootings (4 May 1970), and the Oklahoma City
bombing (19 April 1995). Furthermore, since the September 11 attacks,
events including Hurricane Katrina and the Virginia Tech shooting have

occurred, which hold their own claims to commemoration, and yet have not been accorded a proportion – for their 'size'[22] – of the attention paid to the attacks. The public 'forgetting' of Pearl Harbor et al. serves to raise questions about the very terms in which the September 11 attacks will be remembered in the future, casting doubt on Guiliani's claim in regard to Ground Zero: 'This is going to be a place that is remembered 100 and 1000 years from now, like the great battlefields of Europe and the United States' (quoted in Simpson 2006: 47). (The comparison of Ground Zero with 'battlefields' can itself be considered intriguing – a conception of the site echoed in the notion that the vault that will store the unidentified remains of the dead constitutes, 'our Tomb of the Unknown Soldier').[23] Indeed, the *New York Times* piece, in asking 'What might happen on Sept. 11 a hundred years from now?', compares this anniversary with that of the American Civil War and the way in which the latter has faded from public memory – as this piece asks, 'Does anyone go out on the streets of New York and commemorate the firing on Fort Sumter?'.

At one level the rhetoric of 'war without end' that has come to define the War on Terror can be understood as serving to imply that there will be no diminishment in the attention accorded to the commemoration of the September 11 attacks. Indeed, faced with a process of limitless waiting and the anxiety this gives rise to, the commemoration of the attacks constitutes a vital reference point in drawing attention back to the event that constituted the primary justification for the War on Terror. Indeed, such is the status attributed to the attacks as this conflict's instigating event that a fall in the attention accorded to their commemoration can be taken as an indicator of the decline of the significance of this conflict. In a similar sense, changes to the terms in which the attacks are commemorated can be read as potentially significant markers of changing attitudes to the War on Terror. As such, the future commemoration of the attacks holds the potential to figure as a rich index of the regard in which the War on Terror is held.

Coda: The spectre's return

While the commemoration of the September 11 attacks might then raise profound questions about the course the War on Terror has taken, at the same time it has also played a rather different function – providing a focus for a series of Bin Laden's video appearances, and a means of reminding his supporters and opponents of his role in both the September 11 attacks and the ongoing conflict.

Bin Laden chose the 2007 anniversary of the attacks to make his first 'video' appearance since October 2004 – ending the growing rumours that he had been dead for some time.[24] And yet this appearance took a form quite different from that of his preceding video appearances – an issue largely overlooked in commentaries on and analyses of this video. This video contained no moving image footage of Bin Laden, instead presenting a still image of Bin Laden accompanied by a voice assumed to be his.[25] While discussion of the video pointed to how Bin Laden appeared to look 'younger' (evidence again of his shape-changing capacities) than in previous appearances, and of him seeming to possess a darker beard (prompting speculation that it might be a fake), little mention was made of the unusual nature of the visual presence Bin Laden assumed in this footage, or of the difficulty in attributing the voice heard on the video to Bin Laden (audio material purported to feature the voice of Bin Laden has previously been the subject of inconclusive debate about whether it does or does not belong to him). Instead, the references in the video to recent developments – Nicholas Sarkozy and Gordon Brown were referred to – were focused upon as providing evidence of the recent date of its production.

Such a response is somewhat strange. It is almost as if – after the lengthy absence of video appearances by Bin Laden – the still photograph this footage contained was enough to satisfy the desire for a sighting of him, when the very absence of moving images of Bin Laden might be taken as evidence that he has indeed passed away (or was too sick to appear). Indeed, the very absence of questions about the nature of the visual form Bin Laden assumed in this video can be read as suggestive of a certain desire for Bin Laden to still remain alive. In one respect – as discussed in Chapter 3 – the terms in which Bin Laden has been identified as a supreme source of evil has accorded with him coming to assume a vital position in the War on Terror for the architects and advocates of this conflict. At the same time, Bin Laden has served to provide an otherwise all too often unseen enemy with, at the very least, a semblance of a visible profile – in so doing providing the sense that this enemy can indeed be targeted and destroyed (despite Bin Laden having avoided this himself). This is a role that has come to be imbued with an even greater significance by the expansion of Al Qaeda – as evident, for example, in Al Qaeda in Iraq having been joined by 'Al Qaeda in the Maghreb',[26] with the latter responsible for a series of attacks in Algeria and Morocco. At the same time too evidence of the continued existence of Bin Laden serves to support the phantasy that his capture or killing will result in the enemy-in-general coming to be

defeated. While it is doubtful Bin Laden's capture would make a significant difference to Al Qaeda's operational capacity, the US senate voted
in July 2007 to double the reward for the capture or killing of Bin Laden
to $50 million.[27] (And yet, an increasing number of Americans doubt
Bin Laden will ever be found[28].)

The continuing fascination exerted (at least upon the media) by
Bin Laden is evident in BBC correspondent Matt Frei's response to the
appearance of the video at the time of the 2007 anniversary of the
attacks:

> Who could have predicted six years ago that on the sixth anniversary
> of that day, Osama Bin Laden would not just be alive and free, but
> broadcasting and honing his public relations skills in cyberspace?
> Who, in their most absurd satirical fantasies, could have prophesied
> that the world's most wanted man would be sitting somewhere – in
> a cave, in a TV studio, in a hotel room, we just do not know – calling
> on Americans to convert to Islam and feeling their pain over the
> sub-prime mortgage crisis and the slump in the real estate market?
> Bin Laden, in a new video message, trying to sound like a personal
> finance guru on cable TV – what next?[29]

Evident again here is a sense of Bin Laden's shape-shifting capacities –
however, beyond the type of phantasy form Bin Laden assumes in this
account, there is little evidence to support the contention that Bin
Laden is still alive at all.

And yet, whether Bin Laden is dead or alive perhaps matters very
little, what remains significant is Bin Laden's continued capacity to
haunt the West: his status as spectral metonym for an enemy that
refuses to be exorcised.

Epilogue

Ghosts, spectres, endless waiting, delirious waiting, the Thing, scopic desire, acting out, hostage videos, execution videos, warnings of attacks, the lamella, the unseen, the uncanny, unseen travelling ... – as suggested in the preceding chapters, all significant points of reference that by themselves and together provide a means of re-imagining and re-conceptualising the War on Terror.

Indeed, the need to continue to think and rethink the nature of this conflict is underlined by the sense in which it shows no sign of abating or disappearing from sight, with the prospect of the United States launching an attack on Iran at once coming into view and appearing – at least for a moment – to recede,[1] as this book was being completed in early 2008, and with Pakistan assuming an ever more central position in the future course the War on Terror might take. (And what then? What would be the results of an assault on Iran, or a US intervention in Pakistan?[2])

As has been evident across the preceding chapters, seeing at once promises to reveal this conflict to us – with the centrality accorded to imagery in this conflict and the extent to which it has been photographed and filmed, suggesting that, more than ever before, this is a conflict which we will be able to witness and comprehend. And yet at the same time the visibility of the conflict raises questions around what precisely the value of seeing is – in regard to the type of knowledge it gives rise to, and what is done with this knowledge. In another respect the sense of intimacy with the conflict suggested by its visibility has done little to assuage the anxiety generated by it. Indeed, Lacan's conception of the gaze serves to emphasise how the proliferation of images of the conflict have served to increase the spectator's awareness of their capacity to be seen by the enemy, and to constitute a potential target or victim of a forthcoming attack. In this respect the War on Terror occupies a pivotal position, with – as highlighted in discussing the hostage videos to have come out of Iraq – for the first time in a conflict situation Western publics encountering how the enemy sees as aggressor. (And it is worthwhile reiterating again how the dissemination of this material has been made possible by developments in media technologies.)

Indeed, one of the many intriguing epiphenomena of the War on Terror – and a marker for the sense of horror-without-end this conflict has generated – is the confessions of a certain nostalgia for the Cold War,[3] a nostalgia that raises the question of what type of conflict is it that generates a longing for a confrontation that held the promise of full-scale nuclear confrontation and Mutually Assured Destruction? While nostalgia might always be prey to the comforting distortions of sentimentality, only with reference to the sense of horror and delirium the War on Terror has given rise to can such a nostalgia be begun to be comprehended.

At the same time, this notion that 'more is seen than ever' has done little to alter the sense of uncertainty surrounding the activities of the enemy. While perceptions of the threat level may have altered – rising and falling, coming to the fore and receding – the endless speculation about the whereabouts of Bin Laden and the shape and structure Al Qaeda has come to assume points to the limited knowledge about the type of attacks the enemy might be planning or the details of its broader strategy (beyond quite general assumptions, such as the United States constituting the principal opponent this strategy is directed against). This sense of the unexpected was all too evident in the September 11 attacks, with, as *The 9/11 Report* (2004: 486–498) made clear, a failure of the imagination – born from a failure to engage with or take seriously enough a sense of the unknown and 'what might happen' – underpinning the failure to prevent the attacks. While it is true that there have been numerous 'successes' in halting potential attacks, it is worth highlighting how the enemy in the War on Terror operates with a notion of sacred time, in which the emphasis is upon ultimate victory over short-term successes or setbacks[4] – an outlook that when set alongside the Bush's administrations' declarations of the apparent endlessness of the War on Terror serves to multiply the possibilities of the new horrors this conflict may bring forth.

Without wanting to add unduly to the anxiety associated with the threat of forthcoming attacks, at the same time it is difficult to read assessments of the future forms such threats might take[5] without experiencing a sense of fear. Israel's secretive strike in September 2007 on a Syrian site,[6] purportedly the beginnings of a nuclear facility with parts supplied by North Korea (itself a nascent nuclear power), and more significantly perhaps, the leaking of information from Pakistan about its nuclear technology, point to the expanding, 'uncontrolled' dissemination of such technology, and, at the very least, to the increased possibilities of the enemy obtaining WMDs.[7] While opinion is divided on the desire (and capacity) of terrorist groups in general to make use of this weaponry, the possibility that the enemy in the War on Terror might do so has added significantly to the sense of threat associated with it.

At the same time – as evident in the analysis developed in the preceding chapters – the terms in which the War on Terror has been waged have contributed to the threats faced by the West. This conflict has been misdirected from its earliest stages – as evinced in the aerial assault on Afghanistan, the transporting of suspects to Guantanamo Bay, and the lack of attention accorded to the redevelopment of the country. Subsequently too the conflict has been beset by strategic errors: most noticeably in its extension into Iraq. In so doing the War on Terror has served to not only increase hostility to the United States and its allies in the Muslim world, but, in the case of Iraq, open up a new theatre of operations which the United States has found itself heavily committed to, and yet which adds little to the overall struggle against Islamic terrorism (apart from ensuring the country does not become a haven for the enemy, which it would never have been but for the invasion).

At the same time, as was foregrounded in discussing the experience of awaiting a forthcoming attack, the anxiety generated by this conflict has been enhanced by the very 'cures' proposed for it – in the ways in which Western governments have since the September 11 attacks sought to manage the threats that are faced. 'The paradox of security' – the way in which a focus upon questions of security has given rise to a heightened sense of insecurity – constitutes one source of this heightened anxiety. In another respect though measures taken in the name of security have generated their own fears at the type of societies we in the West have come to inhabit. This derives not just from the most egregious practices deployed against the enemy, as delineated by the matrix 'torture – extraordinary rendition – Guantanamo Bay – Abu Ghraib'. At the same time it emanates from the disregard displayed for those broader values – which might be grouped under the rubric of 'liberty' – put at risk by the prioritising of security, as if they are of little consequence, rather than integral to the identity and status of the West. Indeed, as Davis Hanson notes, 'even' from a realist standpoint, such values have been vital to the West's historical ascendancy. As such these values should be protected precisely for the contribution they can make to ensuring the West's 'victory' in the War on Terror, rather than abandoned and denigrated. One counter to the ever encroaching demands of security (in all its forms – including its 'softest' variants such as 'health and safety') is an acceptance that things may not be secure as they might be, but that this is something that not only has to be lived with, but should be embraced.[8] That this may entail a risk to life has ultimately to be expected and accepted, a contention that has increasingly come to resemble an absolute heresy, and to constitute the kernel of justifications for security über alles.

At the time of the September 11 attacks there were numerous declarations that the world would be changed for good. This has been true – indeed it can be contended that the scale of these changes could hardly have been predicted. What is required for the future course the War on Terror might take is for this conflict to be thought about in terms which entail an imagining of the full extent of its ramifications – not just in regard to the form future attacks might take – but the type of world that is being created by it, and to consider how things might be different. Indeed, to return to the interrogation of the imagination presented in the preceding chapters, the act of imagining constitutes at the very least a starting point, or minimal act, for reconsidering the War on Terror and conceiving of how things could be another way.

Notes

Introduction

1. 'Bush tones down talk of winning terror war', Mike Allen, *The Washington Post*, 31 August 2004, http://www.washingtonpost.com/wp-dyn/articles/A47707-2004Aug30.html.
2. 'New realities in the media age', *Council on Foreign Relations*, 7 February 2006, http://www.cfr.org/publication/9900/.
3. As *The Economist* asked on the front page of its 15 December 2007 issue, 'Must these be wars without end?'. See from the same issue, 'Can a lull be turned into a real peace?', 31–3, and 'Policing a whirlwind', 34–6.
4. For readers seeking further explication of Lacan's work and the concepts drawn upon in this book, Dylan Evans's (1996) guide and Malcolm Bowie's (1988) commentary provide two of the most useful points of reference.

1 September 11, 2001: Spectacularity, the Ruse, the Blot

1. 'Barbican stands by Stockhausen', BBC, 21 September 2001, http://news.bbc.co.uk/2/hi/entertainment/1556137.stm.
2. 'Hirst apologises for Sept 11 Comments', BBC, 19 September 2002, http://news.bbc.co.uk/2/hi/entertainment/2268307.stm. See Hillman (2005: 139–42) for a broader discussion of conflicts perceived as works of art.
3. The original dates for Lacan's seminars refer to the years the seminars were delivered, rather than when they appeared in published form.
4. See also '9/11 in a Movie-Made World', Tom Engelhardt, *Nation*, 25 September 2006, http://www.thenation.com/doc/20060925/engelhardt. Engelhardt surveys the development of these phantasies since the Second World War.
5. 'The Art of Terror', *National Public Radio*, 8 December 2001, http:www.npr.org/programs/wesat/features/2001/groundzero/011208.groundzero.html.
6. 'Expressionists' instant appeal: to Western buyers, brutal punch and mood are selling', Souren Melikan, *International Herald Tribune*, 11–2 February 2006, 9. Melikan contends that 'a major shift in the aesthetic approach to art is under way in Western society' towards expressionist works (with 'expressionist' conceived in a broad sense).
7. 'A cosy, casual chat about mass murder – (edited transcript of the discussion between Osama bin Laden and an unnamed shiekh)', *Guardian*, 14 December 2001, 3. It should be noted though that the attacks also served to turn some away from Al Qaeda, causing a split in the Al Qaeda hierarchy, with Abu al Walid al Masri breaking up with Bin Laden, see 'Osama's spin lessons', John Tierney, *International Herald Tribune*, 13 September 2006, 9.
8. Reinforced by those failures when the full capacity of this firepower has not been drawn upon – as in the Vietnam War, the 1982–4 intervention in Lebanon, and in 1993 in Somalia.

9. 'Full transcirpt of Bin Laden's speech', Al Jazeera, 11 November 2004, http://
english.aljazeera.net/NR/exeres/79C6AF22-98FB-4A1C-B21F-2BC36E87F61F.
htm.

10. 'The roots of Muslim rage', Bernard Lewis, *The Atlantic*, September 1990,
http://www.theatlantic.com/doc/print/199009/muslim-rage.

11. See Kuklick (2002: 565) on the War on Terror salvaging 'an otherwise sagging
presidency'.

12. In this respect Engelhardt's question (op. cit.) 'what if?' the planes had hit
the Towers but neither Tower had collapsed – and thereby the spectacle of
the attacks had been significantly reduced – is intriguing, even if any
response to it must remain highly speculative. Engelhardt wonders if the
reaction to the attacks may then have been very different, with the War on
Terror not having developed on the scale it has, and the Iraq War perhaps
never having taken place.

13. See, for example, Mulvey (2006: 128).

14. Not, it should be added, from a Lacanian or specifically psychoanalytic
standpoint.

15. My emphasis.

16. Dylan Evans (1996: 160) also points towards this aspect of the Real, noting
that 'The real also has connotations of matter, implying a material substra-
tum underlying the imaginary and the symbolic'.

17. It is possible to conceive of a history written around similar great acts of
destruction: the razing of Carthage (146 BC), the sacking of Rome (410) and
Constantinople (1204), the torching of Moscow (1812), the destruction
of Berlin (1945), Hiroshima (1945), and now Ground Zero – a history that
takes as its focus those moments when the material environment – the hard
Real – has become the defining register of the scale which conflict can
assume.

18. Inarritu has to date directed three features: *Amores Perros* (2000), *21 Grams*
(2003), and *Babel* (2006).

19. The collection comprised films from 11 directors of different nationalities,
intended to commemorate the first anniversary of the attacks.

20. 'Interview with Alejandro Gonzalez Inarritu about *11'09"01*', *Artificial Eye*,
http://www.artificial-eye.com/dvd/ART240dvd/inter7.html. This use of a
black space can be traced in the work of other subsequent films about the
attacks – see Michael Moore's *Fahrenheit 9/11* (2004) and Paul Greengrass's
United 93 (2006).

21. For Lacan's unpublished seminars, the years the seminars were delivered
along with dates of specific relevant individual seminar sessions are cited.

22. While Inarritu's film attracted critical praise, it also, among the films that
made up *11'09"01*, garnered the sharpest criticism, with Peter Bradshaw in
the *Guardian* describing it as 'crudely exploitative' ('11'09"01', 27 December
2002, http://film.guardian.co.uk/News_Story/Critic_Review/Guardian_Film_
of_the_week/0,,865490,00.html), and Peter Matthews writing in *Sight and
Sound* judging it 'an unremitting monstrosity', with the glimpses of falling
bodies the film offers identified as 'an abominable variation on the diving
sequence from Leni Riefenstahl's *Olympia* ('One day in September', January
2003, 33). These criticisms can be seen to derive, at least in part, from the
way in which the film attempts to confront the Real. Indeed, they intimate

this in their phraseology ('crude', 'unremitting', 'monstrosity', 'abominable'), which suggests various vulgar conceptions of the Real.

2   'Acting Out': Afghanistan, Autumn 2001 and since

1. Simpson (ibid.: 302) argues that the notion of the Taliban as formidable opponents had more to do with the history of Western perceptions of Islamic fighters than their actual military capacity. See Davis Hanson (2001: 135–69, 231–75) on the history of this perception. The re-emergence of the Taliban as an apparently potent fighting force in the summer of 2006 can be understood in terms of the different requirements of fighting an insurgency (rather than resisting an invasion), and the development they have undergone in the five-year period since the assault.
2. 'We can't do it by bombing', Jonathan Freedland, *Guardian*, G2 section, 19 October 2001, 2.
3. 'Afghanistan "falling into the hands of Taliban"', Richard Norton-Taylor, *Guardian*, 22 November 2007, 19.
4. It might be contended that the assault on Afghanistan constituted a 'Shock and Awe' operation of the type formulated by Harlan Ullman and James Wade, and deployed at the opening of the Iraq War (and discussed in Chapter 3). However, a defining component of such operations are their intended rapid, initial impact – instead the bombardment of Afghanistan developed over an extended time period (see Simpson 2003: 363).
5. George Walden in 'We can't do it by bombing', Jonathan Freedland, *Guardian*, G2 section, 19 October 2001, 2.
6. See, for example, Gray (2006).
7. 'America will never see peace before we live it: Bin Laden statement', *Guardian*, 8 October 2001, 4.
8. 'Rhetoric to arouse the Islamic world' Julian Borger, *Guardian*, 8 October 2001, 4.
9. Ibid.
10. 'Bush al-Jazeera "plot" dismissed', BBC, 22 November 2005, http://news.bbc.co.uk/2/hi/uk_news/politics/4459296.stm; 'Al-Jazeera seeks "US bomb" talks', BBC, 25 November 2005, http://news.bbc.co.uk/2/hi/uk_news/politics/4469044.stm.
11. 'False sense of victory let the Taliban regroup', David Rohde and David Sanger, *International Herald Tribune*, 13 August 2007, 1, 3.
12. 'America's wars rumble on, five years after Kabul attack', *Independent*, 7 October 2006, 34.
13. 'Is Rumsfeld's "revolution in military affairs" finally over?' William Hawkins, *American Economic Alert*, 12 September 2006, http://www.americaneconomicalert.org/view_art.asp?Prod_ID=2548. Hawkins draws attention to the history of developing the US military to achieve quick victories and the persistent failure of such phantasies. The struggle against the insurgency in Iraq has subsequently brought an emphasis on the capacity to fight counter-insurgency operations (Graham 2007).
14. 'Unfriendly fire', *Economist*, 23 June 2007, 70; 'Outside insurgents are redefining Taliban extremism', David Rohde, 31 October 2007, *International Herald Tribune*, 1, 7.

15. 'A war without witnesses', Felicity Lawrence, *Guardian*, 11 October 2001, 21.
16. 'War without witnesses – what the reporters say', Molloy Woodcraft, *The Observer*, 'Review' section, 28 October 2001, 2.
17. 'US buys all satellite war images', Duncan Campbell, *Guardian*, 17 October 2001, 1.
18. See, for example, Collins (2004); Gannon (2004); 'West "must not fail Afghanistan"', BBC, 13 September 2006, http://news.bbc.co.uk/2/hi/south_asia/5340892.stm; 'Delay issue over Afghan mission', BBC, 17 October 2006, http://news.bbc.co.uk/2/hi/uk_news/6060074.stm.
19. In November 2006 German human rights lawyers began moves to attempt to prosecute Donald Rumsfeld for war crimes, including torture, 'Rumsfeld faces legal test', BBC, 14 November 2006, http://news.bbc.co.uk/2/hi/americas/6146058.stm. Speaking on the BBC's *Newsnight* programme on 14 November 2006, one of the lawyers, Wolfgang Kaleck, acknowledged that attempting to bring Rumsfeld to justice would no doubt be a long drawn out process, but that it now had at least been embarked upon.

3   The Bin Laden Tapes

1. For an overview of the video and audio material featuring Bin Laden, see 'Timeline: the al-Qaida tapes', Simon Jeffrey, *Guardian*, http://www.guardian.co.uk/alqaida/page/0,12643,839823,00.html. Accessed 29 December 2007.
2. 'We should have listened to Bin Laden', *Independent*, 2 July 2005, 31.
3. 'Might' as there has been extensive debate over which of these audio recordings actually feature Bin Laden's voice.
4. 'High-tech snooping for bin Laden', CNN, 5 March 2004, http://www.cnn.com/2004/WORLD/asiapcf/03/04/binladen.search/index.html.
5. See, for example, Corbin (2003: 267), Willis (2005: 74), and Matt Frei's report for *BBC News at Ten O'Clock*, 30 October 2004, in which Bin Laden is described as Al Qaeda's 'spectral anchorman'.
6. Susan Willis (2005: 74) speculates that in the wake of the September 11 attacks the quantity of mail addressed to Bin Laden from the United States would have included love letters to him. Pejk Malinovski's *Dreaming of Osama* sound-piece, broadcast on *BBC Radio 3* on 24 November 2007, includes accounts of dreams in which Bin Laden figures as an object of desire.
7. The profile of work was heightened by it being shortlisted for the 2004 Turner Prize for contemporary art.
8. In fact, in the absence of the successful sighting of Bin Laden, the US military has had to make do with practising using Predators to destroy replicas of Bin Laden's house in the Nevada desert (Mayer 2003: 33).
9. My emphasis.
10. 'Intervention that substitutes for a bombing', Ewan MacAskill, *Guardian*, 30 October 2004, 17.
11. Remade in a Hollywood version by Gore Verbinski as *The Ring* (2002).
12. Poll conducted by Harris in January 2003, *Harris Interactive*, http://www.harrisinteractive.com/harris_poll/index.asp?PID=359.
13. 'Top US evangelist targets Islam', BBC, 14 March 2006, http://news.bbc.co.uk/2/hi/americas/4805952.stm.

14. See also 'They seek him here, they seek him there', Justin Huggler, *Independent*, *Review* section, 4 August 2004, 2–3.
15. My emphasis.
16. Quoted in Ali (2005: 53).
17. Specifically on BBC2, 28 March 2004.
18. 'War of words', Rahimuulah Yusufzai, *Guardian*, *G2* section, 9 October 2001, 4–5.

4   'Shock & Awe': Iraq, Spring 2003 and since

1. The show ran from 23 May to 27 June 2007. The ICA is located on the Mall, close to the centres of government and the monarch's principal residence, Buckingham Palace.
2. 'Iraq faces massive missile barrage', David Martin, CBSs, 24 January 2003, http://www.cbsnews.com/stories/2003/01/24/eveningnews/main537928. shtml; 'Iraq: a new kind of war', Jonathan Marcus, BBC, 14 April 2003, http://news.bbc.co.uk/2/hi/middle_east/2946597.stm.
3. This slightly later document provides an effective condensation of Ullman and Wade's 1996 work. Ullman denied that the assault on Iraq had constituted a Shock and Awe operation, 'No shock, no awe: it never happened', Paul Sperry, *WorldNetDaily*, 3 April 2003, http://wnd.com/news/article.asp? ARTICLE_ID=31858.
4. 'Analysis: US "shock and awe" tactic', Steve Schifferes, BBC, 21 March 2003, http://news.bbc.co.uk/2/hi/middle_east/2874075.stm; 'Papers depict "shock and awe"', BBC, 22 March 2003, http://news.bbc.co.uk/2/hi/uk_news/2874833.stm.
5. Dostoyevsky ([1871–1872] 1953: 586) in *The Devils* evokes the particular sense of drama associated with a fire at night and the destruction it brings. It is difficult to come to any clear conclusions about the effectiveness of the assault. As Cockburn (2005: 35–6) highlights though, the speed with which, following the invasion, the insurgency commenced points the limitations of its impact.
6. Greenacre (who died in 1989) was a New York based psychoanalyst, whose work was addressed in part towards questions of child analysis.
7. 'Blair knew US had no post-war plan for Iraq', Nicholas Watt, *Guardian*, 17 June 2007, http://politics.guardian.co.uk/tonyblair/story/0,,2104989,00. html; 'Iraq is not just Blair's dark legacy: it defines the future', Andrew Rawnsley, *Guardian*, 17 June 2007, http://politics.guardian.co.uk/columnist/ story/0,,2104883,00.html.
8. To take the title of the leading neo-conservative thinktank.
9. The BBC correspondent Matt Frei writing in the autumn of 2007 contended, 'America is tearing itself apart over a conflict that would probably never have been fought without the events of 9/11', 'Washington Diary: 9/11's legacy', BBC, 12 September 2007, http://news.bbc.co.uk/2/hi/americas/6990365.stm. This letter echoes that sent by to President Clinton on 26 January 1998, calling for the removal of Saddam Hussein from power, emphasising the sense in which this constituted an ongoing ambition for the United States to transform Iraq, *Project for the New American Century*, http://www. newamericancentury.org/iraqclintonletter.htm.

10. *Project for the New American Century*, 20 September 2001, http://www. newamericancentury.org/Bushletter.htm. The United States' failure in Iraq can be understood as encouraging a further repetition of this process of acting out – with Iran constituting the next possible target in this sequence.

11. Lacan's prioritising Symbolic over Imaginary knowledge accords with Martin Jay's (1994) analysis of 'the denigration of vision' in French twentieth-century thought, in which he discusses Lacan's work.

12. *NASA Earth Observatory*, http://earthobservatory.nasa.gov/NaturalHazards/ natural_hazards_v2.php3?img_id=10149, accessed 20 August 2007.

13. These questions are raised in a similar fashion by Werner Herzog in his film *Lessons of Darkness* (1992) with its depiction of the smoke of burning oil wells from the 1991 Gulf War.

14. 'Unseen pictures, untold stories', James Rainey, *Los Angeles Times*, 21 May 2005, http://www.latimes.com/news/nationworld/nation/la-na-iraqphoto 21may21,0,2732182.story?coll=la-home-headlines.

15. Although by no means entirely so. There has been degree of national variation in this respect. As Christina Konstantinidou (2007) highlights, Greek media has provided far greater coverage of Iraqi casualties.

16. 'One in 40 Iraqis "killed since invasion"', Sarah Boseley, *Guardian*, 12 October 2006, 1; 'Toll as high as 600,000 disputed Iraqi study says', Sabrina Tavernise and Donald McNeil, *International Herald Tribune*, 12 October 2006, 5.

17. 'Aura of fear and death stalks Iraq', Peter Beaumont, *Guardian*, 12 October 2006, 18.

18. 'Baghdad is like Grand Theft Auto', *Alive in Baghdad*, 18 December 2006, http://aliveinbaghdad.org/2006/12/18/baghdad-is-like-grand-theft-auto/.

19. Here then, in contrast to the terms in which, as Duras suggests, film serves to limit the imagination in depicting what might otherwise be imagined, Horror opens up a space for imagining a situation it does not document directly, but which it is suggestive of. These issues will be returned to in Chapter 7.

20. 'Car bomb survivors, no longer statistics', *Alive in Baghdad*, 27 November 2006, http://aliveinbaghdad.org/2006/11/27/car-bomb-survivors-no-longer-statistics/.

21. 'Waiting for the ghost's next move', CJ Chivers, *International Herald Tribune*, 4–5 November 2006, 1, 6.

22. Season one was broadcast in 2004, season two in 2005.

23. 'Multi-National Force Iraq', *YouTube*, http://www.youtube.com/user/MNFIRAQ. This channel was set up in March 2007.

24. 'The uncovered war: air power in Iraq', Tom Engelhardt, *Nation*, 20 November 2006, http://www.thenation.com/blogs/notion?bid=15&pid=142240.

25. 'Guide: armed groups in Iraq', BBC, 15 August 2006, http://news.bbc.co.uk/ 2/hi/middle_east/4268904.stm.

26. 'Outside insurgents are redefining Taliban extremism', David Rohde, 31 October 2007, *International Herald Tribune*, 1, 7.

27. As evident in the arrest in September 2007 of a group planning to launch attacks in Germany, 'The Convert's Zeal', Daniel Benjamin, *Slate*, 7 September 2007, http://www.slate.com/id/2173561/.

28. 'Al Qaeda video taunts Bush, Iran, Shiites', CNN, 5 May 2007, http://www. cnn.com/2007/WORLD/meast/05/05/al.qaeda.tape/index.html.

29. 'President Bush meets his national security team', *The White House*, 28 December 2006, http://www.whitehouse.gov/news/releases/2006/12/20061 228-1.html.
30. 'White House on defensive as US media breaks taboo to declare conflict "civil war"', Julien Borger, *Guardian*, 29 November 2006, 19.
31. 'Press briefing Scott McClellan', *The White House*, 27 June 2005, http://www. whitehouse.gov/news/releases/2005/06/20050627-3.html. Such a claim is parodied in the *Doonesbury* cartoon strip, in a story (that ran in August 2007) in which a US soldier is followed home by an insurgent anxious to launch an attack in the US.
32. 'Militants widen reach as terror seeps out of Iraq', Michael Moss and Souad Mekhennet, *New York Times*, 28 May 2007, 1.
33. 'Iraqi tactics come to Afghanistan', Damian Grammaticas, BBC, 21 June 2007, http://news.bbc.co.uk/2/hi/south_asia/6222574.stm.
34. 'Qaeda group in Iraq tied to UK attacks', Raymond Bonner, Jane Perlez and Eric Schmitt, *International Herald Tribune*, 14 December 2007, 1,8.
35. 'The uniformed kidnappers of Baghdad', Paul Wood, BBC, 16 June 2007, http://news.bbc.co.uk/2/hi/programmes/from_our_own_correspondent/ 6756425.stm.
36. 'The US forces, like the crusaders before them, are prisoners in their own fortresses', *Independent*, 2 April 2005, http://news.independent.co.uk/fisk/ article8930.ece.
37. 'The uniformed kidnappers of Baghdad', op. cit.
38. Chandrasekaran (2006) provides a detailed account of the gap between the two 'zones'.
39. 'A permanent military empire', Tom Englehardt, *Nation*, 8 June 2007, http:// www.thenation.com/doc/20070625/engelhardt.
40. 'Bush ties Iraq to Vietnam, South Korea, Japan', 22 August 2007, *AFP*, http:// www.afp.com/english/news/stories/070822175358.4fzz6pxg.html.
41. See, for example, 'The neocons have finished what the Vietcong started', Martin Jacques, *Guardian*, 8 December 2006, http://www.guardian.co.uk/ comment/story/0,,1967420,00.html; 'How super was our power anyway?', Tom Englehardt, *Nation*, 20 August 2007, http://www.thenation. com/blogs/notion?pid=225033; 'The sole superpower in decline', Dilip Hiro, *TomDispatch.com*, 20 August 2007, http://www.tomdispatch.com/ post/174830.
42. Although the whole notion of Al Qaeda waging 'asymetrical warfare' against the United States has served to raise questions about the signifi- cance of a technologically sophisticated military. Furthermore, as Hiro (op. cit.) notes, China is closing the gap on the United States' technological superiority, as evinced in the test firing of an anti-satellite missile in January 2007.
43. 'Hints of normalcy as Baghdad security improves', Damien Cave and Alissa Rubin, *International Herald Tribune*, 20 November 2007, 1, 4; 'Is Iraq getting better?', Jim Muir, BBC, 11 November 2007, http://news.bbc.co.uk/2/hi/ middle_east/7089168.stm.
44. 'Powell: "We are losing"', *Salon*, 18 December 2006, http://www.salon.com/ politics/war_room/2006/12/18/iraq_detainee/index.html.

5 Hostage Videos: 'scenes of slaughter'

1. In the period from the invasion of Iraq to December 2006, over 280 foreign nationals had been seized there (along with thousands of Iraqis), of which approximately 50 had been killed, 140 released or managed to escape, with the whereabouts of the remaining 90 unknown. See 'Abduction: scourge of Iraqi unrest', Martin Asser, BBC, 30 March 2006, http://news.bbc.co.uk/2/hi/middle_east/4838018.stm. Many more Iraqis have been kidnapped, although they rarely come to appear in Western media coverage.

2. The reference to Gaza is specifically to those non-Israeli hostages whose kidnappers identified with the broader struggle against the United States and its allies.

3. 'Iraq's danger for foreigners', Gordon Corera, BBC, 28 November 2005, http://news.bbc.co.uk/2/hi/uk_news/4479038.stm; 'Letter from al-Zawhiri to al-Zarqawi', *Office of the Director of National Intelligence*, 11 October 2005, http://.fas.org/irp/news/2005/10/dni101105.html. The letter was purportedly dated 9 July 2005, with the contents of the letter released in October.

4. 'Beheading video seen as war tactic', Matthew Stannard, SFGate, 13 May 2004, http://www.sfgate.com/cgi-bin/article.cgi?file=/c/a/2004/05/13/MNG6E6KL791.DTL.

5. The syntax of this phrase is confusing – this is how it appears in the released version of the letter.

6. In regard to which might be read the delay in claiming responsibility for the September 11 attacks.

7. 'Trimmed Bin Laden in media-savvy war', Frank Gardner, BBC, 8 September 2007, http://news.bbc.co.uk/2/hi/middle_east/6985086.stm.

8. Cockburn (2005: 47) has pointed to the lack of desire shown by insurgents in Iraq to cultivate the media.

9. 'Iraq hostage believes ransom paid', BBC, 31 March 2006, http://news.bbc.co.uk/2/hi/middle_east/4864650.stm.

10. An exception might be said to be those of periods of occupation in World War II, where an awareness of the enemy's gaze constituted a defining experience of being occupied. Afterwards may be a different matter: witness the fetish in the UK and US for footage shot by the Nazis for instance. Images that became infamous in showing the US military and its South Vietnamese allies in an unsympathetic light, such as Ron Haeberle's photographs of the 1968 My Lai massacre, or Eddie Adams's photo from the same year of South Vietnamese police chief Nguyen Ngoc Loan about to shoot a Viet Cong prisoner in the head, were typically the work of Western photographers or Vietnamese from the south of the country.

11. In so doing, these videos also present a version of the minor gaze – albeit a macabre one – that in emanating from outside of the realm of media institutions provides a counterpoint to the coverage offered of Iraq.

12. 'Who watches murder videos?', Duncan Walker, BBC, 12 October 2004, http://news.bbc.co.uk/2/hi/uk_news/magazine/3733996.stm, includes comments from viewers of these videos on their experience of watching the videos.

13. Duncan Walker, 'Who watches murder videos?', BBC, 12 October 2004, http://news.bbc.co.uk/2/hi/uk_news/magazine/3733996.stm. *The Northeast*

Intelligence Network is an independent body, whose website is subtitled 'Information on the cutting edge – combating terrorism by investigation, research and analysis', http://www.homlandsecurityus.com.

14. See, for example, 'London Terror attack "inevitable"', BBC, 16 March 2004, http://news.bbc.co.uk/2/hi/uk_news/politics/3515312.stm; 'Peter Clarke, Head of Scotland Yard's Anti-Terrorist Branch, talks to BBC Two', BBC, 1 September 2006, http://www.bbc.co.uk/pressoffice/pressreleases/stories/2006/09_september/01/clarke.shtml; 'British official foresees graver attacks', Alan Cowell, *International Herald Tribune*, 26 April 2007, 3.

15. While the material world – including the built environment, as in the case of the September 11 attacks – might be deemed as constituting as significant a target, the material world is the product of bodily labour which it relies upon to sustain it.

16. The Abu Ghraib images covered acts carried out the preceding autumn, placing their production prior to the first of the videos to feature Western hostages, which did not appear until April 2004.

17. The current affairs site *Salon* has presented a comprehensive archive of these images and footage supported by a series of essays titled 'The Abu Ghraib Files', http:www.salon.com/news/abu_ghraib/2006/03/14/introduction/. Accessed 18 August 2006.

18. Joan Walsh 'Introduction – The Abu Ghraib Files', *Salon*, http:www.salon.com/news/abu_ghraib/2006/03/14/introduction/. Accessed 18 August 2006.

19. 'FBI quiz execution video hoaxer', BBC, 8 August 2004, http://news.bbc.co.uk/2/hi/middle_east/3545822.stm.

20. 'Face to face with death', Jonathan Jones, *Guardian*, *G2* section, 26 September 2006, 18–20, quote from p. 20.

21. See, for example, Amancio (2005); Gatrall (2001); and Lechte (1990).

22. Which has come to assume something of a focus in discussions of the painting.

23. It might be contended that other pictures from the history of Western art bear closer comparison with the videos than Holbein's work. For example, as Honour and Fleming (1995: 468) contend in regard to Matthais Grunewald's *Isenheim altarpiece* (c. 1510–15), 'Of all the tortured Christs in the history of Western art, this makes the most violent impact'. And yet, as Kristeva adds in comparing this work with Holbein's painting, Grunewald's work lacks the sense of isolation of Holbein's image, with Christ's suffering being mediated by the presence of other figures in this painting.

24. 'Britain's neglected wars', *Economist*, 18 August 2007, 26–7.

25. Support for the war had fallen to 30 per cent by summer 2007. Ibid. In this case and in that referred to in the following note 'war' includes the post-invasion occupation.

26. In the United States, support for the war in Iraq had fallen to 30 per cent by summer 2007, with 54 per cent of those polled saying the war was not morally justified, 'Poll: support for Iraq war reaches new low', CNN, 27 June 2007, http://politicalticker.blogs.cnn.com/2007/06/27/poll-support-for-iraq-war-reaches-new-low/.

27. As surveyed by Mair (2006) in regard to the state of contemporary democracy in the West, and as analysed by – amongst others – Badiou (see, for example, 2005: 52–9) and Zizek (1998, 1999a: 198–205, 1999b, 2004).

28. 'Britain's neglected wars', op. cit. See also Anderson (2007: 22) on the 'shallowness' of the movements against the Iraq War.
29. 'How can this bloody failure be regarded as a good war?', Seumas Milne, *Guardian*, 23 August 2007, 33.
30. 'Democracy or imperialism?: ask the experts', BBC, 8 September 2003, http://news.bbc.co.uk/2/hi/talking_point/3085046.stm.
31. For an overview of this issue see, 'The new wars of religion', *Economist*, 3 November 2007, 13–14; 'The rise of mosques becomes catalyst for conflict across Europe', Ian Traynor *Guardian*, 11 October 2007, 23; 'The crescent and the very cross', *Economist*, 15 September 2007, 44.
32. Although it might be added, it is a mistake to regard such a state of affairs as providing further 'evidence' that religion constitutes a 'bad object' that is the cause of wars. Rather, as Freud ([1927] 1991) suggests, the question to be raised is why people seek to believe in religions at all.

6   Endless Waiting

1. 'Videotape supposedly shows suicide bomber "graduation"', CNN, 18 June 2007, http://www.cnn.com/2007/WORLD/meast/06/18/bomber.video/index.html. The footage was shot by a Pakistani journalist invited to observe the ceremony.
2. See, for example, the list of thwarted attacks released by the White House in October 2005, 'US lists 10 foiled terror plots', *BBC*, 7 October 2005, http://news.bbc.co.uk/2/hi/americas/4319714.stm; 'British official foresees graver attacks', Alan Cowell, *International Herald Tribune*, 26 April 2007, 3.
3. 'What novelists reveal about the minds of murderers', Jason Cowley, *Observer*, 13 August 2006, 23.
4. See Derrida's (1994: 4) analysis of this relationship.
5. 'The routine of atrocity', *Guardian*, 15 September 2005, 1–2.
6. '10/8. Was this going to be the next date in the calendar of terror?', *Independent*, 11 August 2006, 1.
7. '9/11 in a Movie-Made World', Tom Engelhardt, *Nation*, 10 September 2006, http://www.thenation.com/doc/20060925/engelhardt.
8. Islamic terrorism has figured as one of the threats faced in *24* and *Spooks*, while constituting the principle threat in *Sleeper Cell*. The first series of *24* was broadcast in the US in 2001 with the seventh planned for 2008; the first of *Spooks* was broadcast in the UK in 2002, with the sixth in 2007; and the first and second of *Sleeper Cell* in the US in 2005 and 2006. *24* and *Spooks* have been hugely popular and have been broadcast in numerous countries.
9. 'Fierce Creature', Jeff McCrory, *Sacremento News and Review*, 13 December 2001, http://www.newsreview.com/sacremento/Content?oid+oid%3A10017.
10. 'London Terror attack "inevitable"', BBCs, 16 March 2004, http://news.bbc.co.uk/2/hi/uk_news/politics/3515312.stm.
11. 'Peter Clarke, Head of Scotland Yard's Anti-Terrorist Branch, talks to BBC Two', *BBC*, 1 September 2006, http://www.bbc.co.uk/pressoffice/pressreleases/stories/2006/09_september/01/clarke.shtml; 'British official foresees graver attacks', Alan Cowell, *International Herald Tribune*, 26 April 2007, 3.
12. *US Department of Homeland Security*, http://www.dhs.gov/index.shtm. Accessed 17 May 2007.

13. 'Citizen guidance on the Homeland Security Advisory System', *US Department of Homeland Security*, http://www.dhs.gov/xlibrary/assets/CitizenGuidanceHSAS2.pdf. Accessed 17 May 2007.
14. See Neocleous (2007) for an overview of this approach.
15. See also from the same issue 'Can a lull be turned into a real peace?', 31–3, and 'Policing a whirlwind', 34–6.
16. The film has itself been viewed as a response to the Vietnam War.
17. See, for example: 'Terror laws targeting criticised', Dominic Casciani, BBC, 3 September 2004, http://news.bbc.co.uk/2/hi/uk_news/3624330.stm; 'Two wheels: good. Two legs: terrorist suspect', David Lister, *Times*, 17 October 2005, http://www.timesonline.co.uk/article/0,,2-1829289,00.html; 'Questions over London terror raid', BBC, 10 June 2006, http://news.bbc.co.uk/2/hi/uk_news/5066846.stm.
18. 'Fear of the unknown', Sean Coughlan, BBC, 21 August 2006, http://news.bbc.co.uk/2/hi/uk_news/magazine/5270500.stm. The two men were found to pose no threat.
19. 'The problem with eyewitnesses', Finlo Rohrer, BBC, 24 August 2005, http://news.bbc.co.uk/2/hi/uk_news/4177082.stm.
20. 'Seeing is believing', Mark Honigsbaum, *Guardian*, 27 June 2006, http://www.guardian.co.uk/attackonlondon/story/0,,1806794,00.html.
21. 'Fake tube safety email spreads', BBC, 28 July 2005, http://news.bbc.co.uk/2/hi/technology/4724101.stm.
22. See, for example, *The Conspiracy Files: 9/11*, BBC2, 18 February 2007.
23. 'Bush tones down talk of winning terror war', Mike Allen, *Washington Post*, 31 August 2004, http://www.washingtonpost.com/wp-dyn/articles/A47707-2004Aug30.html.
24. 'Washington digs in for a "long war"', Simon Tisdall, *Guardian*, 7 February 2006, http://www.guardian.co.uk/Columnists/Column/0,,1703990,00.html.

7 Imagining Kabul

1. 'Blair meets troops in Afghanistan', BBC, 20 November 2006, http://news.bbc.co.uk/2/hi/south_asia/6164252.stm.
2. 'The troops and us', Lawrence Kaplan, *New Republic*, 17 November 2006, https://ssl.tnr.com/p/docsub.mhtml?i=20061127&s=diarist112706.
3. 'Army chief warns of social "gulf"', BBC, 22 September 2007, http://news.bbc.co.uk/2/hi/uk_news/7006720.stm.
4. 'Caught on film: a soldier's agony', Helen Pidd, *Guardian*, 3 September 2007, 12–13.
5. BBC video material on 'Kabul', http://search.bbc.co.uk/cgi-bin/search/results.pl?tab=av&q=kabul&recipe=all&scope=all&edition=i. Accessed 18 December 2007. CNN video material on 'Kabul', http://search.cnn.com/search.jsp?query=kabul&type=video&sortBy=date&intl=false. Accessed 18 December 2007.
6. 'Phantasy' can be said to constitute the psychoanalytic conception of imagining, and yet I have largely steered clear of using this notion in this chapter, due in part to the terms in which it is configured as an emanation of the unconscious.
7. As Lewis (2003), Marash (1995), and Wright (2004) assert.

8. Fixers – whose role is to organise or facilitate multiple aspects of story gathering – have played an important role for Western news teams in Afghanistan and Iraq.

9. McCurry has worked in Afghanistan both prior to and after the September 11 attacks.

10. This is an assessment echoed by Wright (2004: 106) in regard to *Euronews'* 'No comment' feature, which dispenses with any commentary to offer images accompanied only by their unedited sound.

11. The following comment in regard to McCurry's image of 'the green eyed girl', taken in a refugee camp in Pakistan in 1984 – which became *National Geographic's* most requested photograph – is suggestive of the terms which Afghans have been conceived as Other: 'Her name is Sharbat Gula, and she is Pashtun, that most warlike of the Afghan tribes. It is said of the Pashtun that they are only at peace when they are at war, and her eyes – then and now – burn with ferocity', 'A life revealed', Cathy Newman, *National Geographic*, http://ngm.nationalgeographic.com/ngm/afghangirl/index2.html. Accessed 10 December 2007.

12. 'The land that time forgot', Olivia Snaije, *Guardian, G2* section, 10 October 2001, 10–11.

13. It is worth noting how Samira's father, Mohsen Makhmalbaf – whose *Kandahar* (2001) presented an initial attempt to depict an Afghanistan that had become a 'forgotten country' (then still held by the Taliban) – provided extensive support to Siddiq Barmak in making *Osama. At Five in the Afternoon* does depict Kabul in the period since the September 11 attacks from a non-Western standpoint. And yet, it would be wrong to conflate non-Western depictions of the city, when it is the question of how Afghans see which is critical to the development of a democratic visual culture in Afghanistan.

14. 'The Taliban's secret pictures', video essay, *Slate*, http://www.slatev.com/player.html?id=1151557602. Accessed 4 November 2007.

15. *YouTube*, http://www.youtube.com/watch?v=SuBuawtzgMc. Accessed 17 July 2007. Posted by 'Alishah85'.

16. An exception here is the first part of *The Kite Runner* – although the depiction offered of the city is a recreation from 2006 to 2007. The Harrison Forman collection (held at the University of Wisconsin Madison) contains a selection of images of Afghanistan and Kabul from the late 1960s that includes images of such symbols of modernity as the city's university and airport. 'Afghanistan: the Harrison Forman collection', http://www.uwm.edu/Library/digilib/afghan/. Accessed 12 August 2007.

17. http://www.afghanlord.org/. Accessed 8 April 2007. Weblogs can themselves be said to present a distinctly democratic form of news coverage.

18. http://sanjar.blogspot.com. Accessed 20 January 2005.

19. http://www.kabuli.org/. Accessed 17 September 2007.

20. http://www.afghansite.com/. Accessed 17 September 2007.

21. http://www.afghan-web.com/. Accessed 17 September 2007.

22. See, for example, http://www.flickr.com/photos/sohrab_kabuli/with/2117902378/. Accessed 17 September 2007. These images, along with the *Afghan Lord* and *Kabuli* blogs, are the work of Nasim Fekrat – a key figure in the dissemination of images of Kabul.

23. Shulan's piece has no page numbers. See also Sontag (2002: 7, 75, 99, 103) for comments on photography as a democratic medium.
24. 'In pictures: Afghanistan's voters', BBC, 22 July 2005,   http://news.bbc. co.uk/2/shared/spl/hi/picture_gallery/05/south_asia_afghanistan0s_voters/ html/1.stm-10.stm.
25. It would be desirable to expand upon the context in which Stora makes this statement, however, little of his work – which takes Algeria as its focus – has been translated into English.
26. Churchill's statement is relevant here: 'Democracy is the worst form of government compared to all the others that have been tried.' To the accusation that the support for democracy entails an imposing of Western values, I regard democracy in the broadest sense of the term – equality of politico-legal status – as an absolute value, and the notion its development should not be encouraged, as highly problematic.
27. At the same time, depression can manifest itself in terms of a 'shutting down' or diminishment of the subject's imaginative capacities.
28. There are parallels here with Debord's ([1967] 1995) analysis in *The Society of the Spectacle*.
29. Although the anxiety generated in recent years by the possible future effects of global warming suggests a caveat here. And yet it might be argued that given the scale of the threat presented by global warming and the response there has so far been to this threat, Scarry is indeed correct.

8   Phantoms and Jails

1. 'Interview: Iraqi official mourns sons, vows to fight "the ghosts of death"', *Radio Free Europe, Radio Liberty*, 8 February 2005, http://www.rferl.org/featuresarticle/2005/02/70bb0174-012b-483d-a708-467530aaa9ca.html.
2. 'A silent neighbourhood – rigged to explode', Michael Gordon, *International Herald Tribune*, 27 June 2007, 7.
3. 'US sails against ghostly enemy', Peter Beaumont, *Observer*, 23 September 2001, http://observer.guardian.co.uk/waronterrorism/story/0,,556693,00. html. It is revealing to note the Soviet army's reference to the enemy it fought in Afghanistan as 'dukhi' – ghosts, 'Red Army's "ghosts" of Afghnistan', Tom Coghlan, BBC, 24 August 2005, http://news.bbc.co.uk/2/hi/south_asia/4177312.stm.
4. 'Face up to the truth', Nick Cohen, *Observer*, 10 July 2005, http://www. guardian.co.uk/attackonlondon/comment/story/0,,1525261,00.html.
5. Matt Frei's report on the video released just before the 2004 US presidential election, BBC1, *News at 10 O'Clock*, 30 October 2004. Reaching back a little further the title of a study of the pre-September 11 conflicts which gave rise to Al Qaeda is *Ghost Wars* (Coll, 2004).
6. 'Muslims react to Hamza conviction', BBC, 7 February 2006, http://news. bbc.co.uk/2/hi/uk_news/4690132.stm.
7. As evident, to cite just one example, in the film *Ringu / The Ring* (cited in discussing Bin Laden's video appearances) – in which the spirit Shaku multiplies with copies of the fatal tape.
8. 'Taliban "must be included" in Afghanistan', ITN, 25 September 2007, http://itn.co.uk/news/e5f36b369a873dd9b389a5bf8162f4d9.html.

9. 'Taliban sets out demands to Afghan president', Declan Walsh and Sami Yousafzai, *Guardian*, 15 October 2007, 14.

10. 'CIA jails in Europe "confirmed"', BBC, 8 June 2007, http://news.bbc.co.uk/2/hi/europe/6733353.stm.

11. This sense of suspect's understanding little of what is happening to them or where they are being held is illustrated in the UK film *Extraordinary Rendition* (currently awaiting a full release date).

12. While it might be argued that extraordinary rendition simply makes use of facilities that pre-exist the programme, it is still the case that it has sought to detain suspects under these conditions.

13. 'Tenfold rise in terrorism prisoners forecast', Alan Travis, *Guardian*, 8 November 2007, http://www.guardian.co.uk/prisons/story/0,,2207152,00.html.

14. 'Decision Re Application of the Geneva Convention on Prisoners of War to the Conflict with Al Qaeda and the Taliban', 25 January 2002, as reproduced in Greenberg and Dratel (eds) (2005: 118–21).

15. 'No impunity for war crimes: US administration seeks to amend the war Crimes Act', *Amnesty International*, 11 August 2006, http://web.amnesty.org/library/Index/ENGAMR511362006;'Gonzales and the Geneva Conventions', *Human Rights Watch*, 9 December 2004, http://www.humanrightsfirst.com/us_law/etn/gonzales/briefs/brief_20041209_Gonz_%20GC.pdf.

16. Here too Agamben's (1998) sense of 'bare life', constituted as life that stands beyond the law, and is suggestive of life in the Real, is pertinent.

17. 'US judge rules wiretaps illegal', BBC, 18 August 2006, http://news.bbc.co.uk/2/hi/americas/5260892.stm; 'Limiting electronic espionage', *International Herald Tribune*, 22 November 2007, 6; 'The dog ate my evidence', Dahlia Lithwick, *Slate*, 16 October 2007, http://www.slate.com/id/2176017/nav/ais/_.

18. 'Powell: Iraq hiding weapons, aiding terrorists', CNN, 6 February 2003, http://www.cnn.com/2003/US/02/05/sprj.irq.powell.un/index.html.

19. Syria was added to the list of members of the 'Axis of Evil' in May 2002.

20. 'CIA flights controversy here to stay', Stephen Mulvey, BBC, 16 February 2007, http://news.bbc.co.uk/2/hi/europe/6363361.stm. The Parliament's investigation has been accompanied by numerous national investigations.

21. 'Italy halts CIA extradition bid', BBC, 12 April 2006, http://news.bbc.co.uk/2/hi/europe/4903518.stm.

22. See Jacques Alain Miller (2006) for an extended analysis of Lacan's discussion of shame in *Seminar XVII*. 'Late modernity' is not the term used by Lacan, but this is the era his analysis refers to.

23. 'Self-defeating', *Economist*, 7 June 2007, http://www.economist.com/books/displaystory.cfm?story_id=9299100.

24. For Lacan jouissance constitutes the intense experience of pain and pleasure – that dissolves the boundaries between each – and which exists beyond the Symbolic.

25. At the same time, the question of the knowledge produced by torture exposes the uselessness of the 'ticking bomb' scenario, used to justify the use of torture in the War on Terror, in terms of the torture of a prisoner being justified if it would mean saving thousands of lives. Not only is such a scenario of little, if any, relevance to the majority of cases in which torture is used, it ignores the question of the validity of the knowledge produced by torture.

26. Rather than a condition of endless war, as suggested in 'Rudy Giuliani's 'War with Iran' team', John Nichols, *Nation*, 12 November 2007, http://www. thenation.com/blogs/campaignmatters?bid=45&pid=251099, accessed 19 November 2007.

27. This has come increasingly to be acknowledged, as in Attorney General Michael Mukasey declaring he wants Guantanamo Bay closed 'because it's hurting us', with President Bush also stating he wants to see the camp closed at some point, 'Bay watch', *Economist*, 17 November 2007, 51–2.

28. 'Want to torture? Get a warrant', Alain Dershowitz, *San Francisco Chronicle*, 22 January 2002, http://www.sfgate.com/cgi-bin/article.cgi?file=/chronicle/ archive/2002/01/22/ED5329.DTL.

29. 'Arar launches lawsuit against US government', CBC, 22 January 2004, http://www.cbc.ca/world/story/2004/01/22/ararsuit040122.html; '"Torture victim" seeks US justice', Laurence Peter, BBC, 2 February 2007, http://news. bbc.co.uk/2/hi/europe/6325561.stm. Furthermore, Italian prosecutors are still pursuing the case of Abu Omar, 'First CIA rendition trial opens', BBC, 8 June 2007, http://news.bbc.co.uk/2/hi/europe/6732897.stm.

9   The Unseen

1. While some of these images did appear outside the United States in the spring of 2006 not all the images have ever been shown, 'New Abu Ghraib images broadcast', BBC, 15 February 2006, http://news.bbc.co.uk/1/hi/ world/middle_east/4715540.stm.

2. 'Dozens more Abu Ghraib abuse images broadcast', Times, 15 February 2006, http://www.timesonline.co.uk/tol/news/world/iraq/article731027.ece.

3. 'Inquiry into destroyed CIA tapes', BBC, 8 December 2007, http://news.bbc. co.uk/2/hi/americas/7134860.stm.

4. As quoted in 'Return of US war dead kept solemn, secret', Gregg Zoroya, *USA Today*, 31 December 2003, http://www.usatoday.com/news/nation/2003- 12-31-casket-usat_x.htm.

5. 'US concern over war dead photos', BBC, 28 April 2004, http://news.bbc. co.uk/2/hi/americas/3652171.stm; 'No cameras for US war dead's return', Nick Childs, BBC, 4 November 2003, http://news.bbc.co.uk/2/hi/americas/ 3239659.stm. The actor John Cusack identified this ban as one of the 'most cowardly political acts' in his lifetime, with the ban lying behind his desire to make the film *Grace is Gone* (2007), 'Cusack: photo ban one of "most cowardly political acts" in my lifetime', David Edwards and Jason Rhyne, 4 December 2007, *The Raw Story*, http://rawstory.com/news/2007/Bush_ political_cowardice_prompted_new_John_1204.html.

6. Crary (1992: 14) points to the terms in which the emergence of photography supports this 'abstracted' sense of visual experience.

7. Krauss (1994) provides a further discussion of 'the optical unconscious' in regard to conceptions of modernist art.

8. In the collection of the Imperial War Museum, London. Taube translates as 'dove', and refers to a German reconnaissance plane from which bombs could be dropped – (Taub in German also means death). Nevinson's (1889– 1946) paintings of World War I are among his best-known work.

9. One example of the expansion of this blind field is provided by Predator drones flying over Afghanistan being controlled by operators in Las Vegas, 'Hunting the Taliban in Las Vegas', Robert Kaplan, *The Atlantic*, September 2006, http://www.theatlantic.com/doc/200609/taliban-vegas.

10. As suggested by an audience member at Roger Tolson's lecture 'The exploded view – images of the city at war', Louise T Blouin Foundation, London, 21 August 2007.

11. 'What happened at Haditha?', Martin Asser, BBC, 21 December 2006, http://news.bbc.co.uk/2/hi/middle_east/5033648.stm; 'US marines likely to avoid murder charges over killing of Iraqi civilians', Ewan MacAskill, *Guardian*, 5 October 2007, 27.

12. 'Iraq wedding party video backs survivors' claims', *Fox News*, 24 May 2004, http://www.foxnews.com/story/0,2933,120721,00.html.

13. *Iraq Veterans against the War*, http://www.ivaw.org/. Accessed 7 July 2007.

14. 'Far from Iraq, a demonstration of a war zone', David Montgomery, *Washington Post*, 20 March 2007, http://www.washingtonpost.com/wp-dyn/content/article/2007/03/19/AR2007031901558.html.

15. Ibid.

10   New York: A Return

1. 'Where the towers once stood', *Economist*, 8 September 2007, 48.

2. Although as Hugh Sykes's report for the 'The World Today', *BBC World Service*, 12 August 2004, makes clear, the city had already embarked upon such a process of waiting in the wake of the 1993 attacks on the World Trade Center.

3. As has been commented upon more broadly, see Young (1990).

4. It should be added that the differing values attributed to the dead applies to the victims of the September 11 attacks themselves. As William Langewiesche delineates in his account of the clear-up of the Ground Zero – *American Ground* (2004) – the firefighters involved in the clear-up sought to assert the supreme value of their fallen colleagues, to the extent that this resulted in brawls between them and the police. The illegal immigrants rumoured to be living in the basement of the World Trade Center can be seen to have accorded the lowest value among the victims of the attacks – with little attempt made to clarify even the validity of the rumours of their existence.

5. 'Success in Afghan war hard to gauge', Edward Epstein, *San Francisco Chronicle*, 23 March 2002, http://www.sfgate.com/cgi-bin/article.cgi?f=/c/a/2002/03/23/MN218394.DTL&hw=tommy+franks+body+counts&sn=004&sc=643.

6. This contrast is given a further dimension by Simpson's (2006: 29–32) discussion of the history of the United States seeking to record its dead as reaching back to 1757 and the opening of the struggle for independence.

7. 'Where the towers once stood', op. cit.

8. '9/11 families protest cultural plans at Ground Zero', Phil Hirschkorn, CNN, 21 June 2005, http://www.cnn.com/2005/TRAVEL/06/21/ground.zero.plans/index.html.

9. See, for example, Augé (1995).

10. '9/11 families protest cultural plans at Ground Zero', op. cit.

11. That originally appeared in the December 2001 issue of *Harper's* magazine, and was reproduced in the *Guardian*, 22 December 2001, http://books. guardian.co.uk/departments/generalfiction/story/0,,623732,00.html.

12. Indeed the counternarrative can be seen to constitute a variant of Deleuze and Guattari's 'minor voice'.

13. With a selection of images appearing in book form (2002). See also the project's website, http://hereisnewyork.org. Accessed 12 December 2006.

14. A situation which has led to seemingly false claims about who died in the attacks, as in the case of Tania Head, who claimed she was a survivor of the attacks and that her fiancé, 'Dave' died in the North Tower, 'Barcelona paper throws new doubt no 9/11 story', Manny Fernandez, *International Herald Tribune*, 1 October 2007, 6. Such claims point again to the status accorded to the victims (and survivors) of the attacks.

15. 'The New Ground Zero: finding comfort in the safety of names', Michael Kimmelman, *New York Times*, 31 August 2003, http://query.nytimes.com/gst/ fullpage.html?res=9900E5DD133BF937A2575AC0A9659C8B63; 'Remains of 9/11 hijackers identified', BBC, 28 February 2003, http://news.bbc.co.uk/2/ hi/americas/2808599.stm.

16. Plans for the memorial museum still remain unclear, 'Top-secret $510 million Ground Zero museum wallows in grief', James Russell, *Bloomberg*, 1 June 2007, http://www.bloomberg.com/apps/news?pid=20601088&sid=aSKaS78J rzR4&refer=muse.

17. 'Remains of 9/11 hijackers identified', op. cit.

18. The New Ground Zero: finding comfort in the safety of names', op. cit.

19. 'As 9/11 draws near, a debate rises: how much tribute is enough?', N. R, Kleinfield, *New York Times*, 2 September 2007, http://www.nytimes.com/2007/ 09/02/nyregion/02fatigue.html.

20. 'Bush campaign says it won't pull 9/11 ads', CNN, 29 April 2004, http:// www.cnn.com/2004/ALLPOLITICS/03/07/bush.ads/index.html.

21. 'Anger at 9/11 Giuliani fundraiser', BBC, 26 September 2007, http://news. bbc.co.uk/2/hi/americas/7013466.stm.

22. Although following Badiou's (2007: 2) critique of the number of dead providing an index of the significance of an event – how this size is measured is worth thinking about.

23. 'Top-secret $510 million Ground Zero museum wallows in grief', op. cit.

24. 'Trimmed Bin Laden in media-savvy war', Frank Gardner, *BBC News*, 8 September 2007, http://news.bbc.co.uk/2/hi/middle_east/6985086.stm.

25. 'Bin Laden releases video on 9/11 anniversary', James Sturcke, *Guardian*, 11 September 2007, http://www.guardian.co.uk/alqaida/story/0,,2100080,00. html.

26. Al Qaeda in the Maghreb developed out of the Algeria-based Salafist group for Preaching and Combat (active since 2002), announcing its change of name in January 2007. While at one level this change of name can be read as simply that it is also indicative of the group's desire to more firmly identify itself with Al Qaeda.

27. 'Embrace Islam' Bin Laden urges', BBC, 7 September 2007, http://news.bbc. co.uk/2/hi/middle_east/6984102.stm.

28. 'Poll: majority thinks Bin Laden will avoid capture', CNN, 7 September 2007, http://politicalticker.blogs.cnn.com/2007/09/07/poll-majority-thinks-bin-laden-will-avoid-capture/.
29. 'Washington Diary: 9/11's legacy', Matt Frei, BBC, 12 September 2007, http://news.bbc.co.uk/2/hi/americas/6990365.stm.

Epilogue

1. With the appearance in December 2007 of the 'National Intelligence Estimate' in the United States, and its assertion that Iran was not developing a nuclear military capacity, 'US report cools crisis on Iran', Paul Reynolds, BBC, 4 December 2007, http://news.bbc.co.uk/2/hi/americas/7126429.stm.
2. With the possibilities of the latter increasingly discussed, 'US weighs new push by CIA in Pakistan', Steven Lee Myers, David Sanger and Eric Schmitt, *International Herald Tribune*, 7 January 2008, 7.
3. 'The good old days of the Cold War', Paul Kennedy, *Los Angeles Times*, 18 February 2007, http://www.latimes.com/news/opinion/la-op-kennedy-18feb18,0,1483277.story. Kennedy counsels against such nostalgia.
4. 'Still out there', *Economist*, 10 January 2004, 9.
5. See, for instance, Alinson (2006) for a suggestive imagining of future possible attack scenarios.
6. 'Israel admits air strike on Syria', BBC, 2 October 2007, http://news.bbc.co.uk/2/hi/middle_east/7024287.stm.
7. 'A state of denial', Pervez Hoodbhoy, *International Herald Tribune*, 17 January 2008, 8.
8. 'The real price of freedom', *Economist*, 20 September 2007, http://www.economist.com/opinion/displaystory.cfm?story_id=9833041.

References

Abedin, Mahn (2004) 'The essence of Al Qaeda: an interview with Saad Al-Faqih', *Spotlight on Terror*, 2 (2), http://www.jamestown.org/publications_details.php? volume_id=397&&issue_id=2907.

Adorno, Theodor (2003) *Can One Live after Auschwitz?: a philosophical reader*. Rolf Tiedemann (ed.), Stanford: Stanford University.

Agamben, Giorgio (1998) *Homo Sacer: sovereign power and bare life*. London: Stanford University.

Ali, Tariq (2005) *Rough Music: Blair, bombs, Baghdad, London, terror*. London: Verso.

Alinson, Graham (2006) 'Flight of fancy', *The Annals of the American Academy of Political and Social Science*, 607, 162–6.

Amancio, Edson Jose (2005) 'Dostoevsky and Stendhal's syndrome', *Arq Neuropsiquiatr*, 63 (4), 1099–103.

Anderson, Perry (2007) 'Jottings on the conjuncture', *New Left Review*, 48, 5–37.

Armes, Roy (2005) 'Algeria', in D. Rosenthal (ed.), *International Film Guide 2005: the definitive annual review of world cinema*. London: Button. 68–9.

Augé, Marc (1995) *Non-Places: introduction to an anthropology of supermodernity*. London: Verso.

Aumont, Jacques (1997) *The Image*. London: BFI.

Badiou, Alain (2004) 'Fragments of a public diary on the American war against Iraq', *Contemporary French and Francophone Studies*, 8 (3), 223–38.

Badiou, Alain (2005) *Infinite Thought: truth and the return to philosophy*. London: Continuum.

Badiou, Alain (2007) *The Century*. Cambridge: Polity.

Baker, Steve (2000) *The Postmodern Animal*. London: Reaktion.

Barthes, Roland (1989) *The Rustle of Language*. London: California University Press.

Barthes, Roland (1990) *Fragments of a Lover's Discourse*. London: Penguin.

Barthes, Roland (2000) *Camera Lucida: reflections on photography*. London: Vintage.

Basu, Anustup (2003) 'The state of security and warfare of demons', *Critical Quarterly*, 45 (1–2), 11–32.

Baudrillard, Jean (1993) *Symbolic Exchange and Death*. London: Sage.

Baudrillard, Jean (2002) *The Gulf War Did Not Take Place*. London: Indiana University.

Beigbeder, Frederic (2005) *Windows on the World*. London: Harper Perennial.

Benjamin, Walter (1985) *One Way Street and Other Writings*. London: Verso.

Benjamin, Walter (2002) *The Arcades Project*. London: Harvard University.

Bhabha, Homi (1994) *The location of Culture*. London: Routledge.

Black, Jeremy (2004) *War since 1945*. London: Reaktion.

Blanchot, Maurice (1986) *The Writing of the Disaster*. London: University of Nebraska.

Blanchot, Maurice (1995) 'Waiting', in M. Holland (ed.), *The Blanchot Reader*. Oxford: Blackwells. 272–8.

Bodansky, Yossef (1999) *Bin Laden: the man who declared war on America*. Rocklin, CA.: Forum.

Bonitzer, Pascal (1996) 'Hitchcockian suspense', in S. Zizek (ed.), *Everything You Ever Wanted to Know about Lacan ... but Were Afraid to Ask Hitchcock.* London: Verso. 15–30.

Botting, Fred (1999) 'Future horror (the redundancy of Gothic)', *Gothic Studies*, 1 (2), 139–55.

Bowie, Malcolm (1988) *Theory as Fiction: Freud, Lacan and Proust.* Cambridge: Cambridge University.

Bozovic, Miran (1997) 'The man behind his own retina', in S. Zizek (ed.), *Everything You Always Wanted to Know about Lacan ... but Were Afraid to Ask Hitchcock.* London: Verso. 161–77.

Brennan, Teresa (1993) *History after Lacan.* London: Routledge.

Brennan, Teresa (1996) 'The contexts of vision from a specific standpoint', in Teresa Brennan and Martin Jay (eds), *Vision in Context: historical and contemporary perspectives on sight.* London: Routledge. 217–30.

Brophy, Philip (1986) 'Horrality – the textuality of contemporary horror films', *Screen*, 27 (1), 2–13.

Bryson, Norman (1983) *Vision and Painting: the logic of the gaze.* London: Macmillan.

Burke, Edmund (1998) *A Philosophical Enquiry into the Origin of Our Ideas of the Sublime and Beautiful.* Oxford: Oxford University.

Campbell, David (2004) 'Horrific Blindness: images of death in contemporary media', *Journal for Cultural Research*, 8 (1), 55–74.

Chandrasekaran, Rajiv (2006) *Imperial Life in the Emerald City: inside Baghdad's green zone.* London: Bloomsbury.

Chion, Michel (1999) *The Voice in Cinema.* New York: Columbia University.

Cockburn, Alexander (2007) 'Whatever happened to the anti-war movement?', *New Left Review*, 46, 29–38.

Cockburn, Patrick (2005) 'The occupation', *New Left Review*, 36, 35–67.

Coll, Steve (2004) *Ghost Wars: the secret history of the CIA, Afghanistan and Bin Laden.* London: Penguin.

Collins, Joseph (2004) 'Afghanistan: winning a three block war', *The Journal of Conflict Studies*, 24 (2), 61–75.

Copjec, Joan (2002) *Imagine There's No Woman: ethics and sublimation.* London: MIT.

Corbin, Jane (2003) *The Base: Al-Qaeda and the changing face of global terror.* London: Pocket.

Crary, Jonathan (1992) *Techniques of the Observer: on vision and modernity in the nineteenth century.* London: MIT.

Creed, Barbara (1993) *The Monstrous-Feminine: film, feminism, psychoanalysis.* London: Routledge.

Danner, Mark (2006) 'Iraq: the war of the imagination', *The New York Review of Books*, 21 December, 81–8 and 94–6.

Davis Hanson, Victor (2001) *Why the West Has Won: carnage and culture from Salamis to Vietnam.* London: Faber and Faber.

Debord, Guy (1995) *The Society of the Spectacle.* New York: Zone.

Deleuze, Gilles and Guattari, Felix (1986) *Kafka: toward a minor literature.* Minneapolis: University of Minnesota.

DeLillo, Don (1991) *Mao II.* London: Vintage.

Derrida, Jacques (1987) *The Truth in Painting.* London: University of Chicago.

Derrida, Jacques (1994) *Specters of Marx: the state of the debt, the work of mourning and the new international.* London: Routledge.

Devetak, Richard (2005) 'The Gothic scene of international relations: ghosts, monsters, terror and the sublime after September 11', *Review of International Studies*, 31 (4), 621–43.

Dolar, Mladan (1996) 'A father who is not quite dead', in S. Zizek (ed.), *Everything You Ever Wanted to Know about Lacan ... but Were Afraid to Ask Hitchcock.* London: Verso. 143–50.

Dolar, Mladen (2006) *A Voice and Nothing More.* London: MIT.

Dostoyevsky, Fyodor (1953) *The Devils.* London: Penguin.

Dworzak, Thomas (2004) *Taliban.* New York: Trolley.

Eagleton, Terry (2006) 'Political Beckett?', *New Left Review*, 40, 67–74.

Elkins, James (1996) *The Object Stares Back: on the nature of seeing.* London: Harvest.

Evans, Dylan (1996) *An Introductory Dictionary of Lacanian Psychoanalysis.* Hove: Brunner-Routledge.

Fallows, James (2006) 'Declaring victory', The Atlantic, September, 60–73.

Fallows, James (2006a) 'Endgaming the terror war', 8 August, *The Atlantic*, http://www.theatlantic.com/doc/200608u/fallows-interview.

Flower MacCannell, Juliet (2006) 'More thoughts for the times on war and death', in J. Clemens and R. Grigg (eds), *Jacques Lacan and the Other Side of Psychoanalysis: reflections on seminar XVII.* London: Duke University. 195–215.

Freud, Sigmund (1973) 'Thoughts for the times on war and death', in J. Strachey (ed.), *The Standard Edition of the Complete Works of Sigmund Freud Volume XIV.* London: Hogarth. 275–300.

Freud, Sigmund (1975) *The Psychopathology of Everyday Life*, in J. Strachey (ed.), Harmondsworth: Penguin.

Freud, Sigmund (1991) 'The future of an illusion', in A. Dickson (ed.), *The Penguin Freud library: volume 12.* London: Penguin. 183–241.

Freud, Sigmund (1991a) 'Mourning and melancholia', in A. Richards (ed.), *The Penguin Freud Library: volume 11.* London: Penguin. 251–68.

Freud, Sigmund (1993) 'Inhibitions, symptoms and anxiety', in A. Richards (ed.), *The Penguin Freud Library: volume 10.* London: Penguin. 237–315.

Freud, Sigmund (1995) 'The uncanny', in J. Strachey (ed.), *The Standard Edition of the Complete Works of Sigmund Freud: volume XVII.* London: Hogarth. 219–52.

Freud, Sigmund (2001) 'Remembering, repeating and working through', in J. Strachey (ed.), *The Standard Edition of the Complete Works of Sigmund Freud Volume XII.* London: Vintage. 147–56.

Freud, Sigmund (2001a) 'Formulations on the two principles of mental functioning', in J. Strachey (ed.), *The Standard Edition of the Complete Works of Sigmund Freud Volume XII.* London: Vintage. 218–26.

Gannon, Kathy (2004) 'Afghanistan unbound', *Foreign Affairs*, 83 (3), 35–46.

Gatrall, Jeff (2001) 'Between iconoclasm and silence: representing the divine in Holbein and Dostoevskii', *Comparative Literature*, 53 (3), 214–32.

Geertz, Clifford (1977) 'Centers, kings, and charisma: reflections on the symbolics of power', in J. Ben-David and T. Nichols Clark (eds), *Culture and Its Creators: essays in honour of Edward Shils.* Chicago: University of Chicago. 150–71.

Gordon, Avery (1997) *Ghostly Matters: haunting and the sociological imagination.* London: University of Minnesota.

Graham, Stephen (2007) 'War and the city', *New Left Review*, 44, 121–32.
Gray, John (2006) 'The moving target', *The New York Review of Books*, October 5, 22–4.
Greenacre, Phyllis (1956) 'Experiences of awe in childhood', in *The Psychoanalytic Study of the Child: volume XI*. London: Imago. 9–30.
Greenacre, Phyllis (1987) *Trauma, Growth and Personality*. London: Maresfield Library.
Greenberg, Karen and Dratel, Joshua (2005) *The Torture Papers: the road to Abu Ghraib*. Cambridge: Cambridge University.
Grey, Stephen (2006) *Ghost Plane: the story of the CIA's secret rendition programme*. London: Hurst.
Günther, Renate (2002) *Margeurite Duras*. Manchester: Manchester University.
Harraway, Donna (2006) 'When species meet', Pavis Lecture, 11 October 2006, The Open University.
Heath Atchley, J. (2004) 'The loss of language, the language of loss: thinking with DeLillo on terror and mourning', *Janus Head*, 7 (2), 333–54.
here is new york: a democracy of photographs (2002) New York: Scalo.
Hillman, James (2005) *A Terrible Love of War*. New York: Penguin.
Honour, Hugh and Fleming, John (1995) *A World History of Art*. London: Laurence King.
Huchthausen, Peter (2004) *America's Splendid Little Wars: a short history of US engagements from the fall of Saigon to Baghdad*. London: Penguin.
Huppauf, Bernd (1995) 'Modernism and the photographic representation of war and destruction', in L. Devereaux and R. Hillman (eds), *Fields of Vision: essays in film studies, visual anthropology and photography*. London: University of California Press. 94–124.
James, Henry (1975) *The Turn of the Screw and Other Stories*. London: Penguin.
Jay, Martin (1994) *Downcast Eyes: the denigration of vision in twentieth-century French thought*. London: University of California.
Kaldor, Mary (2004) 'The red zone', in R. Bechler (ed.), *Re-Imagining Security*. London: The British Council. 24–40.
Kessler, Oliver and Daase, Christopher (2006) 'The paradox of security', 'Security, Technologies of Risk, and the Political' symposium, Centre for Citizenship, Identities and Governance, The Open University, 23–24 November.
Klein, Melanie (1997) *The Psycho-Analysis of Children*. London: Vintage.
Konstantinidou, Christina (2007) 'Death, lamentation and the photographic representation of the Other during the Second Iraq War in Greek newspapers', *International Journal of Cultural Studies*, 10 (2), 147–66.
Krauss, Rosalind (1994) *The Optical Unconscious*. London: MIT.
Kristeva, Julia (1982) *Powers of Horror: an essay on abjection*. New York: Columbia University.
Kristeva, Julia (1989) *Black Sun: depression and melancholia*. New York: Columbia University.
Kuklick, Bruce (2002) 'The plumber and the professor: or, a primer on how to think about the war', *Diplomatic History*, 26 (4), 559–70.
Lacan, Jacques, (1962–1963) *The Seminar of Jacques Lacan: Anxiety, Book X*. Unpublished. Translated by Cormac Gallagher from unedited French manuscripts.
Lacan, Jacques (1974–1975) *RSI*. Unpublished. French transcript available, http://nosubject.com/Seminar_XXII.

168   *References*

Lacan, Jacques (1992) *The Ethics of Psychoanalysis: the seminar of Jacques Lacan Book VII, 1959–60*. London: Routledge.

Lacan, Jacques (1994) *The Four Fundamental Concepts of Psychoanalysis*. London: Penguin.

Lacan, Jacques (1997) *The Psychoses: the seminar of Jacques Lacan Book III, 1955–56*. London: Norton.

Lacan, Jacques (1999) *Encore, on Feminine Sexuality, the Limits of Love and Knowledge: the seminar of Jacques Lacan, Book XX, 1972–73*. London: Norton.

Lacan, Jacques (2006) *Ecrits*. London: Norton.

Lacan, Jacques (2007) *The Other Side of Psychoanalysis: seminar XVII*. London: Norton.

LaFeber, Walter (2002) 'The Bush Doctrine', *Diplomatic History*, 26 (4), 543–58.

Langewiesche, William (2004) *American Ground*. London: Scribner.

Latimer, John (2003) *Deception in War*. London: John Murray.

Layne, Christopher (2006) *The Peace of Illusions: American grand strategy from 1940 to the present*. London: Cornell University Press.

Lechte, John (1990) 'Kristeva and Holbein, artist of melancholy', *British Journal of Aesthetics*, 30 (4), 342–50.

Lewis, Justin, Jhaly, Sut and Morgan, Michael (1991) *The Gulf War: a study of the media, public opinion and public knowledge*. Amherst: University of Massachusetts.

Lewis, Justin (2003) 'The absence of narrative: boredom and the residual power of television news', in T. Miller (ed.), *Television: critical concepts in media and cultural studies – volume II*. London: Routledge. 322–7.

Lucas, Christopher (1990) 'Exhibitionism', in *The British Journal of Psychotherapy*, 7 (1), 15–24.

Lutticken, Sven (2006) 'Suspense and Surprise', *New Left Review*, 40, 95–109.

Magnum Photographers (2001) *New York September 11*. New York: Powerhouse.

Mair, Peter (2006) 'Ruling the void?: the hollowing of western democracy', *New Left Review*, 42, 25–51.

Marash, David (1995) 'Big story, small screen', *Columbia Journalism Review*, July/August, 9, 9–10.

Mayer, Jane (2003) 'The search for Osama: did the government let bin Laden's trail go cold?', *The New Yorker*, 4 August, 26–34.

McCurry, Steve (2007) *Shadow of the Mountain*. London: Phaidon.

Metz, Christian (1983) *Psychoanalysis and Cinema: the imaginary signifier*. London: Macmillan.

Miller, Jacques Alain (2006) 'On shame', in J. Clemens and R. Grigg (eds), *Jacques Lacan and the Other Side of Psychoanalysis: reflections on seminar XVII*. London: Duke University Press. 11–28.

Mulvey, Laura (2006) *Death 24x a Second: stillness and the moving image*. London: Reaktion.

National Commission on Terrorist Attacks upon the United States (2004) *The 9/11 Report*. New York: St Martin's.

Neocleous, Mark (2005) 'Gothic Fascism', *Journal for Cultural Research*, 9 (2), 133–49.

Neocleous, Mark (2007) 'Security, liberty and the myth of balance: towards a critique of security politics', *Contemporary Political Theory*, 6 (2), 131–49.

Nevinson, Christopher (1937) *Paint and Prejudice*. London: Methuen.

Nietzsche, Friedrich (1994) *Human, All Too Human.* London: Penguin.

Norfolk, Simon. (2002) *Afghanistan: chronotopia.* Stockport: Dewi Lewis.

Nye, David (1994) *American Technological Sublime.* London: MIT Press.

Pape, Robert (2003) 'The Strategic Logic of Suicide Terrorism', *American Political Science Review*, 97 (3), 1–19.

Pfaff, William (2006) 'A disaster by any measure', *The New York Review of Books*, 19 October, 10.

Phillips, Adam (1994) 'On being bored', in *On Kissing, Tickling and Being Bored.* London: Faber and Faber. 71–82.

Portraits 9/11/01: the collected 'Portraits of Grief' from the New York Times (2002) New York: Time.

Retort (2006) 'All quiet on the eastern front', *New Left Review*, 41, 88–91.

Rifkin, Adrian (2003) 'Waiting and seeing', *Journal of Visual Culture*, 2 (3), 325–39.

Robertson, Linda (2003) *The Dream of Civilized Warfare: World War I flying aces and the American imagination.* London: University of Minnesota.

Robinson, Piers (2002) The CNN Effect: the myth of news, foreign policy and intervention. London: Routledge.

Rutherford, John (2005) 'At War', *Cultural Studies*, 19 (5), 622–42.

Salecl, Renata (2004) *On Anxiety.* London: Routledge.

Sartre, Jean Paul (1957) *Being and Nothingness: an essay on phenomenological ontology.* London: Methuen.

Scarry, Elaine (1985) *The Body in Pain: the making and unmaking of the world.* Oxford: Oxford University Press.

Scarry, Elaine (1993) 'Watching and authorizing the Gulf War', in M. Garber, J. Matlock and R. Walkowitz (eds), *Media Spectacles.* London: Routledge. 57–73.

Scarry, Elaine (1999) 'The difficulty of imagining other persons', in C. Hesse and R. Post (eds), *Human Rights in Political Transition: Gettysburg to Bosnia.* New York: Zone. 277–309.

Schivelbusch, Wolfgang (2003) *The Culture of Defeat: on national trauma, mourning and recovery.* London: Granta.

Schmid, Alex (1999) 'Terrorism and the use of Weapons of Mass Destruction: from where to risk?' *Terrorism and Political Violence*, 11 (4), 106–32.

Sconce, Jeffrey (2000) *Haunted Media: electronic presence from telegraphy to television.* London: Duke University Press.

Seawright, Paul (2003) *Hidden.* London: Imperial War Museum.

Shulan, Michael (2002) Untitled introduction in *here is new york: a democracy of photographs.* New York: Scalo.

Sifaoui, Mohamed (2003) *Inside Al Qaeda: how I infiltrated the world's deadliest terrorist organisation.* London: Granta.

Simpson, David (2006) *9/11: the culture of commemoration.* London: Chicago University.

Simpson, John (2003) *News from No Man's Land: reporting the world.* London: Pan.

Smith, Terry (2003) 'The dialectics of disappearance: architectural icon types between clashing cultures', *Critical Quarterly*, 45 (1–2), 33–51.

Sobchak, Vivian (1984) 'Inscribing ethical space: ten propositions on death, representation and documentary', *Quarterly Review of Film Studies*, 9 (4), 283–300.

Sontag, Susan (2002) *On Photography.* London: Penguin.

Sontag, Susan (2004) 'What have we done?', *The Guardian, G2* section, 24 May 2004, 2–4.

Stoichita, Victor and Coderch, Anna Maria (1999) *Goya: the last carnival.* London: Reaktion.

Sun Tzu (2003) *The Art of War.* New York: Barnes and Noble Classics.

Taylor, John (1998) *Body Horror: photojournalism, catastrophe and war.* Manchester: Manchester University.

Toscano, Alberto (2007) '"European nihilism" and beyond', in Alain Badiou, *The Century.* Cambridge: Polity. 179–201.

Ullman, Harlan and Wade, James (1996) *Shock and Awe: achieving Rapid Dominance.* http://www.ndu.edu/inss/books/books%20-%201996/Shock%20and%20Awe% 20-%20Dec%2096/index.html. Washington DC: National Defense University.

Ullman, Harlan and Wade, James (1998) Rapid Dominance – a force for all seasons: technologies and systems for achieving shock and awe: a real revolution in military affairs. London: Royal United Services Institute for Defence Studies.

Venturi, Roberto (1995) *Afghanistan: il nodo del tempo.* Rome: Contrasto.

Vertov, Dziga (1984) *Kino-Eye: the writings of Dziga Vertov.* Annette Michelson (ed.), London: Pluto.

Virilio, Paul (1989) *War and Cinema: the logistics of perception.* London: Verso.

Wallerstein, Immanuel (2006) 'The curve of American power', *New Left Review,* 40, 77–94.

Warner, Marina (2004) 'The desert of the real', *The Guardian, G2* section, 25 September, 13–14.

Warner, Marina (2005) 'Angels and engines: apocalypse and its aftermath, from George W. Bush to Philip Pullman', *The Times Literary Supplement,* August 19 & 26, 14–17.

Weber, Max (1978) *Economy and Society: an outline of interpretive sociology.* London: University of California.

Wigley, Mark (2002), 'Insecurity by design', in M. Sorkin and S. Zukin (eds), *After the World Trade Center.* New York: Routledge. 69–85.

Willis, Susan (2005) *Portents of the Real: a primer for post-9/11 America.* London: Verso.

Willis, Susan (2006) 'Guantanamo's symbolic economy', *New Left Review,* 39, 123–31.

Woodward, Bob (2006) *State of Denial: Bush at war, part III.* London: Simon and Schuster.

Worth, Alexi, (2001) 'Wolfgang Staehle Untitled, 2001', *Artforum,* November, 40 (3), 128–9.

Wright, Terence (2004) 'Collateral coverage: media images of Afghan refugees, 2001', *Visual Studies,* 19 (1), 97–111.

Yeats, William (1990) *Collected Poems.* London: Macmillan.

Young, Robert (1990) *White Mythologies: writing history and the west.* London: Routledge.

Zelizer, Barbie (2004) 'When war is reduced to a photograph', in S. Allan and B. Zelizer (eds), *Reporting War: journalism in wartime.* London: Routledge. 115–35.

Zizek, Slavoj (1993) *Tarrying with the negative: Kant, Hegel and the critique of ideology.* London: Duke University.

Zizek, Slavoj (1995) 'The lamella of David Lynch', in R. Feldstein, B. Fink and M. Jaanus (eds.), *Reading Seminar XI: Lacan's 'Four fundamental concepts of psychoanalysis'*. Albany: SUNY. 205–20.

Zizek, Slavoj (1996) '"I hear you with me eyes"; or, The Invisible Master', in R. Salecl and S. Zizek (eds), *Gaze and Voice as Love Objects*. London: Duke University. 90–126.

Zizek, Slavoj (1997) 'In his bold gaze my ruin is writ large', in S. Zizek (ed.), *Everything You Ever Wanted to Know about Lacan ... but Were Afraid to Ask Hitchcock*. London: Verso. 211–72.

Zizek, Slavoj (1998) 'For a Leftist appropriation of the European legacy', *Journal of Political Ideologies*, 3 (1), 63–78.

Zizek, Slavoj (1999) 'The Hitchcockian Blot', in R. Allen and S. Ishii-Gonzales (eds), *Alfred Hitchcock: centenary essays*. London: BFI. 123–39.

Zizek, Slavoj (1999a) *The Ticklish Subject*. London: Verso.

Zizek, Slavoj (1999b) 'Carl Schmitt in the age of post-politics', in C. Mouffe (ed.), *The Challenge of Carl Schmitt*. London: Verso. 18–37.

Zizek, Slavoj (2000) 'The Thing from Inner Space', in R. Salecl (ed.), *Sexuation*. London: Duke University. 216–59.

Zizek, Slavoj (2001) *On Belief*. London: Routledge.

Zizek, Slavoj (2002) *Welcome to the Desert of the Real*. London: Verso.

Zizek, Slavoj (2002a) 'Are we in a war? Do we have an enemy?', 23 May. *The London Review of Books*, http:lrb.co.uk/v24/n1o/zize01_.html.

Zizek, Slavoj (2003) *The Puppet and the Dwarf: the perverse core of Christianity*. London: MIT.

Zizek, Slavoj (2004) 'A cyberspace Lenin: why not?', *Fraccion Trotskista*, 6 February, http://www.ft.org.ar/notasft.asp?ID=1765&i=3.

Zizek, Slavoj (2005) *Iraq: the borrowed kettle*. London: Verso.

Zulaika, Joseba and Douglass, William (1996) *Terror and Taboo: the follies, fables and faces of terrorism*. London: Routledge.

Index